African Politics of Survival
Extraversion and Informality in the Contemporary World

Edited by

Mitsugi Endo, Ato Kwamena Onoma & Michael Neocosmos

In collaboration

Langaa RPCIG
Mankon Bamenda

CAAS
Kyoto University

Publisher:
Langaa RPCIG
Langaa Research & Publishing Common Initiative Group
P.O. Box 902 Mankon
Bamenda
North West Region
Cameroon
Langaagrp@gmail.com
www.langaa-rpcig.net

In Collaboration with
The Center for African Area Studies, Kyoto University, Japan

Distributed in and outside N. America by African Books Collective
orders@africanbookscollective.com
www.africanbookscollective.com

ISBN-10: 9956-551-68-6

ISBN-13: 978-9956-551-68-2

Notes on Contributors

Toshihiro ABE (PhD) is Professor of Sociology at Otani University in Japan. His research interests principally relate to social reconciliation, transitional justice, migration and social movements in the South African and Cambodian contexts. His publications include *Unintended Consequences in Transitional Justice: Social Recovery at the Local Level* (2018, Lynne Rienner Publishers) and *The Khmer Rouge Trials in Context* (2019, editor, Silkworm Books).

Mitsugi ENDO (DPhil) is Professor of Graduate School of Arts and Sciences at the University of Tokyo, Japan. He is also chair of the Graduate Program on Human Security at the Graduate School. He specialised in comparative politics and international relations, recently focusing on the Greater Horn of Africa. His major works include *Collapsed States and International Security: Experiences of Somalia and New Sovereign Statehood* (2015, Yuhikaku, in Japanese).

Tamara ENOMOTO (PhD) is Professor at Meiji University, Japan. Her most recent works include: *The Arms Trade Treaty: The Self, Sovereignty, and Arms Transfer Control* (2020, Kouyou Shobou, in Japanese), *Weapon Taboos: Genealogies of Pariah Weapons*, (2020, editor, Nihon Keizai Hyouronsha, in Japanese), 'Demarcating Battle Lines: Citizenship and Agency in the Era of Misanthropy' in I. Hazama, K. Umeya and F. B. Nyamnjoh, eds., *Citizenship in Motion: South African and Japanese Scholars in Conversation* (2019, chapter contribution, Langaa RPCIG).

Eisei KURIMOTO is Professor of Anthropology and currently Vice President in charge of student affairs at Osaka University. His research topics are Nilotic ethnography, civil wars and ethnic conflicts, refugee and displacement issues, peacebuilding and humanitarianism. His major works include *People Living through Ethnic Conflict* (1996, Sekai Shisosha, in Japanese), *Primitive and Modern Wars* (1999, Iwanami Shoten, in Japanese), *Conflict, Age and Power in North East Africa* (1998, co-edited, James Currey), *Remapping Ethiopia* (2002, co-edited, Ohio University Press) and *Kyosei Studies Manifesto* (2020, co-edited, Osaka University Press, in Japanese).

Kumiko MAKINO is Director of African Studies Group at the Institute of Developing Economies, Japan External Trade Organization (IDE-JETRO). Her main research field is South Africa. Her research topics include distributional politics, social movement and Africa–Japan relations. Her major works include *Protest and Social Movements in the Developing World* (2009, co-edited with Shinichi Shigetomi and Edward Elgar) and *Economic and Social Transformation in Democratic South Africa* (2013, co-edited with Chizuko Sato, IDE-JETRO, in Japanese).

Motoji MATSUDA is Professor of Sociology and Anthropology, Kyoto University, Japan. His research fields are Nairobi and Western Kenya. His research topics are urbanisation, migration and conflict. His major works include *Urbanisation from Below* (1998, Kyoto University Press), *The Manifesto of Anthropology of the Everyday Life World* (2008, Sekai Shisosha, in Japanese), *African Virtues in the Pursuit of Conviviality: Exploring Local Solutions in Light of Global Prescriptions* (2017, co-edited with Itaru Ohta and Yntiso Gebre, Langaa RPCIG) and *The Challenge of African Potentials: Conviviality, Informality and Futurity* (2020, co-edited with Yaw Ofosu-Kusi, Langaa RPCIG).

Michael NEOCOSMOS is Emeritus Professor in Humanities at Rhodes University in South Africa and Distinguished Visiting Scholar at the University of Connecticut Humanities Institute in the United States. He is the author of many articles and several books including *From Foreign Natives to Native Foreigners: Explaining Xenophobia in South Africa* (2010, CODESRIA) and *Thinking Freedom in Africa: Toward a Theory of Emancipatory Politics* (2016, Wits University Press). This last book was awarded the Frantz Fanon Prize for outstanding work by the *Caribbean Philosophical Association* in 2017. He is currently working on a book provisionally titled *The Dialectics of Emancipation in Africa* to be published by Daraja Press as well as on *An Anthology of African Political Thought from Ancient Egypt to the Present* to be published by CODESRIA.

Artwell NHEMACHENA is a Senior Lecturer at the University of Namibia and has been appointed visiting Associate Professor at Kobe University. He is a Research Fellow at the University of South Africa and is a member of editorial boards of a number of international journals. He holds a PhD in Social Anthropology from the University of Cape Town. He has published over 18 books and over 80 book chapters and journal articles in the areas of security, environment, development, sociology and social anthropology of science and technology studies, relational ontologies and decoloniality. His research interests lie in these areas.

Ato Kwamena ONOMA is a Senior Programme Officer at the Council for the Development of Social Science Research in Africa (CODESRIA). He holds degrees in Philosophy and Political Science. He is the author of *The Politics of Property Rights Institutions in Africa* (2009, Cambridge University Press) and *Anti-refugee Violence and African Politics* (2013, Cambridge University Press). His current work uses epidemics and interment practices to explore mobility, identity and intercommunal relations in Africa.

Akira SATO (PhD) is a Senior Researcher at the Institute of Developing Economies, Japan External Trade Organization (IDE-JETRO). His Research field is Francophone West Africa, especially Côte d'Ivoire. His research topics are political history and conflict resolution. His major works include *Modernity in a Cocoa Republic: History of Associations and Integrative Revolution in Côte d'Ivoire* (2015, IDE-JETRO, in Japanese) and 'Ambiguity and Paradox Finding African Solutions to Africa's Problems: Evaluation of the Unintended Outcomes of the Enhancement of African Regional Organizations' Capacity to Respond to Conflicts', *International Relations*, 194, pp.79–94 (2018, in Japanese).

Shinichi TAKEUCHI (PhD) is Professor at Tokyo University of Foreign Studies and Director of its African Studies Center. He is also a Senior Research Fellow at the Institute of Developing Economies, Japan External Trade Organization (IDE-JETRO) with a cross-appointment status. He has a PhD from the University of Tokyo. With a background of political economy, he has been interested in topics related to conflicts and land problems in Africa. His major publication includes *Confronting Land and Property Problems for Peace* (2014, editor, Routledge).

Table of Contents

African Potentials for Convivial World-Making

Motoji Matsuda

1. The Idea of 'African Potentials'

The *African Potentials* series is based on the findings since 2011 of the African Potentials research project, an international collaboration involving researchers based in Japan and Africa. This project examines how to tackle the challenges of today's world using the experiences and wisdom (ingenuity and responsiveness) of African society. It has identified field sites across a variety of social domains, including areas of conflict, conciliation, environmental degradation, conservation, social development and equality, and attempts to shed light on the potential of African society to address the problems therein. Naturally, such an inquiry is deeply intertwined with the political and economic systems that control the contemporary world, and with knowledge frameworks that have long dominated the perceptions and understanding of our world. Building on unique, long-standing collaborative relationships developed between researchers in Japan and Africa, the project suggests new ways to challenge the prevailing worldview on humans, society and history, enabling those worldviews to be relativised, decentred and pluralised.

After the rose-coloured dreams of the 1960s, African society entered an era of darkness in the 1980s and 1990s. It was beleaguered by problems that included civil conflict, military dictatorship, national economic collapse, commodity shortages, environmental degradation and destruction, over-urbanisation and rampant contagious disease. In the early 21st century, the fortunes of Africa were reversed as it underwent economic growth by leveraging its abundant natural resources. However, an unequal redistribution of wealth increased social disparities and led to the emergence of new forms of conflict and discrimination. The challenges facing African society appear to be more profound than ever.

The governments of African states and the international community have attempted to resolve the many problems Africa has experienced. For example, the perpetrators of crimes during times of civil conflict have been punished by international tribunals, support for democratisation has been offered to states ruled by dictators and despots and environmental degradation has been tackled by scientific awareness campaigns conducted at huge expense.

Nonetheless, to us – the Japanese and African researchers engaging with African society in this era – the huge monetary and organisational resources expended, and scientifically grounded measures pursued, seem to have had little effect on the lives of ordinary people. The punishment of perpetrators did not consider the coexistence of perpetrators and victims, while the propagation of democratic ideals and training to raise scientific awareness was far removed from people's lived experiences. Nevertheless, while many of these 'top-down' measures prescribed to solve Africa's challenges proved ineffective, African society has found ways to heal post-conflict communities and to develop practices of political participation and environmental conservation.

Why did this happen? This question led us to examine ideas and practices African society has formulated for tackling the contemporary difficulties it has experienced. These were developed at sites where ordinary Africans live. 'African Potentials' is the name we gave to these home-grown ideas and the potential to engender them.

2. African Forum: A Unique Intellectual Collaboration between Japan and Africa

As the concept of African Potentials emerged, it required further reflection to develop ideas that could be applied in the humanities and social sciences. The context for these processes was the African Forum: a meeting held in a different part of Africa each year where African researchers from different regions and Japanese researchers studying in each of those regions came together to engage in frank discussion. The attendance of all core members of the project sympathetic to the idea of African Potentials ensured the continuity of the discussions at these African Forums. The core members who drove the project forward from the African side included Edward Kirumira (Uganda), Kennedy Mkutu (Kenya), Yntiso Gebre (Ethiopia), the late Samson Wassara (South Sudan), the late Sam Moyo (Zimbabwe), Michael Neocosmos (South Africa), Francis B. Nyamnjoh (Cameroon and South Africa) and Yaw Ofosu-Kusi (Ghana). The researchers from Japan specialised in extremely diverse fields, including political science, sociology, anthropology, development economics, education, ecology and geography. As they built creative interdisciplinary spaces for interaction across fields over the course of a decade, project members have produced many major outcomes that serve as research models for intellectual and academic exchange between Japan and Africa, and experimental cases of educational practice in the mutual cultivation and guidance of young researchers.

African Forums have been held in Nairobi (2011), Harare (2012), Juba (2013), Yaoundé (2014), Addis Ababa (2015), Kampala (2016), Grahamstown (now Makhanda, 2017), Accra (2018) and Lusaka (2019). These meetings fostered deeper discussion of the conceptualisation and generalisation of African Potentials. This led to the development of a framework for approaching African Potentials and its distinguishing features.

3. What are African Potentials?

The first aim of African Potentials is to 'de-romanticise' the traditional values and institutions of Africa. For example, when studying conflict resolution, members of African Potentials are not interested in excessive idealisation of traditional means of conflict resolution and unconditional endorsement of a return to African traditions as an 'alternative' to modern Western conflict-resolution methods, because such ideas fix African Potentials in a static mode as they speak to a fantasy that ignores the complexities of the contemporary world; they are cognate with the mentality that depreciates African culture.

Rendering African culture static displaces it from its original context and uses it to fabricate 'African-flavoured' theatrical events, as we have seen in different conflict situations. Typical of this tendency is the 'theatre' of traditional dance by performers dressed in ethnic costume and the ceremonial slaughter of cows in an imitation of the rituals of mediation and reconciliation once observed in inter-ethnic conflicts. In our African Forums, we have criticised this tendency as the 'technologisation' and 'compartmentalisation' of traditional rituals.

Naturally, a stance that arbitrarily deems certain conflict-resolution cultures to be 'subaltern', 'backward' or 'uncivilised' needs to be critiqued and it is important to re-evaluate approaches that have been written off in this way. This does not mean that we should level unconditional praise on a fixed subject. With globalisation, African society is experiencing great changes brought about by the circulation of diverse ideas, institutions, information and physical goods. African Potentials can be found in the power to generate cultures of conflict-resolution autonomously under these fluid conditions, while re-aligning elements that were previously labelled 'traditional' and 'indigenous'. In the African Potentials project, we call this the power of 'interface function': the capacity to forge combinations and connections within assemblages of diverse values, ideas and practices that belong to disparate dimensions and different historical phases. In one sense, this is a kind of 'bricolage' created by dismantling pre-existing values and institutions and recombining them freely. It is also a convivial process in the sense that it involves enabling the coexistence of diverse, multi-dimensional elements to create new strengths that are used in contemporary society. The terms 'bricolage' and 'conviviality' are apt expressions characterising the 'interface functions' of African Potentials.

Following this outline, we can identify two features distinguishing African Potentials. First, African Potentials comprise not fixed, unchanging entities but, rather, an open process that is always dynamic and in flux. To treat African traditions and history as static is to fall into the trap of modernist thinking, in which Africa is scorned as barbaric and uncivilised, and the knowledge and practices generated there treated as subaltern and irrational – or a diametrically opposed revivalist mindset that romanticises traditions unconditionally and imbues them with exaggerated significance.

The second feature of African Potentials is its aspiration to pluralism rather than unity. For example, a basic principle of modern civil society is that conflict resolution should occur in accordance with law and judicial process. This principle is deemed to be based on common sense in our society, which means that any resolution method that runs counter to the principle is regarded as 'mistaken' from the outset. This constitutes an aspiration toward unity. It supposes that there is a single way of thinking in relation to the achievement of justice and deems all other approaches peripheral, informal and inferior. The standpoint of Africa's cultural potential, however, renders untenable the idea of a single absolute approach that represents all others as mistaken or deserving of rejection. Here, we can identify a pluralist aspiration that embraces both legal/judicial approaches and extrajudicial solutions.

An aspiration to unity, reduced to the level of dogma, can find eventual culmination in beliefs about 'purity'. In other words, thoughts, values and methods can be regarded as an absolute good, while any attempt to incorporate other (impure) elements is stridently denounced as improper behaviour that compromises purity and perfection. In direct contrast, African Potentials affirm the complexity and multiplicity of a range of elements, and attach value to that which is incomplete. This signifies a more tolerant, open attitude to ideas and values, one that differs from those of the more developed world. African Potentials are grounded in this kind of openness and tolerance.

As we have seen, African cultural potentials are distinguished by their dynamism, flexibility, pluralism, complexity, tolerance and openness. These features are completely at odds with the notion that there is a perfect, pure, uniquely correct mode of existence that competes with others in a confrontational, non-conciliatory manner – one that repels, subordinates and controls them, and occupies the position of an absolute victor. African Potentials can lead us to worldviews on humans, society and history that differ from the hegemonic worldviews that dominate contemporary realms of knowledge.

4. The African Potentials Series

In this way, the concept of African Potentials has enabled researchers from Japan and Africa to organise themselves and pursue activities in multidisciplinary research teams. The products of these activities have been classified into seven different fields for publication in this series. The authors and editors were selected by and from both Japanese and African researchers, and the resulting publications advance the research that has grown out of discussion in the African Forums. The overall structure of the series is as follows:

Volume 1

Title: *African Politics of Survival: Extraversion and Informality in the Contemporary World*

Editors: Mitsugi Endo (The University of Tokyo), Ato Kwamena Onoma (CODESRIA) and Michael Neocosmos (Rhodes University)

Volume 2

Title: *Knowledge, Education and Social Structure in Africa*

Editors: Shoko Yamada (Nagoya University), Akira Takada (Kyoto University) and Shose Kessi (University of Cape Town)

Volume 3

Title: *People, Predicaments and Potentials in Africa*

Editors: Takehiko Ochiai (Ryukoku University), Misa Hirano-Nomoto (Kyoto University) and Daniel E. Agbiboa (Harvard University)

Volume 4

Title: *Development and Subsistence in Globalising Africa: Beyond the Dichotomy*

Editors: Motoki Takahashi (Kyoto University), Shuichi Oyama (Kyoto University) and Herinjatovo Aimé Ramiarison (University of Antananarivo)

Volume 5

Title: *Dynamism in African Languages and Literature: Towards Conceptualisation of African Potentials*

Editors: Keiko Takemura (Osaka University) and Francis B. Nyamnjoh

(University of Cape Town)

Volume 6

Title: *'African Potentials' for Wildlife Conservation and Natural Resource Management: Against the Images of 'Deficiency' and Tyranny of 'Fortress'*

Editors: Toshio Meguro (Hiroshima City University), Chihiro Ito (Fukuoka University) and Kariuki Kirigia (McGill University)

Volume 7

Title: *Contemporary Gender and Sexuality in Africa: African-Japanese Anthropological Approach*

Editors: Wakana Shiino (Tokyo University of Foreign Studies) and Christine Mbabazi Mpyangu (Makerere University)

Acknowledgement

This publication is based on the research project supported by the JSPS KAKENHI Grant Number JP16H06318: 'African Potential' and Overcoming the Difficulties of Modern World: Comprehensive Area Studies that will Provide a New Perspective for the Future of Humanity.

Introduction

African Politics of Survival: Extraversion and Informality in the Contemporary World

Mitsugi Endo, Ato Kwamena Onoma and
Michael Neocosmos

In this research project, the Nation and Citizenship Research Team has raised two primary research concerns. The first is the consideration of extraversion (or extroversion) as a possible African Potential. The second examines competing systems and strategies – the subtitle of a book published in 2016 as the second in a five-volume series on African Potentials – with a focus on the relationship between formal and informal institutions in terms of collaboration and conflict.

Extraversion, deployed by the Beninese philosopher Paulin Hountondji (1995) as a form of inordinate orientation toward elsewhere, especially the Global North for meaning and value in the scientific and economic pursuits of Africans and African societies, has for obvious reasons been portrayed as problematic. One of the main pursuits of this volume is an investigation of some of the positive potentials of extraversion. This exercise is undertaken in the spirit of efforts to further explore the concept and its multiple meanings for African life by scholars that include Bayart (2000), Brett and Gissel (2018) and Clark (2018). Bayart defined the strategy of extraversion as 'mobilizing resources from their (possibly unequal) relationship with the external environment' (Bayart 2000: 218). He identified six characteristics of forms of action seen in African political organisations: coercion, trickery, flight, intermediation, appropriation and rejection (ibid.: 254–5), which are not mutually exclusive. Hagman (2016), who invokes the conceptual framework of Bayart's extraversion in his own research, discusses the importance of the following two points: 'First, these modes of extraversion are

1

not mutually exclusive but may draw on other modes or combine. Second, extraversion modes are not equally distributed through time. They have a life of their own' (Hagman 2016). Such an approach demands critical reconsideration of the concept of African Potentials. Hagman (2016) also provided a detailed analysis of the six forms of action using a case study in Somalia. In each chapter in this book, the authors explore topics of interest in relation to the six forms of action.

This book also explores the emerging concept of competing systems and strategies, with a particular focus on relationships between formal and informal institutions in terms of collaboration, conflict and more ambivalent interactions that straddle these domains. This has been examined in recent years by researchers including Cheeseman (2018) and aligns with work that insists on serious consideration of African contexts or what Mamdani (1996: 8) refers to as the need to move beyond 'history by analogy' in the study of the continent. In dominant literatures in political economy there has been a tendency to neglect or even criticise creativity by actors while emphasising the salutary effects of institutionalisation and the streamlining of processes in the march to societies that are (supposedly) more propitious for human life and wellbeing. Constraining the options of actors and rendering the future predictable are important goals of this effort. In Africa, institutionalisation is said to be considerably limited compared to advanced industrialised societies, a Manichaean view that Mkandawire (2001) has criticised as it concerns discussions of the African state. More recently work in historical institutionalism (cf., Mahoney and Thelen (eds) 2015) on institutional ambiguity and its creative exploitation by ingenious agents in advanced industrialised countries, further questions this dichotomy between what is said to be institutionalised and non-institutionalised worlds. Avoiding such Manichaean juxtapositions, this volume examines the extent to which the ability of Africans to envisage and pursue survival strategies in the interstices of the multiple formal and informal institutions on the continent allows for choice among difficult options of a formal as well as of an informal hue.

Exploring the reality of these capabilities and potentials offers a perspective from which to reconsider the meaning that formal institutions may have in the African context. That is, the idea of competing systems and strategies may offer more promising ways of discussing neopatrimonialism, and the destabilisation of organised systems in Africa as defects. The utility of the concept of neopatrimonialism has been questioned by Mkandawire (2015) in a move whose spirit coincides with Cheeseman's (2018: 354–5) urging that 'The study of African politics must therefore take seriously both the significance of formal institutions and the complex ways in which formal and informal institutions interact.' This book explores topics such as how advancement in the formalisation of African land systems is related to existing informal systems.

In addition to these two research topics, this volume contains three chapters focused on Africa's ongoing response to the COVID-19 pandemic. This volume is, therefore, one of the earliest academic contributions to the analysis of African Potentials and resilience in the post-COVID-19 era. The final part of this volume presents an important contribution to the concept of African Potentials that allows intellectual access to alternative ways of thinking about latent ideas of universality.

In the first chapter, 'A Legitimate Proxy? The United Nations Operation in Côte d'Ivoire from the Perspective of African Regional Organisations', Akira Sato focuses on military action taken by the United Nations Operation in Côte d'Ivoire (UNOCI) peacekeeping operation in April 2011, discussing how international legitimacy was established to support military intervention in Africa. According to Sato, the UNOCI was endorsed by the Security Council's resolution to nullify the military capacity of former President Laurent Gbagbo's troops with a view to stopping their attacks on civilians and United Nations' personnel. In this sense, the UNOCI action can be considered as an intervention legitimised by the idea of the 'responsibility to protect (R2P)'.

Sato points out, however, that the UNOCI military action had a highly political outcome that made it more than an R2P type intervention. In the UNOCI's immediate aftermath, former Prime Minister Alassane Ouattara's troops, making use of the altered military situation, successfully captured Gbagbo, thereby ending the political and military struggle between the 'two presidents' that had been ongoing since the presidential election in November 2010. Ouattara was officially sworn in as president of the Republic in May 2011.

Sato's research question is: why would the UNOCI engage in such a daring intervention? He tries to find an answer in the attitudes of regional African organisations, specifically, the Economic Community of West African States (ECOWAS) and the African Union (AU). According to Sato, the ECOWAS expressed its desire for military intervention as early as December 2010. It reiterated this intent at the end of March 2011 and required the Security Council to endorse deployment of the ECOWAS force in Côte d'Ivoire. Sato points out that the AU, having at first sought solutions through negotiations, abandoned them in March 2011 because of Gbagbo's stubbornness. For the UNOCI, strong military action that could produce a desired political outcome would ultimately produce less criticism.

Through this interpretation, the chapter sets out two implications. First, in Côte d'Ivoire's case, the legitimacy of the United Nations Peacekeeping Operation (UN PKO) in taking military action was guaranteed by regional African organisations. In other words, according to Sato, the Security Council's decision to intervene was made multilaterally, not unilaterally. Secondly, from the standpoint of the ECOWAS, military action was taken by the UN PKO on behalf of the ECOWAS. In this sense, Sato argues that West African countries successfully realised their will to intervene by making use of proxies in a case of 'extraversion/extroversion' (Bayart 2000) in which African countries externally drew upon necessary resources.

In the second chapter, 'Overcoming the Dichotomy Between Africa and the West: Norms and Measures for Arms Transfers to Non-State Actors (NSAs)', Tamara Enomoto presents an in-depth historical analysis of international policy debates on arms transfers to NSAs, calling for a cautious examination of the dynamic relationship between Africa the 'West'.

Since the 1990s, arms transfers to NSAs have been at the centre of international policy debates on how the international community should respond to the 'new wars' (Kaldor 1999) in the Global South.

In these debates, African NSAs who have acquired arms have been criticised for committing atrocities, threatening human security and undermining the fruits of development. Urgent efforts to address this issue have been called for, and several international agreements have established regulations for arms transfers to NSAs. Such international debates and agreements have often been challenged by Africanists as imposing 'modern, Western' ideas and systems on African societies rather than considering 'African' concepts and mechanisms.

Enomoto shows that Western ideas and problem-solving mechanisms have in fact changed significantly over the course of history, such that it is difficult to determine which ideas and mechanisms should be regarded as Western. Moreover, independent African states have actively created, modified and fragmented internationally dominant Western ideas and mechanisms, adjusting them to fit their needs and interests.

As Jean-François Bayart has pointed out, more attention should be paid to the relationships that African elites are trying to establish between Africa and the rest of the world (Bayart 2000). At the same time, the stereotypical, static image of Western concepts and systems needs to be overcome. Portraying the West as a self-evident static category and over-simplifying the dichotomy between the West and Africa may hinder analyses of the ambivalence and dynamism that characterises the relationship between Africa and the rest of the world. This chapter presents the need for an in-depth analysis of the organic interaction between African elites and the international community as well as a more nuanced exploration of what are often referred to as Western ideas and mechanisms.

In Chapter 3, entitled 'Competing Local Knowledges of Indigenous Plants: Social Construction of Legitimate Rooibos Use in Post-Apartheid South Africa', Abe focuses on the dynamism of politics and discourse in terms of benefit attribution, allocation and sharing in South African rooibos production.

What crucial local knowledge informs the plant's cultivation? To what extent is the rooibos plant wild as opposed to domesticated? Who should be identified as a legitimate rights-holder? What options exist for coping with the expanding global market?

Abe begins with the debate surrounding the historical origins of rooibos use in South Africa. Though scholars have examined written records, critical information about its origins has long vanished from indigenous oral history. Various actors, including Khoisan/coloureds, Afrikaners and Russian immigrants, were involved in the agricultural cultivation of rooibos. After the end of apartheid, with a new stakeholder in the mix – the majority African National Congress (ANC) party – local knowledge about rooibos use was replaced by legislative terms and ideas imported from around the world. Rooibos has been characterised as a national plant and has faced repetitive challenges by foreign enterprises seeking to acquire patent rights. Rooibos has, therefore, emerged as possessing a dual role: it is part of a unique indigenous tradition while also being a sought-after global commodity. Such 'management of diversity' (Gebre et al. 2017: 21), with particular focus on the wild rooibos species, is discussed from a more symbolic perspective in view of African Potentials.

Wild rooibos is treated as superior to cultivated rooibos and satisfies the needs of global consumers who desire evocative images and stories. Few consumers will undertake a pilgrimage to areas of rooibos production. Competing local knowledge about rooibos use in post-apartheid South Africa generates a multilayered, dynamic discourse involving indigenous plants, indigenous ethnic groups and indigenous knowledge systems in the context of global politics. Referring to the words of Edward Kirumira (2017), Abe concludes that competing discourses on the origins of, and contributions to, current rooibos use demonstrate how rooibos indigeneity functions to create a social assemblage in a pluralistic society.

In Chapter 4, entitled 'The Working Collapsed State as a Resilient Reaction in the Contemporary World: The Case of Somalia', Mitsugi Endo describes how a collapsed state can continue to exist while not necessarily functioning, using Somalia as a representative example. Here, the concept of 'working' is the same as that used by Chabal and Daloz (1999) in the context of sub-Saharan Africa; that is, in the sense of a non-institutionalised informality of politics. The interface of a collapsed state with international or external aid is examined with respect to 'extraversion' as defined by Bayart (2000).

The concept of a collapsed state is clearly defined as a type of state without a responsible central government in an international context. Thus, the concept of a collapsed state exists only with respect to externally or internationally defined sovereignty. A collapsed state is still a legally recognised state, although collapse or failure conflates the absence of a central government with anarchy. The problem is that a collapsed state is not expected to control its territory as required internationally.

Endo discusses the dynamism of a collapsed state, drawing on an anecdote that appeared in a UN Monitoring Report (UNSC 2010) examining the role of businesspeople, including those engaged in criminal activities (i.e., actors concerned primarily with economic, rather than political or military, gain). By utilising the conceptualisation of 'interdependence sovereignty' originally developed by Krasner (1999), Endo analyses the case of the Adaani family, pointing out that sovereignty was in part effectively utilised and controlled by NSAs who eventually increased their authority by monopolising transborder transactions.

By referring to state-building activities in the context of Somalia, Endo reveals that extraversion, especially appropriation, provides the basis for the working of a collapsed state within a contemporary international system in which different groups of people seek to ensure their own survival. Paradoxically, Endo concludes that Somalian society nonetheless demonstrates resilience in the contemporary world.

In Chapter 5, 'When African Potentials Fail to Work: The Background to Recent Land Conflicts in Africa', Shinichi Takeuchi examines the reasons for land conflicts that have recently proliferated in rural Africa. The continent has witnessed fierce competition for land marked by intensifying conflict. Although land conflicts are among the more common types of conflict worldwide, recent features of land conflicts in Africa have prompted serious reflection. Increasing violence in rural areas indicates rising tensions over customary lands, which account for a significant part of the continent.

Importantly, management of customary land has been characterised by such features as negotiability, flexibility and ambiguity. These saliencies, reflecting the society's inclusiveness and egalitarian tendencies, considerably overlap with those of African Potentials as illustrated by authors such as Gebre, Ohta and Matsuda. Why, then, have land conflicts intensified in recent years despite the virtues and art of conflict management? This chapter identifies reduced availability of customary land as a crucial root cause, emphasising the importance of two structural factors: population growth and legal land reform.

Most Africans still live in rural areas, in which population size continues to increase. Demand for African land has been boosted by liberalisation policies in the context of 'Africa rising'. Huge swathes of customary land were put under deals with private companies in a short period after the 2000s. This was facilitated and further accelerated by the legal land reforms that African countries launched in the 1990s with significant donor assistance. While structural factors have increased pressures on the land, institutional factors have facilitated the legalisation and officialisation of customary land tenure, thus promoting land tenure security for specific actors while ruling it out for others. The availability of customary land in Africa has been rapidly reduced over the last several decades, contributing to the intensification of land conflicts. Examining concrete cases of recent land conflicts, this chapter shows that tension has arisen between those who used to constitute the community, such as the chief and his subjects, and those who used to establish complementary relations, such as farmers and herders. The loss of customary lands has resulted in a loss of the features – negotiability, flexibility and ambiguity – that have epitomised land management in Africa, creating tension in rural African communities.

In Chapter 6, '"Peace from Below" as an African Potential: Wars and Peace in South Sudan', Eisei Kurimoto uses a case study of South Sudan to highlight 'peace from below' (i.e. indigenous and endogenous) – as opposed to 'peace from above', which is external and imposed through war – as an exemplar of the African people's capacity for reconciliation and restoration of co-existence even under extremely difficult conditions. Kurimoto criticises the peace from above approach with regard to a massive intervention by the UN and international community between 2005 and 2013, and reconsiders

8

why peace-building programmes in South Sudan have failed.

Kurimoto details the long process of reconciliation, peace-making and peace-building efforts in South Sudan that were initiated by the Wunlit Dinka-Nuer West Bank Peace and Reconciliation Conference held deep inside the war-torn country for nine days at the end of February 1999. Kurimoto was one of 1,500 people in attendance, including people from different Dinka and Western Nuer sections, and observers and facilitators from abroad.

Kurimoto evaluates peace from below as demonstrating people's capacity to resolve conflicts and restore peaceful co-existence from an African Potentials perspective. He also cites its flexibility and creativity. In contrast, peace from above is evaluated as exogenous; conceived and planned somewhere else and transplanted into conflict zones or post-conflict areas. Kurimoto does not reject peace from above, rather, he advocates for bridging the gap and harmonising it with peace from below, particularly since the latter approach sometimes requires outside support for mediation and logistics.

In Chapter 7, 'Institutional Bricolage in Responses to Public Health Crises in South Africa: Between Path Dependency and Flexibility', Kumiko Makino first examines the ways in which African Potentials are realised in the context of the COVID-19 pandemic from the perspective of 'path dependency'. Makino notes Africa's experience in dealing with diverse infectious diseases such as HIV, tuberculosis (TB), malaria and ebola. While some argue that COVID-19 may be a critical juncture disrupting the status quo, she observes less of an abrupt change than a flexible adaptation of existing institutions in Africa's response to COVID-19, which can be understood as an example of 'institutional bricolage'.

Specifically, Makino focuses on South Africa, which had the highest cumulative number of confirmed COVID-19 cases on the African continent at the end of August 2020. South Africa also has the highest disease burden of HIV/AIDS in the world along with an active social movement comprising people living with HIV fighting for access to life-saving antiretroviral therapy. These people who have had no choice but to rely on public health care organised a group called the Treatment Action Campaign (TAC). With the support of international non-governmental organisations (NGOs) advocating

9

for equitable access to medicine, the TAC succeeded in changing the South African government policy in the early 2000s.

South African AIDS activism has had a significant impact on global AIDS governance. Over the past two decades, access to AIDS treatment in low- and middle-income countries has grown dramatically. The fight against HIV/AIDS has enabled South Africa to respond swiftly to the COVID-19 pandemic by adapting existing HIV/AIDS-related institutions and networks to combat the new public health crisis. The activities of community health workers are a notable example of how systems that were shaped in the context of HIV/AIDS and TB have been adapted for the COVID-19 response. Tens of thousands of community health workers (CHWs), whose primary duties were to respond daily to HIV/AIDS and TB, went to resource-limited communities to conduct proactive mass community screening for early COVID-19 detection.

In Chapter 8, '*Kusina Amai Hakuendwe*: Diasporan Zimbabweans, COVID-19 and Nomadic Global Citizenship', Artwell Nhemachena builds on the Shona saying *kusina amai hakuendwe* (do not wander off too far from your mother) to critique deportations and repatriations of foreign citizens in the context of COVID-19 by interrogating notions of nomadic subjectivity, nomadic citizenship and the notion of nomadic global citizenship.

Taking note of struggles that former colonies are engaged in, demanding (from imperial centres) the repatriation of centuries-old skulls and skeletons of their African anticolonial heroes and heroines, Nhemachena argues that empire, paradoxically, delights in retaining dead African anticolonial heroes while deporting living Africans in the context of COVID-19.

In developing this argument, Nhemachena posits that empires prefer dead over living Africans and, thus, it would prefer Africa to be populated by dead Africans (what this chapter calls necrozenship) who are currently being repatriated. Noting the ways in which colonial citizenship was premised on colonial dispossession and exploitation of indigenous people, Nhemachena suggests the term 'conizenship' to mark colonial modes of citizenship that were premised on dispossessing and exploiting indigenous people.

By situating the Shona saying in the context of the emergent

Global State and global citizenship that is being ushered in by COVID-19, Nhemachena argues for a delicate balance between change and stasis. By postulating the theories of conizenship and necrozenship, Nhemachena anticipates a world in which the dead and death are celebrated as life is destroyed. By arguing that such an emergent world, which Nhemachena names the post-binary world, is one that dwells on the philosophy of brinkmanship between death and life, he wonders about the fate of human citizens in a world that dispenses with the binary distinction between the dead and the living.

In Chapter 9, entitled 'Epidemics, Negotiability and Futurity in Africa and Beyond', Ato Kwamena Onoma invokes the manipulation of hardships caused by the 2013–2016 ebola virus disease epidemic and the ongoing COVID-19 pandemic in intra-communal interactions to highlight the pervasiveness of negotiability in African social interactions. This constant negotiability points to the limited weight the past exerts on future social dynamics on a continent that has all too often been portrayed as a place of tradition where the past exerts an overwhelming influence on the future. While this chapter is significantly rooted in Onoma's ongoing research into the interactions between epidemics and xenophobia, he also draws on earlier and current work on a broad range of issues, including land rights, refugee–host relations and interment practices.

By referring to recent advances in the new institutionalism, Onoma indicates the limited capacity of institutions to structure the future in definitive ways. Thus, room for negotiations by individual agents is a peculiarity of the African continent. Negotiability may not only be more pervasive than it is often portrayed but it may also have positive potentials that are not always acknowledged in the rush to decry the African continent's weak institutions.

From this perspective, Onoma makes two insightful observations. First is the fact that structures have a limited bearing on the future. That all things are constantly negotiated provides greater room for recalibrating social relations and structures and correcting social inequalities; inequalities borne out of one moment of negotiation can always be overturned in the future. Second, is the impact of constant negotiability on the nature of conflicts. The possibility of future negotiations transforms conflicts from one-off, do-or-die

11

events to open-ended processes in which there are potentially no permanent losers or winners. Today's losers can harbour hope of winning the next round, just as the winners of one round are mindful that they may lose the next round. Losing ceases to be a moment of permanent loss that must be avoided at all costs, and winning ceases to be a moment of triumph that should be exploited to the worst disadvantage of the losers.

In the last chapter of the volume, 'African Potentials and the Thought of Universal Humanity: Latent Universalism in African Popular Cultures', Michael Neocosmos points out that the conceptualisation of African Potentials has proven to be an important innovation that provides intellectual access to alternative conceptions of the universal, which are of central importance for the world today. Neocosmos aims to contribute to a shift in academic discourse from a focus on identity (which has been the case over the past 20 years) to a focus on humanity; from a focus on difference to shared commonality.

Neocosmos examines latency in the context of Southern Africa – for example, in popular sayings such as 'a chief is a chief by his people' – that are common in all Southern African cultures. For such sayings to be meaningful and effective they need to be embodied within collective political practices. Neocosmos expands on the following three points: (1) colonial domination and the transformation of cultures, the destruction of the common and the introduction of state-regulated hierarchies through dehumanisation and 'thingification' (Césaire, 1972); (2) resistance against colonialism and its institutions as a way of re-introducing the idea of collective humanity; and (3) the idea of *uBuntu* and other similar cultural prescriptions as *potentially* of universal import.

Neocosmos suggests that the contradiction between inequalities within cultures and the latent potential universalism inherent in popular traditions constitutes a dialectic at the core of all human struggles for emancipation from oppression. Therefore, what is arguably common to African popular conceptions is the latency, or potentiality, of the idea of universal humanity which has the possibility of being actualised. Yet the idea of universal humanity cannot be enacted simply via the exercise of power, but only actualised through popular self-organisation.

In this way, Neocosmos argues for the necessity of shifting the discussion of African cultures from an exclusive emphasis on identity to what he believes are latent ideas of universality. Their latency suggests they must be activated, and it is his contention that this can only happen through collective struggle in which the oppressed are the main contributors to the development of new theoretical concepts toward the development of a new universal history.

Acknowledgement

This work was supported by JSPS KAKENHI Grant Number JP16H06318.

References

Bayart, J-F. (2000) 'Africa in the World: A History of Extraversion', *African Affairs* No. 99, pp. 217–67.

Brett, P. and Gissel, L. E. (2018) 'Explaining African Participation in International Courts', *African Affairs* No. 117/467, pp. 195–216.

Césaire, A. (1972) *Discourse on Colonialism*, New York: Monthly Review Press.

Chabal, P. and Daloz, J.-P. (1999) *Africa Works: Disorder as Political Instrument*, London: James Currey.

Cheeseman, N. (2018) 'Conclusion – Political Institutions and Democracy in Africa: A Research Agenda', in Nic Cheeseman (ed.) *Institution and Democracy in Africa: How the Rules of the Game Shape Political Developments*, Cambridge: Cambridge University Press, pp. 351–75.

Clark, P. (2018) *Distant Justice: The Impact of the International Criminal Court on African Politics*, Cambridge: Cambridge University Press.

Gebre, Y., Ohta, I. and Matsuda, M. (2017) 'Introduction: Achieving Peace and Coexistence through African Potentials', in Y. Gebre, I. Ohta and M. Mtasuda (eds) *African Virtues in the Pursuit of Conviviality: Exploring Local Solutions in Light of Global Prescriptions*,

Langaa RPCIG, pp. 3–37.

Hagman, T. (2016) *Stabilization, Extraversion and Political Settlements in Somalia*, Nairobi: Rift Valley Institute.

Hountondji, P. J. (1995) 'Producing Knowledge in Africa Today the Second Bashorun M. K. O. Abiola Distinguished Lecture', *African Studies Review,* Vol. 38, No. 3, pp. 1–10. https://www.jstor.org/stable/524790?seq=1#metadata_info_tab_contents (accessed: 14 December 2020).

Kaldor, M. (1999) *New and Old Wars: Organized Violence in a Global Era*, Stanford: Stanford University Press.

Kirumira, E. (2017) 'Revisiting Indigeneity: African Potentials as a Discourse for Sustainable Development in Africa', in Y. Gebre, I. Ohta and M. Mtasuda (eds) *African Virtues in the Pursuit of Conviviality: Exploring Local Solutions in Light of Global Prescriptions*, Langaa RPCIG, pp. 379–97.

Mahoney, J. and Thelen, K. (eds) (2015) *Advances in Comparative-Historical Analysis*, Cambridge: Cambridge University Press.

Mamdani, M. (1996) *Citizen and Subject: Africa and the Legacy of Late Colonialism*, Princeton: Princeton University Press.

Mkandawire, T. (2015) 'Neopatrimonialism and the Political Economy of Economic Performance in Africa: Critical Reflections', *World Politics*, Vol. 67, No. 3, pp. 563–612, https://doi.org/10.1017/S004388711500009X.

_____(2001) 'Thinking about Developmental States in Africa', *Cambridge Journal of Economics, Vol. 25, No. 3, pp. 289–314,* https://doi.org/10.1093/cje/25.3.289.

UNSC (United Nations, Security Council) (2010) *Report of the Monitoring Group on Somalia Pursuant to Security Council Resolution 1853 (2008)*, New York: United Nations.

Chapter 1

A Legitimate Proxy? The United Nations Operation in Côte d'Ivoire from the Perspective of African Regional Organisations

Akira Sato

1. Introduction

In this chapter, I discuss the conditions that enabled the United Nations Peacekeeping Operation (UN PKO) military operation in Côte d'Ivoire (officially, the United Nations Operation in Côte d'Ivoire) in April 2011. This military operation brought about the ouster of former President Laurent Gbagbo, who had refused to resign. As such, the operation was extremely political in nature. The question examined here is why a military intervention of a clear political nature was implemented. The answer to this question is highly important to peace and security in Africa.

The thesis of this chapter is that the attitudes of African regional organisations played important roles in the realisation of this military operation. The regional organisations associated with this issue were the Economic Community of West African States (ECOWAS) and the African Union (AU), which were engaged in active initiatives to solve the post-election crisis in Côte d'Ivoire. Noteworthy was the ECOWAS's attitude, which made clear the organisation's preference for military intervention. From the perspective of the United Nations (UN), the fact that Africans were showing a desire to work aggressively toward a solution created an environment that made it easy for the UN to engage in a military operation that could have major political consequences.

In this chapter, I discuss this issue in detail and make suggestions regarding the thesis's contribution to the concept of 'African Potentials', which forms the basis of the project. To this end, I utilise

Bayart's concept of 'extraversion/extroversion' (Bayart 2000). Through this concept, Bayart presented a perspective that he described as follows: For the political elites of Africa, '[t]he external environment thus turned into a major resource in the process of political centralisation and economic accumulation' (Bayart 2000: 218–9). I believe it is beneficial to examine the case of Côte d'Ivoire from this vantage point.

In this case, African countries facilitated military operations by the UN PKO, one of the main external forces in the region, by expressing their preferences through regional organisations. This led to actions that ultimately concluded the post-election crisis in Côte d'Ivoire. This can be understood as a situation wherein African countries successfully extracted the benefits of maintaining peace and security on the continent from powers outside Africa. Although efforts are being made to create the institutional environment necessary for the realisation of 'African solutions to Africa's problems', the fact that African nations are still lacking in military capacity and global legitimacy prevents this from being realised at this point in time. Thus, the nations of Africa successfully compensated for this lack through operations conducted by the UN PKO, which acted as their proxy.

In this chapter, I attempt to develop each of the above ideas. First, I describe the influence of external parties on the domestic politics of Côte d'Ivoire. Next, I contend that the reason for this highly political military operation lay in the legitimacy entrusted to the UN through the clearly expressed desires of African regional organisations to act as their agent. Thus, I argue that African countries demonstrated that it is possible to obtain resources from external sources even in the domain of peace and security and that this process provides a glimpse of 'African Potentials'.

2. The Political Trajectory of Côte d'Ivoire Leading up to Intervention by the UN PKO

Côte d'Ivoire, which has been praised as a rare 'model of stability and development' in sub-Saharan Africa since gaining independence in 1960, fell into political instability after the death of President Félix

Houphouët-Boigny (1993), the leader of the country since it achieved independence. His successor, President Henri Konan Bédié, pursued authoritarian policies and continued on a course of relentless oppression in which he employed ethnic discrimination and xenophobia against his greatest rival, former Prime Minister Alassane Dramane Ouattara. In December 1999, the Bédié regime was toppled after it failed to stop a revolt by the military, which was dissatisfied with its treatment by the regime. In the wake of the Bédié government's collapse, a military regime was established, with former Chief of Staff Robert Guéï installed as its leader. During the presidential election in October 2000, a protest movement against purported election tampering instigated by Guéï developed into a massive riot that led to the deaths of several hundred people. Although President Laurent Gbagbo, who finally won the election, pursued a policy of resuming dialogue with major politicians and pursuing national reconciliation, civil war broke out in September 2002 when a rebel force composed mainly of remnants of the military regime took up arms against the Gbagbo government. Based in the north of the country, the rebel force was prevented from advancing into the south by the continued presence of the French military, which had intervened to protect French citizens in Côte d'Ivoire. Thus, a military front was established, and a stalemate quickly ensued.

The fact that the rebel force, which had failed in its original goal of seizing political power, turned its attention to establishing peace contributed to the relatively rapid peace agreement reached in January 2003 (the Linas–Marcoussis Agreement). Also, in 2003, the ECOWAS deployed a military force to Côte d'Ivoire, and in April 2004, the UN PKO force was added to these troops. Thus, the United Nations Operation in Côte d'Ivoire (UNOCI)[1] was born. Any resumption of large-scale military conflict was suppressed by the presence of international troops; however, the peace process suffered a major period of stagnation for the first several years. The main cause of this was the non-cooperative stance of President Gbagbo, who opposed the reduction of presidential powers called for in the Linas–Marcoussis Agreement. The turning point came in March 2007. The peace agreement reached at that time (the

Ouagadougou Agreement) called for the restoration of presidential powers, which made the president more supportive of the peace process. Thereafter, progress was made on important elements of the peace process, such as the reunification of national territory; re-deployment of necessary administrative personnel; disarmament, demobilisation and reintegration (DDR); and revision of the election process. In October 2010, the country was finally able to hold a presidential election.

The election, which was important as the culmination of the peace process, started in October 2010 with the first round of voting. Since no single candidate won a clear majority of votes, in November of that year, the two candidates who had received the highest number of votes in the first round – the incumbent Gbagbo and the challenger, former Prime Minister Ouattara – advanced to the decisive round of voting. Upon counting the votes, the *Commission Électorale Indépendante* (CEI) [Independent Electoral Commission] announced that Ouattara had won the election. The CEI's announcement was certified by the Special Envoy of the UN Secretary General,[2] who held all certification authority over the election under the peace process. The result was subsequently widely supported by the countries of Africa. However, Gbagbo refused to accept the decision of the CEI and, instead, declared his own victory. He then held his own inauguration ceremony and formed a cabinet.[3] In response, Ouattara held his own inauguration ceremony and formed his own independent cabinet. The result was that Côte d'Ivoire had two presidents and two governments. Gbagbo refused to abide by the request of other African countries to resign, and he used military force to quell domestic movements demanding that he step down. Arbitration by the AU reached a dead end in mid-March 2011. At that point, Ouattara issued a presidential decree creating a new military force known as the *Forces Républicaines de Côte d'Ivoire* (FRCI) [Republican Forces of Côte d'Ivoire], which began operations to topple Gbagbo, on 29 March.[4]

On 30 March 2011, UN Security Council Resolution 1975 was adopted. This resolution reconfirmed that the UNOCI was 'to use all necessary means to carry out its mandate to protect civilians under imminent threat of physical violence' based on Chapter VII of the

United Nations Charter.[5] It also emphasised the UN's complete support of this effort. The mandate to 'protect civilians under imminent threat of physical violence' was originally established in 2004 in the early stages of the UNOCI deployment. However, it was reconfirmed at this stage as a means to stop President Gbagbo, who continued to use heavy weaponry against civilians and UN facilities. At the time, Gbagbo displayed no intention of relinquishing political power despite his growing international isolation. Therefore, it could be anticipated that Gbagbo would use the heavy weaponry he possessed to continue his resistance.[6]

On 31 March 2011, the day after Resolution 1975 was adopted, Ouattara's and Gbagbo's forces clashed in urban warfare in the country's largest city, Abidjan. This led to a humanitarian crisis, when all essential services were cut off for the several million residents of that city. The UNOCI then began its operations. On two occasions, 4 April and 11 April, the UNOCI conducted air strikes against Gbagbo's bases with the assistance of the French military, destroying heavy weaponry such as tanks and rocket launchers. Immediately following the airstrike of 11 April, Gbagbo was arrested by Ouattara's newly formed FRCI, marking the end of the 4½-month-long post-election crisis and the end of the transition period that had persisted since the outbreak of civil war in September 2002.[7]

3. How Was This Intervention Possible?

With the announcement of the CEI, the UNOCI's military operation made the result of the presidential election come true, garnering wide international support. This played a role in stopping political forces from deviating from the peace process; the importance of this became clear in the following events. UN Security Resolution 1975 of 30 March 2011 sanctioned multiple leaders including Gbagbo, naming them as 'individuals who obstruct[ed] peace and reconciliation in Côte d'Ivoire, obstruct[ed] the work of UNOCI and other international actors in Côte d'Ivoire, and commit[ted] serious violations of human rights and international humanitarian law'.[8] Naturally, these sanctions included measures such as freezing the named persons' assets and prohibiting them from

19

travelling abroad, but they did not recommend the physical removal of Gbagbo and the others named in the sanctions. Nevertheless, the sanctions meant that the UN, which was firmly committed to the peace process, concluded that Gbagbo was no longer a part of that peace process but an 'obstruction' and 'disruptor'. Specifically, the sanctions accepted a 'peace process without Gbagbo'. Even though he had already been removed as a result of the UNOCI military operations, this would pre-emptively prevent the peace process from becoming mired in an impasse.

The UNOCI intervention rendered the military force of Gbagbo, one of the actors in the civil war, powerless, eventually breaking the existing stalemate. It was also the deciding factor in the military victory (in the form of the confinement of Gbagbo) of Ouattara, Gbagbo's opponent. The UNOCI did not 'participate in hostilities' with the intention of expressly supporting Ouattara, but the timing of their intervention played a role in settling the conflict between the two men. Thus, it can be considered that a form of external military intervention had had a major consequence in the political history of Côte d'Ivoire.

The question that arises then is whether the UN PKO should be engaged in military operations that have such major political impacts. The offensive undertaken by the UN PKO was conducted under the authority of Chapter VII of the United Nations Charter, which was invoked by the UN Security Council Resolution. Its purpose was to stop attacks by the Gbagbo administration on civilians and UN personnel. Researchers have noted that this military operation is an example of intervention based on the 'responsibility to protect' (Bellamy 2009). However, the political effects (such as those described in this chapter) of such action were not originally implicated in the notion of the 'responsibility to protect'. Rather, they should be considered secondary effects.

It is impossible to think that an actor such as the UN PKO, which was closely observing the political situation on site, was unaware of the outcome a military action would produce. The problematic behaviour targeted by this military action was orchestrated exclusively by Gbagbo. Had it been based on the circumstances unfolding at the time, namely the military engagement in Abidjan between Gbagbo's forces and the opposing military organisation formed by Ouattara, then it would have been obvious that UN PKO intervention would benefit Ouattara.

Moreover, an examination of modern African history highlights frequent examples of military action by extra-regional actors – not only the UN but also superpowers and former colonial powers – that have had a major influence on the political circumstances of African nations. In many cases, this action took the form of unilateral intervention and, as a result, it was harshly criticised by African countries. The UN military operation in Côte d'Ivoire also carried the potential risk of harsh criticism by Africans. Why, then, was the UN PKO able to engage in this military operation despite this risk? What was the background against which the decision was made to accept such risks by undertaking the UNOCI military operation?

4. The Response of African Regional Organisations to the Post-Election Crisis in Côte d'Ivoire

The key to answering these questions is found in the position statements issued by African regional organisations. The main points addressed in this chapter are as follows. The ECOWAS, of which Côte d'Ivoire is a member, indicated as early as December 2010, when the so-called 'period of two presidents' began, that it would be willing to carry out military intervention if necessary. At the end of March 2011, just before the UN PKO military intervention, the ECOWAS requested that the UN Security Council approve its own military operation. Several countries in the AU supported Gbagbo and, although attempts were made to develop a mediation plan that considered his position, these attempts were eventually abandoned. By March 2011, the AU's position had shifted to one that saw no viable option but for President Gbagbo to resign. The fact that the major regional organisations in Africa took these positions greatly reduced the possibility that the anticipated secondary consequences of military action would include harsh criticism by the nations of Africa.

I now refer to documents as I reconstruct the specific processes through which each of the above events developed.[9] The African

Union Peace and Security Council (AUPSC) met on 4 December, 2010, immediately after the post-election crisis occurred. With reference to President Gbagbo, who refused to accept the CEI's announcement of the election results, it stated, 'Council expressed AU's total rejection of any attempt to create a *fait accompli* to undermine the electoral process and the will of the people'. At a meeting held five days later on 9 December, the AUPSC accepted the final statement issued by the ECOWAS indicating that Ouattara had won the election and was therefore president. It also announced the suspension of Côte d'Ivoire's participation in all AU activities until the duly elected president had complete control of all national authority. Furthermore, the AUPSC issued the following formal statement: 'Council reaffirms its determination to take, if necessary, other measures against those who undermine the popular will as expressed on 28 November and duly certified by the Special Representative of the United Nations Secretary-General, incite violence, and commit violations of human rights'.[10]

These announcements and statements indicate that the AUPSC was aware of the problems related to the 'responsibility to protect' and that the incumbent's re-inauguration in Côte d'Ivoire was not dependent on the procedures outlined in the Constitution (unconstitutional regime change). Their deep concern over this was thus made apparent. Nevertheless, some member nations, such as South Africa and Angola, were intent on developing a solution that would consider Gbagbo's demands;[11] consequently, the AUPSC took no further measures.[12]

The ECOWAS had a more deeply rooted political stance than the AUPSC. The final statement of the ECOWAS Extraordinary Summit Meeting on 24 December 2010 stated that the 'status of Mr Alassane Ouattara as the legitimate president of Côte d'Ivoire is non-negotiable' [originally in French]. If Gbagbo were to refuse demands that he step down, then the 'ECOWAS would have no choice but to use all necessary means including measures such as the legitimate use of military power to ensure the will of the people of Côte d'Ivoire' [originally in French]. This statement mentions the possibility of military intervention, indicating that the ECOWAS had abandoned hope of a solution through peaceful mediation.[13] As a result, the AU took on the role of mediator.

The AUPSC continued to express its desire for a solution through peaceful means. A high-level panel was established, and a policy on determining procedures for resolving the crisis through discussion with representatives of Côte d'Ivoire was adopted. Among the members of this panel was South African President Jacob Zuma, whose position considered Gbagbo's claims. The fact that President Zuma was included on the panel reflects the discretion of the AUPSC.[14] However, despite this, the AUPSC's statement on 11 March 2011, issued during a meeting about receiving the proposal submitted to it by the high-level panel held on the previous day, did not mention acceptance of Gbagbo's maintaining his claim to the presidency. Instead, the AUPSC statement recommended that talks with representatives of Côte d'Ivoire to resolve the crisis begin as soon as possible. Furthermore, the AUPSC statement included the phrase 'the outgoing President' to refer to Gbagbo, suggesting that those in the AU who were involved in the decision-making process had reached the *de facto* conclusion that Gbagbo had to resign as President.[15] This was a decisive event, as it came when Gbagbo had become completely isolated from the rest of Africa.

Nevertheless, Gbagbo maintained his hard-line stance. As a result, there were few indications that any discussions among stakeholders such as those proposed by the high-level panel would take place. This also meant that the AU's attempts to act as a mediator in reaching a peaceful solution had collapsed. Consequently, the ECOWAS saw this as an opportunity to issue another position statement. At the ECOWAS Summit Meeting held on 24 March 2011, the following official statement was issued to the UN Security Council: '[ECOWAS] requests the UN Security Council to authorise the immediate implementation of the Authority Decisions of December 2010.' This statement referenced the statement issued on 24 December 2010 by the Extraordinary Summit Meeting, which mentioned the 'use of legitimate military force in order to ensure the will of the people of Côte d'Ivoire'.[16] Furthermore, the aim of the statement issued by the ECOWAS Summit Meeting in March was not only 'to protect life and property', which could be interpreted as being included in their intention to protect civilians but also 'to facilitate the immediate transfer of power to Mr Alassane Ouattara'. In other words, the purpose of the ECOWAS proposal regarding military intervention was explicitly 'regime change'. This differed starkly from the response of the AUPSC, which made public mention of Gbagbo's resignation but lacked a clear plan for achieving this goal.

Upon receiving the ECOWAS proposal, the Security Council convened on 30 March, but no agreement was reached regarding a military operation aimed at bringing about 'regime change', as requested by the ECOWAS. As indicated above, Security Council Resolution 1975, which was ratified on that day, reaffirmed the UNOCI mandate to protect civilians and again emphasised the 'use of all necessary means' under Chapter VII of the UN Charter. During the debate over its ratification, the representative from India expressed the following view: 'Those peacekeepers could not be agents of regime change.'[17] This was an attempt to reaffirm the position that PKO activities should be politically neutral. In other words, this view emphasised that a line was to be drawn between future UNOCI activities and the ECOWAS proposal and that the sole objective of UNOCI activities would be to protect civilians. Five days after this debate, the UNOCI operation began.

5. The Legitimacy Underpinning the UN PKO Military Operation

As seen from the above progression of events, the positions of the AUPSC, the ECOWAS and the UN Security Council regarding the post-election crisis in Côte d'Ivoire were not in agreement. The AUPSC indicated that it would examine all possible measures designed to encourage Gbagbo to resign and that its sole objective was a peaceful resolution. The ECOWAS was originally open to the idea of military intervention to remove Gbagbo from power and expressed the desire for military intervention. The Security Council increased pressure on Gbagbo through sanctions that targeted him individually but at the same time indicated that these sanctions did not express support for regime change but opposition to the 'obstruction of the peace process' based on previously existing resolutions.[18] Finally, the Security Council approved the UN PKO military operation, but the only expressed objective of this operation was to protect civilians. Thus, the differences among the intentions of these three actors are clear.

However, examining how events unfolded over time, one sees that the initiatives of these three actors gradually inched toward a military operation. The initial position of the AU was to reject the legitimacy of the Gbagbo regime as reflecting an 'unconstitutional regime change'. Based on this premise, the ECOWAS and the AU successively attempted to mediate through peaceful means. Although these efforts were ultimately fruitless, through the process, political consensus in the AU was reached on rejecting the legitimacy of the Gbagbo regime. In response, the Security Council issued designated sanctions that acknowledged Gbagbo's 'obstruction' and his role as a 'disruptor'. This created an international environment in which Gbagbo had no choice but to resign. Specifically, even if military action were subsequently to begin and the consequence of that action were Gbagbo's resignation, the three actors could avoid blame for the political consequences of military action.

Furthermore, by supporting a military action whose purpose, according to the ECOWAS, was to remove Gbagbo, the UNOCI would be shielded from any criticism by the ECOWAS and the nations of Africa even if carrying out the action had political consequences outside the scope of its mandate. The fact that the AU had clearly defined the scope of such action under the law as the 'responsibility to protect' removed all barriers to the UNOCI's engaging in military operations. In other words, as each of these three actors responded in accordance with the limits of its authority and circumstances within its own organisation, they could all agree that there was no option other than Gbagbo's removal. By cooperating and distributing the ethical responsibilities among themselves, they created an environment in which they were all in *de facto* support of the military action that would lead to the removal of Gbagbo.

6. Was the United Nations a 'Proxy' for the Nations of Africa?

After the many conflicts that occurred in the 1990s, initiatives to realise the historically shared concept of 'African solutions to Africa's problems' gradually progressed. In short, the establishment of the AU, which embodied two new principles that did not exist during the time of the Organisation of African Unity (OAU), represented a major step (Williams 2007; Murithi 2007). One of these new principles involved criticism of 'unconstitutional regime change', and the other was the 'responsibility to protect'. To facilitate initiatives that would lead to conflict resolution based on these two principles, the AUPSC and the African Standby Force (ASF), among other institutions, were founded. These organisations were the physical embodiments of these principles, and they functioned to create a comprehensive African Peace and Security Architecture (ASPA) (Sato 2019).

As the above events unfolded, the efforts of actors outside Africa to contribute to resolving this conflict were not opposed. The activities of extra-regional actors to maintain peace in Africa, for which there had been little enthusiasm up to the mid-1990s, rapidly increased in the latter half of the 1990s, mainly in the form of UN PKOs. This led to dramatic increases in the number of personnel in Africa (Takeuchi 2008). Specifically, the nations of Africa simultaneously engaged in aggressive initiatives on their own to resolve conflicts and pursued the 'strengthening of cooperation' centred on the UN, the most important mediator in the region (Takizawa 2010).

The 2011 UN PKO operation in Côte d'Ivoire could be considered one of the consequences of these efforts to strengthen cooperation. Through this cooperation, the nations of Africa sought to establish the legitimacy of military intervention. By consolidating this general attitude across Africa, the AU supported resolving the crisis through the emergence of a regime rooted in the election process. Through its consolidation of the attitudes prevalent in West Africa, the ECOWAS showed active support for the military option as a method of resolving the crisis. Thus, various actors in Africa used the announcement of their stances regarding the issue as a way to guarantee the legitimacy of potentially delicate military actions by the UN PKO that could have significant political consequences. Thus, as became evident, the case of Côte d'Ivoire coincided with the development of an international cooperative relationship beginning in the late 1990s for the purpose of guaranteeing peace and security in Africa.

In addition, however, a new factor was also apparent. With Bayart's extraversion/extroversion in mind, this factor is revealed when considering how this case looks from the standpoint of the ECOWAS.

Since the 1990s, the ECOWAS has engaged several times in military intervention among its member nations. The statements of intent issued by the ECOWAS regarding these military actions were not empty words, but were supported by its ability to take action. Thus, if the endorsement of the Security Council could be obtained, the ECOWAS could consider implementing military action in Côte d'Ivoire. However, the Security Council did not approve military action by the ECOWAS and, instead, implemented its own military operation via the UN PKO, with the assistance of the French military already on site. Assuming that intervention by the ECOWAS was possible, it would seem that the UN PKO was acting as a 'proxy' of the ECOWAS when it undertook this military intervention. If we describe this in light of the extraversion/extroversion concept, we see that the ECOWAS skilfully took advantage of the external environment to drive international actors to engage in military action. This, in turn, was beneficial to the peace and security of West Africa. In other words, the ECOWAS achieved its military objective through a 'proxy', the UN PKO.

Naturally, the reasons why the Security Council and the UNOCI, stationed on the ground, decided it would be more appropriate for the UNOCI than for the ECOWAS to carry out the military operation will have to be determined through historical examination of the perceptions at the time and the chronology of the decision-making process. It is likely that the Security Council believed at the time that the ECOWAS' military capability was not great enough to realise their political intentions. It is also possible that the Security Council was afraid that if the ECOWAS became a participant in the conflict, it might develop into an international conflict among nations in West Africa. If the ECOWAS forces were deployed in addition to the UN PKO and the French troops already engaged, then the cost of coordinating the various headquarters may have become excessive. I look forward to further research on this issue.

Until such research is conducted, however, we can only rely on our present observations, which in my case, include the following. The fact that it seems as though the UN PKO was acting as a representative of the ECOWAS is paradoxical. The ambitious measures against regional conflicts, undertaken mainly by the UN and developed countries of the world immediately following the end of the Cold War – measures, which, as mentioned, occurred against the background of demands for increased international cooperation and coordination – were soon tested by the events that unfolded in Bosnia and Somalia, which forced their reconsideration. Subsequently, there was an international trend of praising Africa for taking the initiative to resolve local conflicts on its own. In the midst of this, the United States and major nations of Europe did not become directly involved in the conflicts, but engaged in a policy through which they focused their efforts on logistic support to improve the peacekeeping capability of the nations of Africa when they deployed troops. Following this, a peace-building mission by the nations of Africa developed. Entering the 2000s, peace-building missions that included troops deployed by the AU after its establishment were carried out multiple times. Considering these as extensions of the international environment that had emerged over the preceding 20 years, we can understand that it should have been possible to consider the option of an intervention mission into Côte d'Ivoire led by the ECOWAS, in other words, by Africans. Nevertheless, the opposite actually occurred. The intervention was not led by Africans but by actors representing a broad segment of the international community.

The example of military action in Côte d'Ivoire elucidates the process by which the relationship of actors from Africa with those outside Africa regarding conflict resolution on the continent is currently being dynamically reorganised, even though it includes these paradoxical elements.

7. Conclusion

In this chapter, I focused on the UN PKO military operation

conducted in response to the post-election crisis in Côte d'Ivoire and examined the conditions that made this military action possible despite its potential political consequences. The stances of the ECOWAS and the AU during the process of responding to the crisis were important to the creation of the unshakable legitimacy of the implementation of UN Security Council Resolutions and the UN PKO intervention. This is one of the assertions made in this chapter. In addition, the close cooperation between African and extra-regional actors can be praised as a culmination of the conflict resolution initiatives that have continually been undertaken in Africa in the post-Cold War era.

Furthermore, in this chapter, I highlighted that one of the intriguing aspects of the relation between the ECOWAS and the UN PKO in the Côte d'Ivoire case was how the latter played the role of 'proxy' for the former. This relationship resulted from the success of the ECOWAS in taking advantage of the external environment. Considered from the stance of the African political elite, one in which '[t]he external environment thus turned into a major resource in the process of political centralisation and economic accumulation', which Bayart has utilised in his concepts of extraversion/ extroversion, this phenomenon has important implications for 'African Potentials'.

This suggests another idea discussed in this chapter, namely, the relationship of cooperation between the nations of Africa and extra-regional actors in the field of conflict resolution. Here, one can imagine a new phenomenon in which 'Africa delegates to extra-regional actors'. If this were to happen, the nations of Africa could conceive of the possibility that they might be successful in utilising the behaviour of external actors for their own benefit. Although some have criticised the concept of 'African solutions to Africa's problems' as simply an excuse used by the developed countries of the world to evade responsibility for the important duty of resolving conflicts in Africa, I assert in this chapter that when examining the situation carefully, one sees that the nations of Africa have actually utilised external resources to resolve conflicts. The diplomatic skill that led to this conclusion is certainly an important element of 'African Potentials'.

Endnotes

[1] The ECOWAS military missions and activities of the French troops were approved under Chapter VII of the United Nations Charter in Security Council Resolution 1464 dated 4 February 2003. The UNOCI was created by Security Council Resolution 1528 dated 27 February, 2004, and was also empowered to operate under Chapter VII of the United Nations Charter.

[2] This authority, which is held by the Special Envoy of the UN Secretary General, is specified under Security Council Resolution 1765 dated 16 July 2007 (S/RES/1765, para. 6), which constrains all parties in the peace process.

[3] Gbagbo was unhappy with the CEI announcement and filed a complaint with the Constitutional Court, claiming irregularities in voting. The Constitutional Court holds ultimate authority to approve election results under the law of Côte d'Ivoire. In line with Gbagbo's complaint, the Constitutional Court ruled that all votes in several districts (hundreds of thousands of votes in total) were invalid, and because Gbagbo was ahead after these votes were eliminated, he was declared the winner. However, the legal process states that if the Constitutional Court decides that a vote is invalid, another election should be held. Therefore, the Constitutional Court's decision to skip this step and declare a winner lacked legal grounding. For details, see Sato (2011).

[4] The FRCI was composed mainly of former rebels.

[5] S/RES/1975, para. 6.

[6] On 7 April 2011, Gbagbo-aligned mercenaries stormed the residence of the Japanese ambassador in Abidjan. The residence is close to the presidential palace where Gbagbo was hiding, and it is believed that Gbagbo's supporters wanted to build a defensive base. This incident clearly demonstrates the hard-line stance of Gbagbo's side, who continued to resist, even if that meant putting foreign diplomats in danger.

[7] Ouattara was sworn in on 6 May 2011, and on 21 May, the UN Secretary General attended a large inauguration ceremony in the capital, Yamoussoukro. The FRCI's operation to clear out the remaining Gbagbo supporters hiding in Abidjan was also completed in May. The Ouattara government was fully launched with the formation of a cabinet on 1 June. On 23 November 2011, the International Criminal Court issued an arrest

warrant for former President Gbagbo on charges of 'crimes against humanity (murder, rape, other inhumane acts or—in the alternative—attempted murder, and persecution)' committed in Abidjan and other parts of the country by government security forces and by Gbagbo's militias and mercenaries in the post-election crisis phase. Gbagbo was later imprisoned in The Hague, where a trial was held. He was released in 2019. ICC prosecutors are currently filing an appeal.

[8] S/RES/1975, para. 12, Annex I.

[9] An earlier draft of this section was presented in Sato (2012).

[10] PSC/PR/COMM. 1 (CCLII), 9 December 2010, para. 6.

[11] A proposal was made to recount votes or repeat the election in the constituencies in question. However, Gbagbo's side, which considered him the legitimate winner, refused these proposals.

[12] The AU's 2000 document AHG/Decl., 5, which lays out a response to the 'unconstitutional changes of government', suspended the government from the organisation and issued a statement of condemnation, then gave the perpetrators of the unconstitutional change up to six months to restore constitutional order. However, no grace period has been specified.

[13] ECOWAS, N° 193/2010, 24 December 2010, para. 6, 10. Based on this final statement, the ECOWAS held a meeting of the general staff of its member states from 28 December 2010 to 18 January 2011, to discuss plans for military action and preparations for logistics and deployment. At this meeting, Burkina Faso, Senegal, Nigeria and others expressed their intention to send troops (ISS 2011: 10).

[14] Other members were Mauritania President Abdel Aziz (chairman), Burkina Faso President Compaore, Tanzania President Kikwete and Chad President Deby.

[15] PSC/AHG/COMM. 1 (CCLXV), 10 March 2011, para. 8.

[16] The AUPSC was unable to appoint a senior envoy to persuade Gbagbo to accept the final high-level proposal by the March 24 deadline. The statement from the ECOWAS summit meeting was issued at this time. ECOWAS, N° 043/2011, 25 March 2011, Resolution A/RES. 1/03/11.

[17] Security Council, SC/10215, 30 March 2011.

[18] S/RES/1572, 15 November 2004, para. 9.

Acknowledgement

This work was supported by JSPS KAKENHI Grant Number JP16H06318.

References

Bayart, J.-F. (2000) 'Africa in the world: A history of extraversion', *African Affairs*, Vol. 99, No. 395, pp. 217–67.

Bellamy, A. J. (2009) *Responsibility to Protect: The Global Effort to End Mass Atrocities*, Cambridge and Malden: Polity.

ISS (Institute for Security Studies) (2011) 'Country analysis: Côte d'Ivoire update', *Peace and Security Council Report*, No. 21, pp. 7–12.

Murithi, T. (2007) 'The responsibility to protect, as enshrined in article 4 of the constitutive act of the African Union', *African Security Review*, Vol. 16, No. 3, pp. 14–24.

Sato, A. (2011) 'Post-Election Conflict in Côte d'Ivoire and the Challenges for Ouattara's Presidency', *Ajiken World Trend [IDE World Trend]*, No. 193, pp. 48–57 (in Japanese).

_____ (2012) 'African countries' "agreement" on the United Nations' military intervention in Côte d'Ivoire', *Paper presented at the 2012 Annual Convention of the Japan Association of International Relations (JAIR)*, 20 October 2012, Nagoya.

_____ (2019) 'Ambiguity and paradox of finding African solutions to Africa's problems: Evaluation of the unintended outcomes of the enhancement of African regional organizations' capacity to respond to conflicts', *Kokusai Seiji (International Relations)*, No. 194, pp. 79–94 (in Japanese).

Takeuchi, S. (2008) 'The international society and conflicts in Africa', in S. Takeuchi (ed.) *In Between War and Peace: The International Society in African Peace Processes*, Chiba: Institute of Developing Economies, pp. 3–56 (in Japanese).

Takizawa, M. (2010) 'Partnership between the United Nations and African regional organizations in conflict resolution', in M. Kawabata, S. Takeuchi and T. Ochiai (eds) *Conflict Resolution: African Experiences and Perspectives*, Kyoto: Minerva Shobo, pp. 169–

94 (in Japanese).

Williams, P. D. (2007) 'From non-intervention to non-indifference: The origins and development of the African Union's security culture', *African Affairs*, Vol. 106, No. 423, pp. 253–79.

UN DOCUMENTS

S/RES/1464 (4 February 2003).

S/RES/1528 (27 February 2004).

S/RES/1572 (15 November 2004).

S/RES/1765 (16 July 2007).

S/RES/1975 (30 March 2011).

Security Council, SC/10215 (30 March 2011).

Security Council, SC/10223 (13 April 2011).

S/2011/387 (24 June 2011), Twenty-eighth Report of the Secretary-General on the United Nations Operation in Côte d'Ivoire.

AU DOCUMENTS

AHG/Decl.5 (10–12 July 2000).

Constitutive Act of African Union (11 July 2000).

PSC/PR/Comm.2 (CCL) (30 November 2010) (African Union Peace and Security Council, 250TH Meeting, Press Statement).

PSC/PR/BR (CCLI) (4 December 2010) (African Union Peace and Security Council, 251ST Meeting, Press Statement).

PSC/PR/COMM.1 (CCLII) (9 December 2010) (African Union Peace and Security Council, 252ND Meeting, Communiqué).

PSC/PR/COMM.1 (CCLIV) (21 December 2010) (African Union Peace and Security Council, 254TH Meeting, Press Statement).

PSC/AHG/COMM (CCLIX) (28 January 2011) (African Union Peace and Security Council, 259TH Meeting, Communiqué).

PSC/PR/COMM (CCLXIII) (28 February 2011) (African Union Peace and Security Council, 263RD Meeting, Communiqué).

PSC/AHG/COMM.1 (CCLXV) (10 March 2011) (African Union Peace and Security Council, 265TH Meeting, Communiqué).

PSC/PR/BR.1 (CCLXX) (5 April 2011) (African Union Peace and Security Council, 270TH Meeting, Press Statement).

PSC/PR/COMM.1 (CCLXXIII) (21 April 2011) (African Union Peace and Security Council, 273RD Meeting, Communiqué).

PSC/PR/2 (CCLXXIII) (21 April 2011) (African Union Peace and Security Council, 273RD Meeting, Report of the Chairperson of the Commission on the Situation in Côte d'Ivoire).

ECOWAS DOCUMENTS

N° 193/2010, 24 décembre 2010 (Abuja - Nigeria), Session extraordinaire de la conférence des chefs d'Etat et de gouvernement sur la Côte d'Ivoire, Communiqué final.

N° 043/2011, 25 March 2011 (Abuja - Nigeria) Resolution A/RES.1/03/11 of the Authority of Heads of State and Government of ECOWAS on the Situation in Côte d'Ivoire.

N° 058/2011, 12 April 2011 (Abuja-Nigeria), Press Release, ECOWAS Wants Dignified Treatment of Ex-President.

Chapter 2

Overcoming the Dichotomy between Africa and the West: Norms and Measures for Arms Transfers to Non-State Actors (NSAs)[1]

Tamara Enomoto

1. Introduction

Since the 1990s, arms transfers to non-state actors (NSAs) have been at the centre of international policy debates. In those discussions, African NSAs who have acquired arms from various sources have been criticised for committing atrocities, threatening human security and undermining the fruits of development. Urgent efforts to address this issue have been demanded, and various international agreements have been adopted to regulate arms transfers to NSAs. At the same time, international debates and agreements on matters pertaining to armed violence in African countries have been challenged by Africanists for imposing 'modern, western' ideas and systems on African societies (Ohta 2016) rather than considering 'African' concepts and systems for solving problems.

What precisely are these modern, Western ideas and systems? This chapter presents an in-depth analysis of international policy debates on arms transfers to NSAs, from the time of the emergence of the sovereign-state system to the present, and argues for a cautious examination of the dynamic relationship of Africa with the West. The historical analysis presented herein shows that Western ideas and problem-solving mechanisms regarding arms transfers to NSAs have changed significantly since the formation of the sovereign state system and have not necessarily been monolithic or uniform. Rather, they have been re-created continually over the course of history, such that it is currently difficult to determine which ideas and systems should be understood as Western. Moreover, post-independence African states have been actively involved in the process of developing, changing and fragmenting dominant ideas on the matter of arms transfers to NSAs. Thus, what may ostensibly appear to be Western ideas and problem-solving methods may, in fact, have been at least partly created, revised and promoted by African actors. Consequently, the boundary between Western and African ideas and mechanisms is, in many respects, ambiguous.

As Jean-François Bayart pointed out, more attention should be paid to the active roles that African elites have played in establishing a relationship between Africa and the rest of the world (Bayart 2000). At the same time, the stereotypical and static imagery of Western concepts and mechanisms needs to be addressed and overcome. To address the ambivalence but also the dynamism that characterises the relationship between Africa and the rest of the world requires not only an in-depth analysis of the organic interaction of African elites with the international environment but also a more nuanced exploration into what are often referred to as Western ideas and systems.

2. Modern State Formation, 'Standards of Civilisation' and NSAs

It has not been uncommon throughout history to problematise arms possession by, or arms transfers to, individuals and groups outside the ruling authority. It was, however, only after the formation of the sovereign state system that arms transfers from one state to NSAs (i.e. actors other than sovereign states) in another state emerged as an issue of concern.[2] In general, NSAs can include armed rebel groups, private military companies, private security companies and arms brokers, but also civil institutions, such as museums and civilians, including sports shooters, hunters and gun collectors (Biting the Bullet Project 2006). The term 'non-state actor' is relatively new, and policymakers have not necessarily agreed upon its precise definition.[3] Nevertheless, since the emergence of the sovereign state system, there have been many efforts at an international agreement controlling arms transfers to NSAs.

Until the first half of the 20th century, the problem of arms transfers to NSAs tended to be framed as the inadmissibility of arms transfers to people regarded as not having the will or ability to form and manage a sovereign state. For instance, a treaty of friendship and alliance signed in 1814 between his Britannic Majesty and his Catholic Majesty, Ferdinand the 7th., stipulated that the former would 'take the most effectual measures for preventing his subjects from furnishing arms, ammunition, or any other warlike article' to the American rebels against Spanish rule, so that the 'subjects of those provinces' would 'return to their obedience to their lawful sovereign'.[4] On the other hand, the United Kingdom (UK) and other European states supplied arms to American entities recognised as 'lawful sovereign' (Gillespie 2011: 18). Another example is a convention signed in 1852 by the UK and the Boers (Voortrekkers), settlers of Dutch descent who had moved to the interior of southern Africa.[5] The convention recognised the Boers' right to govern themselves and permitted them access to arms and ammunition while prohibiting 'all trade in ammunition with the native tribes'.[6]

This framing of 'the problem' with an added touch of late-19th-century imperialism, also manifested itself in the first multilateral agreement adopted by most of the great powers to control arms transfers since the formation of the sovereign state system: the 1890 Brussels Act.[7] Formally titled the 'General Act of the Brussels Conference Relative to the African Slave Trade', the Brussels Act prohibited the transfer of firearms and ammunition to much of the African continent,[8] which was already flooded with a substantial number of European-made arms (Atmore, Chirenje and Mudenge 1971; Beachey 1962; Guy 1971). As the formal name of this treaty indicates, the main subject of the conference was the slave trade from Africa to other parts of the world, especially to the Arab world (Berlioux 1872: 1, 3–4, 72–3, 75–6; Clarke 1889: 246–9, 250–2, 254, 332–4, 344; Pasha 1892: 84–5).

In the policy debates leading up to the adoption of the Brussels Act, African people were generally not viewed as autonomous, rational subjects capable of managing a sovereign state, of exercising treaty-making powers or of engaging in diplomatic relations with other sovereign states (Matthews 1959; Miers 1975). Rather, they were seen as 'barbaric' contributors to the slave trade who were unable and unqualified to further the collective social good. Violence or resistance against their colonisers – the 'civilised states' – was regarded as irrational rejection of the benefits of civilisation (Kurimoto 1999: 148). Wars between African groups were considered a source of humanitarian catastrophe and slave hunting (Berlioux 1872: 1, 76; Casati 1891: 289, 291; Clarke 1889: 250–2, 254, 332–4, 344; Pasha 1892: 84–5). Therefore, the prohibition of arms transfers to such 'backward' people was seen as necessary to stop their 'barbaric' infighting and slave hunting and to bring them the benefits of civilisation under the protection of 'civilised states' (Bain 2003: 68; Louis 1966; Matthews 1959).

The prevailing doctrine at the time of the Brussels Act was the sovereign right of a state to determine for itself whether and when to resort to war (Joyner 2005: 163). Beginning in the latter half of the 18th century, the ultimate prerogative of a state to wage war came to be regarded as a legitimate and fundamental element of state sovereignty. As such, arms transfers to 'civilised sovereign states', were largely considered legitimate, unless the recipient was a potential or actual enemy of the exporting state (Enomoto 2020: 44–5). By the late 19th century, the *laissez-faire* policy of minimum governmental interference in the economic affairs of individuals and society had become prevalent (Onozuka 2012: 6–11).[9] As a result, governments rarely sought to regulate arms production and transfers by private companies, except in times of war or when they recognised the urgent need to secure supplies of weapons for their own armies (Krause and MacDonald 1993: 711–2).[10]

3. Interwar Period: 'Standards of Civilisation' Continued

The interwar period included a series of negotiations aimed at creating a modified version of the Brussels Act. Joined by the newly independent small states, the Convention for the Control of the Trade in Arms and Ammunition was adopted in 1919,[11] and the Convention for the Supervision of the International Trade in Arms and Ammunition and in Implements of War in 1925.[12] These treaties literally became dead letters even before their ink was dry, due to the unwillingness of many states to ratify them.[13] Nevertheless, the policy debates leading up to the adoption of these treaties – as well as the actual text of the documents – reveal the dominant perception of the times regarding arms transfers to NSAs. The negotiations were led by the 'great powers', who insisted that it was the moral duty of 'civilised states' to prevent arms from falling into the hands of those who did not meet the 'standards of civilisation' and who were therefore not entitled to sovereign equality (Stone 2000: 218). As a result, the great powers proposed a broader prohibited zone that included not only parts of Africa but also Transcaucasia, Persian lands and/or waters, Gwadar, the Arabian Peninsula and the continental regions of Asia that were part of the Turkish Empire.

The logic behind the prohibition was made apparent in the treatment of Iran throughout the negotiations for these two treaties. During the 1910s, Iran underwent a series of occupations and invasions by Britain, Russia and other forces (Daniel 2001: 127–9), and it was not part of the negotiations for the treaty adopted in 1919, which designated Iran and its waters (the Persian Gulf and the Sea of Oman) as being in the 'prohibited zone'.[14] In 1921, the newly emerged Reza Khan regime sought to re-establish Iran's sovereignty under a strong modern central government (Daniel 2001: 133–5). Iran thus took part as a 'civilised sovereign state' in the negotiations for the treaty adopted in 1925. During this round of negotiations, Iran argued that, as a 'civilised sovereign state', it would not accept being included in the 'special zone'[15] and refused to be treated in an unequal and discriminatory manner (Stone 2000: 224–5). This led to the exclusion of Iranian land from the 'special zone'.[16] However, Britain vehemently insisted that the Persian Gulf and Sea of Oman must remain in this zone, and many other states either took Britain's side or avoided taking any position at all.[17] In the end, Iran walked away from the negotiations, claiming that banning arms transfers to its gulf would, in practice, prevent the country from importing arms via the sea.[18]

The logic that Britain used to justify the inclusion of Iranian waters in the 'special zone' merits closer examination. Britain did not argue for the need to prevent arms flows to Iran itself, but asserted that Iranian waters constituted a hotbed of arms traffic to the 'backward' peoples living in the surrounding regions, especially to those disturbing the 'public order' in India, which was under British control.[19] Regardless of whether this logic fully reflected the real intent of Britain,[20] it clearly embodied the view that transferring arms to sovereign states should not be prohibited, whereas transferring arms to 'backward' peoples who did not meet the standards of civilisation was problematic and should be prevented.

It should be noted that these interwar treaties included a degree of control over arms transfers between states, which had been entirely outside the scope of the 1890 Brussels Act. On both sides of the Atlantic, a growing public outcry to regulate 'merchants of death'[21] drove efforts to control arms transfers (Anderson 1994; Cortright 2008: 98–100; Harkavy 1975: 215; Onozuka 2012; Stone 2000: 217), and the idea of war as legitimate violence between equal, sovereign states was increasingly called into question (Cortright 2008: 62–3).[22] Thus, the treaties of this period included the prohibition of arms transfers, except those sanctioned by both the exporting and importing states.[23] They also included reporting mechanisms for licensed arms exports and imports. Their aims were to place the 'merchants of death' under some control of governments and to limit arms transfers to NSAs not authorised by the state in which they were located, thus facilitating public scrutiny over authorised arms transfers.

However, these licensing and reporting measures were criticised by smaller arms-importing states, which saw them as infringements on their sovereignty and security. These critics claimed that licensing would put smaller importing states at the mercy of producers who might choose to recognise a rebel group over the legitimate government of an importing state.[24] They also argued that publishing arms imports and exports meant that the armaments of importing states would be revealed, while those of producing states would remain secret (Stone 2000: 226–8). Thus, while at the insistence of the great powers these measures were included in the treaties, few importing states rushed to ratify the treaties.[25]

Despite the divergent positions among participant states regarding both the scope of the prohibited ('special') zone and the licensing and reporting measures, the view that states should not transfer arms to people considered unable or unqualified to form and manage a sovereign state and to pursue the collective good was widely shared throughout the negotiations.

4. Post-WWII: From Positive to Negative Sovereignty

The decades following the end of the Second World War saw a significant shift in policy debates on arms transfers to NSAs. Against the backdrop of the independence of most former colonies, the dominant conception of sovereignty changed, as did views on arms transfers to NSAs. As Robert Jackson argues, the game of international relations shifted after the Second World War from one based on positive sovereignty, or a demonstrated ability for effective self-governance and the fulfilment of the 'standards of civilisation', to a new game based on negative sovereignty, i.e. the formal and legal entitlement to freedom from outside interference (Jackson 1990). In the new rules of the game, the principles of sovereign equality and non-intervention were to be respected for all states, regardless of their empirical capabilities as organised political systems. For instance, the Declaration on the Granting of Independence to Colonial Countries and Peoples, adopted by the United Nations General Assembly (UNGA) in 1960, stated that all peoples have the right to self-determination and that inadequacies in political, economic, social or educational preparedness should never serve as pretexts for delaying independence.[26] That the principles of sovereign equality and non-intervention, formulated through the development of the sovereign state system (Krasner 2001), should be respected for any state, regardless of its condition, was a tenet strongly defended by newly independent states and confirmed by UNGA resolutions in the 1960s and 1970s.[27]

The new negative sovereignty norms were emphasised by states in the Global South[28] between the 1950s and 1970s, when Western states sought to regulate international arms transfers, including to states. At the UNGA, Western states proposed resolutions to examine the matter of international arms transfers in order to consider the possibility of developing an international arms transfer registration and publicity system (Catrina 1988: 138; SIPRI 1971: 100–8; Wulf 1991: 230).

Malta, for example, submitted a draft UNGA resolution in 1965 that invited the Eighteen-Nation Committee on Disarmament to consider the question of arms transfers between states 'with a view to submitting to the General Assembly proposals for the establishment of a system of publicity through the United Nations'.[29] Malta argued for the need to address the problem of local arms races in the Third World, expressing concern that by diverting scarce resources they hindered economic and social development. It also stressed that an effective system of international arms transfer registration and publicity would build confidence among states (SIPRI 1971: 101–2). Similar draft resolutions were proposed by Denmark, Ireland, Malta and Norway in 1968 (SIPRI 1971: 103–5), and again by 18 states, including Ireland, Denmark, Japan and Norway, in 1976 (Catrina 1988: 138). However, states in the Global South, including post-independence African states, generally criticised the proposals, insisting that they were based on discriminatory ideas against smaller arms-importing sovereign states and could be used as an instrument for 'the haves' to intervene in the internal affairs of 'the have-nots' (Krause 1993: 1030; Muni 1988: 203–7). As a result, the proposed resolutions were never adopted in the UNGA.

The dominant argument at the time regarding arms transfers to NSAs also reflected a shift in the concept of state sovereignty. This is exemplified by one of the best-known legal cases for students of international law: the case brought to the International Court of Justice (ICJ) by Nicaragua against the United States (US) concerning military and paramilitary activities in and against Nicaragua. In 1979, the Sandinista National Liberation Front (FSLN) established a revolutionary government in Nicaragua. In the following years, the US suspended its aid to Nicaragua and, instead, provided assistance, including in the form of arms, to the Contra rebel militants.[30] In April 1984, the Nicaraguan government brought its case against the US to the ICJ, arguing that the US had resorted to the use of force against Nicaragua, intervened in its internal affairs and threatened its sovereignty, territorial integrity and political independence.[31]

In its 1986 judgement, the ICJ held that the principle of non-intervention and the prohibition of the threat or use of force had been established in customary international law.[32] On the matter of arming NSAs within the territory of another state, the ICJ concluded that it might amount to intervention in the internal or external affairs of another state and could be regarded as a threat or use of force.[33] Moreover, the court ruled that, by arming the Contras, the US had acted in breach of its obligations under customary international law with respect to the principles of non-intervention and the prohibition of the threat or use of force.[34] Thus, when considered historically, the ICJ's judgement in 1986 reflected the view of statehood predominant during that era: that regardless of whether a state is viewed as having met the 'standards of civilisation', both its sovereignty and the principle of non-intervention should be respected.

It should be remembered, however, that the ICJ also recognised that there had been a number of previous instances of foreign intervention for the benefit of forces opposed to the government of another state.[35] In fact, both the Western and Eastern blocs, as well as newly independent states in the Global South, supplied arms to Southern anti-colonial movements and anti-government groups during the Cold War (Garcia 2009; Smith 2008: 46). For instance, the Soviet Union supplied arms to 'socialist-oriented' NSAs, such as anti-colonial movements in Angola and Mozambique and anti-government groups in El Salvador (Shultz 1988). As Stephen Krasner argues, the principles associated with both Westphalian sovereignty, such as the exclusion of external actors from domestic authority configurations, and international legal sovereignty, such as mutual recognition, have in reality been violated frequently since the formation of the sovereign state system (Krasner 2009: 197).[36] Nevertheless, it is clear that 'the problem' of arms transfers to NSAs was framed and defined differently during the Cold War from that during previous periods, reflecting the dominant ideas of statehood and the game of negative sovereignty which states ostensibly played during this time. States in the Global South, including post-independence African states, supported and emphasised this idea of statehood and the game of negative sovereignty and, thereby, justified their military build-up, prevented interventions in 'internal' matters, such as military budgets and arms procurement, and criticised arms transfers to NSAs.

5. Post-Cold War: Three Approaches to Arms Transfer

Since the 1990s, three approaches have emerged regarding the legitimacy and admissibility of arms transfers to NSAs, and international norms concerning NSAs have diversified and fragmented accordingly. These three approaches are examined individually below.

The first could be called a *blanket ban approach*. In the 1990s, the problem of wars not necessarily fought between states but within or beyond states began to draw the interest of policy circles (Kaldor 1999). These so-called 'new wars' often involved a number of NSAs who used arms obtained from other states. To address this problem, during the 1990s and early 2000s Canada and several European states proposed that states agree on a blanket ban on all non-state-sanctioned arms transfers to NSAs; that is, arms transfers to parties not authorised by the states in which they are located (Canada, Ministry of Foreign Affairs 1998; Capie 2004: 10–1; Holtom 2012: 7; Poitevin 2013: 17; Yihdego 2007: 150–1). Many Southern states, especially those in Africa, have supported the blanket ban approach.[37] They cite anti-government activities, acts of terror and organised crime to claim that non-state groups and individuals constitute the roots of evil, misusing the procured arms to bring enormous suffering to their populations. They also insist that non-state-sanctioned arms transfers to NSAs constitute a violation of the principle of non-intervention and hence should be banned altogether.

However, it is not only acts of violence by NSAs that have been problematised since the 1990s; both in the literature on new wars and in policy debates, violations of international human rights law and/or international humanitarian law by national military and security forces, especially those of states in the Global South, have been treated as a source of concern (Anderson 1996; Collier 2009; Kaldor 1999). That is, the ability and will of states, especially states in the Global South, to ensure human security, respect human rights and pursue the collective social good have been seriously questioned, along with the legitimacy of state violence. Since the latter half of the 1990s, the notion of a 'responsibility to protect' has received a certain degree of support from governments, scholars and non-governmental organisations (NGOs), especially in the Global North (Clapham 2014: 167–8). According to this notion, Westphalian sovereignty and international legal sovereignty are not inherent rights of states but are contingent on a state's positive sovereignty. In other words, they are conditional upon a state's capacity and will to protect its population. Failure to fulfil this responsibility may lead to intervention by outside actors. Some of these outside actors may interpret this responsibility as including the supply of weapons to NSAs, such as rebel groups (Holtom 2012: 13–4; Stavrianakis, Xinyu and Binxin 2013).

As the ability and will of states to protect their own populations and pursue the collective good rapidly came under suspicion, in 1991 an UNGA resolution to establish an international arms transfer registry system, a measure that never materialised during the Cold War period, was adopted.[38] Subsequently, the idea of requiring that exporting states assess the risk of misuse before deciding whether arms transfers should be authorised to other states gained support. In the 1990s and 2000s, the permanent members of the United Nations Security Council (P5),[39] the European Council,[40] the European Union (EU),[41] the Organisation for Security and Cooperation in Europe (OSCE),[42] the United Nations Disarmament Commission (UNDC),[43] the Wassenaar Arrangement,[44] the Organisation of American States (OAS),[45] East and Central African states,[46] the Central American Integration System (SICA)[47] and the Economic Community of West African States (ECOWAS)[48] developed and agreed upon common criteria against which the potential risks of misuse were to be evaluated on a case-by-case basis before arms transfers could be authorised.

At the same time, from within the policy circles of governments, NGOs and academics, especially those in the Global North, there emerged what could be called a *hard-case approach* to the issue of arms transfers to NSAs. It was argued that in some specific cases non-state-sanctioned arms transfers to NSAs were indeed legitimate (Biting the Bullet Project 2006). For example, if a group was facing repression or genocide by its state and was seeking to acquire arms to protect itself, then non-state-sanctioned arms transfers to the group could be considered legitimate. In such cases, the group's prospects for success in achieving its just cause would have to be high and the group would have to be trusted to have the will and ability to use the arms with proper restraint and, through safe storage, to prevent their diversion (Biting the Bullet Project 2006).

During the 2000s and 2010s, a third approach, the *criteria approach*, gradually evolved, which advocated the application of uniform criteria to all arms transfers, regardless of whether the recipient was a state actor.

By the time of the final negotiation stages of the Arms Trade Treaty (ATT), between 2010 and 2013, all three approaches were available for consideration. The following section discusses the different approaches followed by states within the context of international agreements made since the 1990s.

6. Post-Cold War International Agreements

Some agreements prohibit arms transfers to NSAs. These include United Nations Security Council (UNSC) resolutions adopted under the authority of Chapter VII, Article 41, of the Charter of the United Nations, which impose arms embargoes on entire territories of particular states or against NSAs and groups operating in particular territories.[49] For example, UNSC resolution 1373 prohibits arms transfers to entities or persons involved in terrorist acts,[50] UNSC resolution 1540 prohibits transfers of weapons of mass destruction to NSAs[51] and UNSC resolution 1390 prohibits arms transfers to individuals, groups, undertakings and entities associated with Al-Qaida and the Taliban, whose scope is not limited to the territory of a particular state.[52] Multilateral forums, such as the EU and the OSCE, have also imposed arms embargoes against the entire territories of certain states or against certain NSAs.[53] Non-state-sanctioned transfers of man-portable air-defence systems (MANPADs) are prohibited by other agreements, such as UNGA resolutions,[54] documents adopted at the Wassenaar Arrangement in 2000, 2003 and 2007,[55] an Action Plan adopted by the Group of Eight (G8) in 2003,[56] an agreement at the Asia-Pacific Economic Cooperation (APEC) in 2003[57] and documents adopted at the OSCE in 2004 and 2008.[58] These prohibition measures single out particular NSAs and/or the provision of particular weapons to them; they do not relate to arms transfers to NSAs in a general sense. Consequently, the scope of the weapons and/or NSAs included in these agreements is substantially limited. Nevertheless, they generally reflect increasing concern over the atrocities and disturbances brought about by NSAs in the age of 'new wars'.

Several regional agreements have sought to develop an international consensus on the need to prohibit non-state-sanctioned arms transfers to NSAs. The EU joint action adopted in 1998, and updated in 2002, stated that the EU would aim to build consensus in the relevant international forums, and in a regional context as appropriate, for the realisation of a commitment by exporting countries to supply small arms and light weapons only to governments in accordance with appropriate international and regional restrictive arms export criteria.[59] In 2000, ministers of the member states of the Organisation of African Unity (OAU) adopted the 'Bamako Declaration', in which they agreed that they would strongly appeal to the wider international community and, in particular, to arms supplier countries to accept that trade in small arms should be limited to governments and traders who are authorised, registered and licensed.[60] The Inter-American Convention of 1997,[61] the 'Nairobi Protocol' adopted by east and central African states in 2004[62] and a document agreed upon at the OSCE in 2000[63] included clauses that require participating states to ensure the permission of the importing state before authorising arms transfers, whether the recipient is a state actor or not. A few African regional agreements, such as the ECOWAS Convention adopted in 2006[64] and the Central African Convention adopted in 2010,[65] more clearly oblige states parties not to transfer arms to NSAs. Article 3 (2) of the ECOWAS Convention states that 'Member States shall ban, without exception, transfers of small arms and light weapons to Non-State Actors that are not explicitly authorised by the importing Member'.[66] Article 4 of the Central African Convention specifies that, 'States Parties shall prohibit any transfer of small arms and light weapons, their ammunition and all parts and components that can be used for their manufacture, repair and assembly to, through and from their respective territories to non-State armed groups'.[67]

During negotiations for the United Nations Firearms Protocol, which was adopted in March 2001,[68] some states, especially African states, argued that the protocol's provision should be applied to arms transfers to NSAs, while other states sought an exemption for such transfers (McDonald 2002: 239). Article 10 (2) of the adopted text stated that before issuing export licences or authorisations for shipments of firearms, their parts and components, and ammunition, each state party should verify that 'the importing States have issued import licences or authorizations'.[69] However, Article 4 (2) of the protocol included compromise language proposed by the US: 'This Protocol shall not apply to state-to-state transactions or to state transfers in cases where the application of the Protocol would prejudice the right of a State Party to take action in the interest of national security consistent with the Charter of the United Nations.'[70] While exporting arms to NSAs without explicit permission of the importing state would be contrary to Article 10 (2), Article 4 (2) in effect allows states parties to determine for themselves whether the protocol should be applied to a specific transfer from a state to an NSA (McDonald 2002: 240).

Arms transfers to NSAs again became a thorny issue during the negotiation of the United Nations Small Arms Programme of Action, finally adopted in July 2001. Negotiating states diverged sharply in their views on whether the document should prohibit non-state-sanctioned arms transfers to NSAs. Many states, especially African states, supported the blanket ban approach, which the US firmly opposed (Garcia 2009: 156–7; Holtom 2012: 7–8). In the end, the issue was not clearly addressed in the adopted programme.[71] During the review conference of the Programme of Action in 2006, the issue was raised again but never settled (Holtom 2012: 9; McDonald, Hassan and Stevenson 2007: 123–4).

The language of the 2002 Wassenaar Arrangement Best Practice Guidelines for Exports of Small Arms and Light Weapons (SALW)[72] was vague but indicated a more permissive approach than a blanket ban. It stated that 'participating States will take especial care when considering exports of SALW other than to governments or their authorised agents'.[73] This implied that such transfers might be permitted after they were considered with 'especial care'.

The final negotiation stages of the ATT, between 2010 and 2013, thus unfolded amid competing approaches regarding arms transfers to NSAs. During the negotiations, African states were among the many Southern states that continued to support the blanket ban approach,[74] which the US continued to oppose (Holtom 2012: 6). European states and the NGOs and academics involved in the negotiation tended to avoid furthering this issue. Although in the 1990s and early 2000s European states had supported the blanket ban approach, by the early 2010s states such as France and the UK were willing to consider engaging in transfers of arms, security equipment and other related materials to opposition movements in the Middle East and North Africa (MENA) following the upsurge of the Arab Spring (Poitevin 2013: 17–8).[75] Thus, some states preferred to keep their options open (Clapham 2014: 164), while many others avoided discussing the issue altogether, possibly fearing a delay or breakdown in the ATT negotiations.

In the end, the adopted text of the ATT did not include an explicit reference to arms transfers to NSAs.[76] It simply stipulates that all arms transfers, with the exceptions clarified in Article 2 (3),[77] are subject to the common criteria enshrined in the treaty. That is, transferring arms to NSAs without the permission of importing states is not clearly prohibited in the treaty. While the claim can be made that arming NSAs without the consent of the importing state constitutes a violation of the Charter of the United Nations and is thus prohibited by Article 6 (2) of the ATT,[78] a more prevalent interpretation is that states parties of the ATT have the obligation to assess the potential risk of arms transfers against the criteria on a case-by-case basis, regardless of whether the recipient of the arms is a state actor or not (Casey-Maslen, Giacca and Vestner 2013: 9; Da Silva and Nevil 2015: 90, 96–7; Henderson 2013; ICRC 2016: 11).

As such, some states parties of the ATT may assess arms transfers to NSAs on a case-by-case basis against the criteria enshrined in the ATT and may authorise transfers without the permission of the importing state, when they deem that the risk of misuse is not 'overriding'.[79] However, since the criteria approach leaves the decision to transfer or deny the transfer of arms to the discretion of each state, the decision regarding whether to transfer arms to a certain actor may differ between one state party of the ATT and another.

In a sense, the criteria approach is not based on the premise that certain actors are capable of defining the collective good of others or of the international community, which was the assumption embedded in the Brussels Act of 1890. Instead, it presumes that any actor has a lesser or greater degree of risk of falling into dysfunction, irrationality and immorality and thus requires an external risk assessment. At the same time, no actor is assumed to be capable of providing any universal judgement as to the level of risk of a specific actor or of defining the collective good on behalf of the potentially affected population or of the international community. As a result, some states parties of the ATT may conclude that the risk of arms being used to commit or facilitate serious violations of international humanitarian law is 'overriding', should they authorise certain arms to a certain NSA at a certain time, but other states parties may find that the risk is not sufficiently 'overriding' to reject the licence for a transfer.

7. Diversification and Fragmentation of International Norms

Based on this review of the policy debates on arms transfers to NSAs, it is clear that the ATT's language on this matter is characteristic of the present era. From the time of the emergence of the sovereign state system until the interwar period, policymakers tended to frame the problem of arms transfers to NSAs as the inadmissibility of arms transfers to peoples regarded as unable and unqualified to further the collective social good. The framing was premised on the idea that people had to fulfil the 'standards of civilisation' to be recognised as a sovereign state. In the late 19th century, arms transfers between 'civilised' states were rarely problematised except in times of war, and the interwar initiatives to regulate such transfers failed, in part due to the lack of support by smaller states, which viewed them as infringements on their sovereignty and security. During the Cold War period, the dominant argument against arms transfers to NSAs, articulated in the ICJ's judgement on military and paramilitary activities in and against

Nicaragua, was based on the idea that the principles of sovereign equality and non-intervention should be respected for all states regardless of their empirical capabilities as organised political systems. At the same time, within the UNGA, Western states proposed international registration and publicity measures for arms transfers between states, but this initiative met fierce criticism by importing states, which considered them as an instrument for exporting states to illegitimately intervene in the internal affairs of importing states.

Since the 1990s, as much as the atrocities and disturbances caused by non-state actors concerned policy circles, the ability and will of states themselves to protect their own populations and pursue the collective good came under increasing suspicion. Governments, NGOs and academics, most often those in the Global North, sought to develop common criteria against which exporting states should assess the potential risks of misuse before authorising arms transfers to other states. Their efforts culminated in the negotiation of the ATT, but the ability and will of states, especially states in the MENA region, to ensure the security of their own populations and to protect their human rights were cast in serious doubt. That the international community should be able to provide military assistance to peoples fighting against oppressive regimes also gathered support and sympathy, especially from states, NGOs, academics and the media in Europe and North America. In a sense, the language of the ATT was developed against a background in which the right to Westphalian sovereignty and international legal sovereignty was increasingly seen as contingent on a state's ability and will to protect its own population.

However, some of the states that have not ratified the ATT, such as the US, are likely to decide whether to authorise arms transfers to NSAs based on their own rules and regulations. In addition, the ATT's inability to address the issue of arms transfers to NSAs has been criticised by many of the states that abstained or voted against the adoption of the ATT, as well as by some that voted for it, including those in Africa.[80] Such states may prohibit the export of arms to NSAs without the explicit permission of the importing state, although their actual practices may not necessarily conform to the principles they claim to espouse.[81] Several prominent individuals have also voiced doubts about the approach taken in the ATT. Notably,

Ben Emmerson, United Nations Special Rapporteur on human rights and countering terrorism, insisted at the time that the ATT entered into force that 'further consideration on the issue of prohibiting the sale of weapons to non-state entities is needed'.[82] Therefore, it is difficult to conclude that the criteria approach embodies a consolidated international norm. Rather, international norms on arms transfers to NSAs have diversified since the end of the Cold War, leading to what Martti Koskenniemi and Päivi Leino call the 'fragmentation of international law' that reflects uneven normative and institutional development and evolution in inter-state relations (Koskenniemi and Leino 2002). In particular, all agreements adopted by African states that addressed the issue of arms transfers to NSAs, i.e. the Bamako Declaration in 2000, the Nairobi Protocol in 2004, the ECOWAS Convention in 2006 and the Central African Convention adopted in 2010, have differed substantially from agreements in other regions, in that all of them were based on the blanket ban approach.

8. Conclusion

Since the 1990s, arms transfers to NSAs have been at the centre of international policy debates, particularly as a factor that has instigated, fuelled or prolonged post-Cold War armed violence in the Global South, especially in Africa. Various international conferences have addressed the issue of arms transfers to NSAs, some of which yielded treaties and non-legally binding agreements. On the other hand, international debates and agreements on matters pertaining to armed violence in Africa have often been criticised for their inclination to perceive modern, Western ideas and systems as universal and to impose them on African societies. For such critics, the issue of arms transfers to NSAs may serve as yet another example of the imposition of Western ideas and systems. However, an analysis of international policy debates on arms transfers to NSAs from the time of the emergence of the sovereign state system to the present indicates that such policy debates have a rather contingent and fluid nature. Over time, discussions of the problem of arms transfers to NSAs in prominent cases have reflected the concept of statehood that dominated during the respective period. Thus, even basic Western ideas, such as those related to state sovereignty and the self, have changed substantially in the last few centuries. Both the recent hard case approach and the criteria approach evolved against a backdrop in which the right to Westphalian sovereignty and international legal sovereignty were increasingly seen as contingent upon a state's ability and will to protect its own population.

This transformation of ideas and systems has yielded conflicting conceptions of the issue of arms transfers to NSAs and the means to address it. The difference between the blanket ban and criteria approaches is so profound that their reconciliation or their integration into unified policy measures is inconceivable. Internal norms and measures on arms transfers to NSAs have diversified and fragmented since the end of the Cold War, with differences in opinion among Western actors on the most effective approach. It is therefore difficult to determine which idea and system should be seen as 'Western' with regard to arms transfers to NSAs.

Post-independence African states have been actively involved in the process of developing, modifying and fragmenting ideas on the matter of arms transfers to NSAs. In the process, they have extracted and promoted some Western ideas and systems, adjusting them to fit their needs and interests. During the Cold War, the principles of sovereign equality and non-intervention came to be respected for all states regardless of their empirical capabilities as organised political systems. African states strongly supported and promoted this transformation of both the concept of sovereignty and the framing of the issue of arms transfers to NSAs. African states emphasised this refurbished concept of sovereignty and deployed it to criticise arms transfers to NSAs. They also sought to suppress the move by Western states to form and develop systems to register and supervise international arms transfers, while justifying military build-ups within their own states. In other words, African state elites sought to maintain power and political control domestically and a certain degree of autonomy internationally through a strategy of what Bayart called 'extraversion' (Bayart 2000), selectively appropriating and mobilising Western ideas that fit their purposes. The ideas and policies supported by African states ultimately became dominant in international policy debates during the Cold War.

After the 1990s, African states have been deeply involved in international policy debates on arms transfers to NSAs, which led to repeated disputes with the US. At the same time, governments, NGOs and academics, mainly in the Global North, increasingly came to support either the hard case or the criteria approach to controlling arms transfers to NSAs, both of which are based on the view that sees the right to Westphalian sovereignty and international legal sovereignty as contingent on a state's ability and will to protect its own population. While this interpretation may seem to indicate a revival of the colonial logic of intervention and domination, present-day African states have their own international legal sovereignty, participating in treaty negotiations and UN general assembly meetings as sovereign states, and negotiate and agree to regional treaties and other documents with neighbouring states. African states have, in fact, emphasised the principles of sovereign equality and non-intervention in internal affairs, arguing that the blanket ban approach should be the universal norm. As a result of the strong resistance of African states, the 2001 United Nations Firearms Protocol and the 2001 United Nations Small Arms Programme of Action did not include any language that implied the possibility to permit arms transfers to NSAs. Moreover, African regional agreements have sharply differed from agreements in other regions, in that all of them either implicitly or explicitly are based on the blanket ban approach. Thus, African states have clearly extracted and utilised the ideas, values and systems that fit their needs and interests and have adopted them in their own regional agreements (while not always abiding by those agreements themselves). Consequently, Western ideas and problem-solving methods have, in fact, been at least partially created, re-created and promoted by African actors. Moreover, due in part to the actions taken by African states, international norms on arms transfers to NSAs have diversified and fragmented in the last few decades, further complicating an understanding of what exactly constitutes Western ideas and mechanisms.

Overall, this review has shown that imagining and constructing the West as a self-evident static category and over-simplifying the dichotomy between Western and African may hinder an analysis of the dynamic relationship between Africa and the rest of the world. There is clearly a need for a nuanced appreciation of Africa's historical embeddedness in the international arena and African elites' active involvement in the formulation of international ideas and mechanisms. In a world where myriad ideas and measures are promoted at multiple on-line and off-line international conferences, and a diverse range of actors are involved in quotidian decision making at the international level, we may benefit more than ever from concerted efforts in 'studying-up' (Nader 1969); that is, in conducting in-depth studies not only of the powerless but also of elites, African or otherwise.

Endnotes

[1] The analysis contained in this chapter, especially on the details of international agreements in sections 1–5, is largely based on my previous articles, while the aim and central argument has been changed (Enomoto 2017a, 2017b). The author would like to thank Keith Krause, Nicholas Marsh and Owen Greene for extensive advice and comments. The views expressed herein are based in part on my experience as a staff member in charge of arms control and humanitarian issues at an international NGO between 2003 and 2015 and as a consultant to other NGOs since 2015. The views expressed in this chapter are mine and do not represent those of the organisations for which I have worked.

[2] The Peace of Westphalia in 1684 is generally seen as a key moment in the gradual formation of the sovereign-state system, a system of political authority based on territory, mutual recognition, autonomy and control (Krasner 2001: 17).

[3] For instance, there is currently no shared view as to whether sub-national militaries or security agencies, such as the Peshmerga and Asayish in the Kurdistan region of Iraq, should be considered NSAs. A more contentious issue is whether entities that have not been recognised by many states, such as Palestine, Somaliland and Taiwan, should be regarded as NSAs. See Holtom (2012: 9–10) and McDonald, Hassan and Stevenson (2007: 123).

[4] Treaty of Friendship and Alliance between His Britannic Majesty and His Catholic Majesty, Ferdinand the Seventh, 5 July 1814, Article 3.

[5] Sand River Convention, 16 January 1852.

[6] Sand River Convention, 16 January 1852.

[7] General Act of the Brussels Conference Relative to the African Slave Trade, 2 July 1890.

[8] Article 8 of the Brussels Act states as follows: 'The importation of firearms, and especially of rifles and improved weapons, as well as of powder, ball and cartridges, is ... prohibited in the territories comprised between the 20th parallel of North latitude and the 22nd parallel of South latitude, and extending westward to the Atlantic Ocean and eastward to the Indian Ocean and its dependencies, including the islands adjacent to the coast within 100 nautical miles from the shore'.

[9] It should be kept in mind that European states generally sought to control the arms trade prior to the shift in the underlying economic ideology of trade from mercantilism to capitalism. Most of the previous control measures had been characterised by unilateral initiatives and designed to protect technological lead or to safeguard scarce weapons. See Krause (1992: 37–48, 59–61) and Krause and MacDonald (1993: 708–11).

[10] Whether a neutral state could legitimately supply arms to belligerents of war was fiercely debated between the UK and the US over the case of the Confederate commerce raider *Alabama* in the 1860s and 1870s. The case reaffirmed the idea of international law that prevailed at the time, that there was no general obligation of neutral states to prevent private arms transfers to belligerents of war. Several decades later, the Hague Convention (V) Respecting the Rights and Duties of Neutral Powers and Persons in Case of War on Land of 18 October 1907 and the Hague Convention (XIII) Concerning the Rights and Duties of Neutral Powers in Naval War of 18 October 1907 prohibited the supply of arms by a neutral state to a belligerent state. Yet, arms transfers by private suppliers were outside of the scope of the prohibition. See Garcia-Mora (1958) and Stone (2000: 214–7).

[11] Convention for the Control of the Trade in Arms and Ammunition, 10 September 1919.

[12] Convention for the Supervision of the International Trade in Arms and Ammunition and in Implements of War, 17 June 1925.

[13] The treaty adopted in 1919 did not specify a fixed number of states that must express their consent for its entry into force; instead, its Article

26 stated that it 'would come into force for each Signatory Power from the date of the deposit of its ratification'. Therefore, the treaty did enter into force for a small number of states that had deposited their instruments of ratification. However, it was widely seen as a dead letter by 1923, which prompted the next round of negotiation. See Stone (2000: 219–20).

[14] Convention for the Control of the Trade in Arms and Ammunition, 10 September 1919, Article 6.

[15] This expression was used to sound less aggressive during this round of negotiation. See LNA, A.13.1925.IX, pp. 254–5.

[16] LNA, A.13.1925.IX, p. 12.

[17] LNA, A.13.1925.IX, pp. 380–1; TNA ADM 1/8699/113.

[18] LNA, A.13.1925.IX, pp. 12, 375–80, 401, 704, 709, 711.

[19] LNA, A.13.1925.IX, pp. 399–400; TNA ADM 1/8699/113.

[20] Britain, in fact, faced repeated uprisings and resistance against British rule in the regions surrounding Iran, especially in India, during negotiation of the treaty. See Chew (2012).

[21] This term refers to arms manufacturers and dealers accused of having instigated and perpetuated the First World War to maximise their profits from arms sales.

[22] There were other sets of initiatives that sought to control arms transfers to particular states during this period. For instance, the 1920s peace treaties with the defeated states (Germany, Austria, Hungary, Turkey and Bulgaria) in the First World War imposed prohibition of imports and exports of arms on these states. There were also unilateral and multilateral arms embargoes in specific conflicts, such as those in China in the 1910s and 1920s, and the Chaco war between Bolivia and Paraguay between 1932 and 1935. See Krause and MacDonald (1993: 714, 720–22).

[23] Convention for the Control of the Trade in Arms and Ammunition, 10 September 1919, Article 1; Convention for the Supervision of the International Trade in Arms and Ammunition and in Implements of War, Articles 2–5.

[24] LNA, A.13.1925.IX, pp. 178–82, 583–5.

[25] The interwar negotiations did not yield any tangible agreement, but they facilitated the institutionalisation of peacetime licensing mechanisms for arms transfers by many of the great powers. See Stone (2000); Krause and MacDonald (1993).

[26] A/RES/15/1514.

[27] A/RES/20/2131; A/RES/25/2625.

[28] In this chapter, the categories of North and South are not premised on prior existence but are treated as imagined spaces that are produced and reproduced through discourse and practice.

[29] Draft resolution submitted by Malta. See SIPRI (1971: 102).

[30] It is known as the 'Iran-Contra affair', a scandal that occurred during the second term of Ronald Reagan's administration. The administration secretly supplied weapons to Iran in hopes of securing the release of American hostages held in Lebanon by *Hezbollah*, a group linked to the Iranian government, and then diverted a portion of the proceeds from the weapon sales to arm the Contras. See Busby (1999).

[31] Military and Paramilitary Activities in and against Nicaragua (Nicaragua v. United States of America). Merits, Judgment. I.C.J. Reports 1986, para. 15.

[32] Military and Paramilitary Activities in and against Nicaragua (Nicaragua v. United States of America). Merits, Judgment. I.C.J. Reports 1986, paras. 188–90, 192, 193, 195.

[33] Military and Paramilitary Activities in and against Nicaragua (Nicaragua v. United States of America). Merits, Judgment. I.C.J. Reports 1986, para. 195.

[34] Military and Paramilitary Activities in and against Nicaragua (Nicaragua v. United States of America). Merits, Judgment. I.C.J. Reports 1986, paras. 228, 238, 242, 292.

[35] Military and Paramilitary Activities in and against Nicaragua (Nicaragua v. United States of America). Merits, Judgment. I.C.J. Reports 1986, para. 206.

[36] On the other hand, arms transfers to NSAs generally took place covertly, which may be interpreted as implicit acknowledgement of the illegality of such acts (Henderson 2013: 643).

[37] There are exceptions, such as the Arab countries that, along with Iran, export arms to Palestine (Garcia 2009: 154–7; Holtom 2012: 9).

[38] A/RES/46/36L. It must be recalled that the resolution was based on a report prepared by a UN Group of Government Experts (A/46/301), which was set up by an UNGA resolution adopted before the end of the Cold War in 1988 (A/RES/43/75I).

[39] Guidelines for Conventional Arms Transfers. Communique issued following the meeting of the P5 in London, 18 October 1991.

[40] Conclusions of the Presidency: Declaration on Non-Proliferation and Arms Exports, adopted at the European Council Meeting in Luxembourg, 28–29 June 1991; Conclusions of the Presidency: Non-Proliferation and Arms Exports, adopted at the European Council Meeting in Lisbon, 26–27 June 1992.

[41] 8675/2/98, Rev. 2.

[42] FSC/3/96; FSC.DOC/1/00/Rev.1.

[43] Guidelines for International Arms Transfers in the Context of General Assembly Resolution 46/36 H of 6 December 1991.

[44] Best Practice Guidelines for Exports of Small Arms and Light Weapons, 11–12 December 2002.

[45] Draft Model Regulations for the Control of Brokers of Firearms, Their Parts and Components and Ammunition, approved at the 34th Regular Session of the Inter-American Drug Abuse Control Commission (CICAD), 17–20 November 2003.

[46] Best Practice Guidelines for the Implementation of the Nairobi Declaration and the Nairobi Protocol on Small Arms and Light Weapons, approved at the Third Ministerial Review Conference of the Nairobi Declaration on the Problem of the Proliferation of Illicit Small Arms and Light Weapons in the Great Lakes Region and the Horn of Africa, 20–21 June 2005.

[47] Code of Conduct of Central American States on the Transfer of Arms, Ammunition, Explosives and Other Related Material, 2 December 2005.

[48] ECOWAS Convention on Small Arms and Light Weapons, Their Ammunition and Other Related Materials, 14 June 2006.

[49] See the list of UN arms embargoes targeting non-state actors, 1991–2011, in Holtom (2012: 11).

[50] S/RES/1373.

[51] S/RES/1540. The resolution defines a non-state actor as an 'individual or entity, not acting under the lawful authority of any State in conducting activities which come within the scope of this resolution'.

[52] S/RES/1390.

[53] See SIPRI's website for the list of arms embargoes agreed at the UN and other multilateral forums, (https://www.sipri.org/databases/embargoes) (accessed: 5 October 2020).

[54] A/RES/59/90; A/RES/60/77.

[55] Elements for Export Controls of Man-Portable Air Defence Systems (MANPADS), 1 December 2000. Amended versions were adopted on 12 December 2003 and at the plenary meetings held between 4 and 6 December 2007.

[56] Enhance Transport Security and Control of Man-Portable Air Defence Systems (MANPADS): A G8 Action Plan, 2 June 2003.

[57] APEC Guidelines on Controls and Security of Man-Portable Air Defense Systems (MANPADS), 17–18 November 2004.

[58] FSC.DEC/3/04; FSC.DEC/5/08.

[59] 1999/34/CFSP; 2002/589/CFSP.

[60] Bamako Declaration on an African Common Position on the Illicit Proliferation, Circulation and Trafficking of Small Arms and Light Weapons, 1 December 2000.

[61] Inter-American Convention against the Illicit Manufacturing and Trafficking in Firearms, Ammunition, Explosives and other Related Materials, 14 November 1997.

[62] The Nairobi Protocol for the Prevention, Control and Reduction of Small Arms and Light Weapons in the Great Lakes Region and the Horn of Africa, 21 April 2004.

[63] FSC.DOC/1/00/Rev.1.

[64] ECOWAS Convention on Small Arms and Light Weapons, Their Ammunition and Other Related Materials, 14 June 2006.

[65] Central African Convention for the Control of Small Arms and Light Weapons, Their Ammunition, Parts and Components that Can be Used for Their Manufacture, Repair and Assembly, 30 April 2010.

[66] It defines non-state actors in Article 1 (10).

[67] Its scope for non-state actors is limited to a 'non-State armed group', which is defined in Article 2 (n).

[68] A/RES/55/255.

[69] A/RES/55/255, Article 10 (2).

[70] A/RES/55/255, Article 4 (2).

[71] A/CONF.192/15.

[72] Best Practice Guidelines for Exports of Small Arms and Light Weapons, 11–12 December 2002.

[73] Best Practice Guidelines for Exports of Small Arms and Light Weapons, 11–12 December 2002.

[74] According to Holtom, Brazil, China, Côte d'Ivoire, Cuba, India,

Indonesia, Liberia, Mali, Nigeria, Turkey and Zimbabwe supported the blanket ban. Statements from the African Group (a group of 54 African states that are UN Members), CARICOM, ECOWAS, and a joint statement from Argentina, Chile, Colombia, Guatemala, Jamaica, Mexico, Peru, Trinidad and Tobago and Uruguay were also in favour of the blanket ban. See Holtom (2012: 4–5). The common position agreed at the African Union also called for the blanket ban. See African Union, African Union Common Position on an Arms Trade Treaty, 2011, para. 19.

[75] It should be noted that some arms deliveries, such as those supplied by France to the National Interim Council (NIC) of Libya, took place after the exporting state recognised the opposition movement as the legitimate government of the importing state, although recognition of an opposition movement when it does not have effective control of most of the country can be of dubious legality. The author thanks Nicholas Marsh for pointing this out. See Henderson (2013: 665–8) and Holtom (2012: 13–5).

[76] A/Conf. 217/2013/L.3; A/67/L.58 and Add.1. Article 11 of the ATT stipulates that the 'exporting State Party shall seek to prevent the diversion of the transfer of conventional arms covered under Article 2 (1) through its national control system'. Yet, the term 'diversion' is not clearly defined in the treaty. See Olabuenaga and Gramizzi (2015: 194), Parker (2016: 348–50). It is generally understood that 'if a state deliberately authorises the transfer of arms to an illicit end user (such as an armed group operating in another state), this would not constitute "diversion"'. See Parker (2016: 349).

[77] Article 2 (3) of the ATT says, 'This Treaty shall not apply to the international movement of conventional arms by, or on behalf of, a State Party for its use provided that the conventional arms remain under that State Party's ownership'.

[78] Article 6 (2) of the ATT states, 'A State Party shall not authorise any transfer of conventional arms covered under Article 2 (1) or of items covered under Article 3 or Article 4, if the transfer would violate its relevant international obligations under international agreements to which it is a Party, in particular those relating to the transfer of, or illicit trafficking in, conventional arms'. Clapham argues that arming non-state actors may constitute a violation of the UN Charter and thus may come within the purview of Article 6 (2). See Clapham (2016: 195–9).

[79] The term 'overriding' was used in Article 7 (3). For the implications

of this term, see Casey-Maslen (2016: 274–6).

[80] GA/11354.

[81] For instance, Russia was one of the states that criticised the ATT for its failure to explicitly prohibit non-state sanctioned arms transfers to NSAs at the time the treaty was adopted, on 2 April 2013. See ibid. However, the country was reported to have transferred arms to Ukrainian opposition forces, the Donetsk People's Republic, in the following year. See Anthony (2015: 59).

[82] The Office of the United Nations High Commissioner for Human Rights (2014).

Acknowledgement

This work was supported by JSPS KAKENHI Grant Number JP16H06318.

References

Anderson, D. G. (1994) 'British rearmament and the "merchants of death": The 1935-36 royal commission on the manufacture of and trade in armaments', *Journal of Contemporary History*, Vol. 29, Issue 1, pp. 5–37.

Anderson, M. (1996) *Do No Harm: Supporting Local Capacities for Peace Through Aid*, Cambridge: Local Capacities for Peace Project, Collaborative for Development Action.

Anthony, I. (2015) 'The Ukraine crisis: From popular protest to major conflict', in J. Batho, A. Mash, K. Millett and A. Sailsbury (eds) *SIPRI Yearbook 2015: Armaments, Disarmament and International Security*, Oxford: Oxford University Press, pp. 57–67.

Atmore, A., Chirenje, J. M. and Mudenge, S. I. (1971) 'Firearms in southcentral Africa', *Journal of African History*, Vol. 12, Issue 4, pp. 545–56.

Bain, W. (2003) *Between Anarchy and Society: Trusteeship and the Obligations of Power*, Oxford: Oxford University Press.

Bayart, J. F. (2000) 'Africa in the world: a history of extraversion',

African Affairs, Vol. 99, No. 395, pp. 217–67.

Beachey, R. W. (1962) 'The arms trade in East Africa in the late nineteenth century', *Journal of African History*, Vol. 3, Issue 3, pp. 451–67.

Berlioux, E. F. (1872) *Slave Trade in Africa in 1872: Principally Carried on for the Supply of Turkey, Egypt, Persia And Zanzibar*, London: Edward Marsh.

Biting the Bullet Project (2006) *Developing International Norms to Restrict SALW Transfers to Non-State Actors*, London: Biting the Bullet Project.

Busby, R. (1999) *Reagan and the Iran-Contra Affair: The Politics of Presidential Recovery*, Basingstoke: Macmillan Press.

Canada, Ministry of Foreign Affairs (1998) 'A proposed global convention prohibiting the international transfer of military small arms and light weapons to non-state actors', Discussion Paper.

Capie, D. (2004) 'Armed groups, weapons availability and misuse: An overview of the issues and options for action', *Background paper for the meeting organized by the Centre for Humanitarian Dialogue in Bamako (Mali), 25 May 2004*.

Casati, G. (1891) *Ten Years in Equatoria and the Return with Emin Pasha*, Volume 2, London: Frederick Warne.

Casey-Maslen, S. (2016) 'Article 7. export and export assessment', in A. Clapham, S. Casey-Maslen, G. Giacca and S. Parker (eds) *The Arms Trade Treaty: A Commentary*, Oxford: Oxford University Press, pp. 244–85.

Casey-Maslen, S., Giacca, G. and Vestner, T. (2013) *The Arms Trade Treaty*, Geneva: Geneva Academy of International Humanitarian Law and Human Rights.

Catrina, C. (1988) *Arms Transfers and Dependence*, London: Taylor and Frances.

Chew, E. (2012) *Arming the Periphery: The Arms Trade in the Indian Ocean During the Age of Global Empire*, New York: Palgrave Macmillan.

Clapham, A. (2014) 'Weapons and armed non-state actors', in S. Casey-Maslen (ed.) *Weapons under International Human Rights Law*, Cambridge: Cambridge University Press, pp. 163–96.

_____ (2016) 'Article 6. prohibitions', in A. Clapham, S. Casey-Maslen, G. Giacca and S. Parker (eds) *The Arms Trade Treaty: A*

Commentary, Oxford: Oxford University Press, pp. 177–243.

Clarke, R. F. (1889) *Cardinal Lavigerie and the African Slave Trade*, London: Longmans.

Collier, P. (2009) *Wars, Guns, and Votes: Democracy in Dangerous Places*, New York: Harper Collins.

Cortright, D. (2008) *Peace: A History of Movements and Ideas*, Cambridge: Cambridge University Press.

Da Silva, C. and Nevil, P. (2015) 'Article 6 prohibitions', in C. Da Silva and B. Wood (eds) *Weapons and International Law: The Arms Trade Treaty*, Brussel: Larcier, pp. 88–115.

Daniel, E. L. (2001) *The History of Iran*, Westport: Greenwood Press.

Enomoto, T. (2017a) 'Controlling arms transfers to non-state actors: From the emergence of the sovereign-state system to the present', *History of Global Arms Transfer*, No. 3, pp. 3–20.

⸺ (2017b) 'Western modernity and Africa: Norms and measures on arms transfers to non-state actors', *Africa Report*, Vol. 55, pp. 116–27 (in Japanese).

⸺ (2020) *The Arms Trade Treaty: The Self, Sovereignty and Arms Transfer Control*, Kyoto: Koyo Shobo (in Japanese).

Garcia, D. (2009) 'Arms transfers beyond the state-to-state realm', *International Studies Perspectives*, Vol. 10, Issue 2, pp. 151–69.

Garcia-Mora, M. R. (1958) 'International law and the law of hostile military expeditions', *Fordham Law Review*, Vol. 27, Issue 3, pp. 309–31.

Gillespie, A. (2011) *A History of the Laws of War: Volume 3, the Customs and Laws of War With Regards to Arms Control*, Oxford and Portland: Hart Publishing.

Guy, J. J. (1971) 'A note on firearms in the Zulu Kingdom with special reference to the Anglo-Zulu war, 1879', *Journal of African History*, Vol. 12, Issue 4, pp. 557–70.

Harkavy, R. E. (1975) *The Arms Trade and International Systems*, Cambridge: Ballinger.

Henderson, C. (2013) 'The provision of arms and "non-lethal" assistance to governmental and opposition forces', *University of New South Wales Law Journal*, Vol. 36, No. 2, pp. 642–81.

Holtom, P. (2012) 'Prohibiting arms transfers to non-state actors and the Arms Trade Treaty', *UNIDIR Resources*, Geneva: United

Nations Institute for Disarmament Research.

ICRC (International Committee of the Red Cross) (2016) *Arms Transfer Decisions: Applying International Humanitarian Law Criteria — A Practical Guide*, Geneva: ICRC.

Jackson, R. H. (1990) *Quasi-States: Sovereignty, International Relations and the Third World*, Cambridge: Cambridge University Press.

Joyner, C. (2005) *International Law in the 21st Century: Rules for Global Governance*, Lanham: Rowman & Littlefield.

Kaldor, M. (1999) *New and Old Wars: Organized Violence in a Global Era*, Stanford: Stanford University Press.

Koskenniemi, M. and Leino, P. (2002) 'Fragmentation of international law?: Postmodern Anxieties', *Leiden Journal of International Law*, Vol. 15, pp. 553–79.

Krasner, S. (2001) 'Rethinking the sovereign state model', in M. Cox, T. Dunne and K. Booth (eds) *Empires, Systems and States: Great Transformations in International Politics*, Cambridge: Cambridge University Press.

_____ (2009) *Power, The State and Sovereignty: Essays on International Relations*, London: Routledge.

Krause, K. (1992) *Arms and the State: Patterns of Military Production and Trade*, Cambridge: Cambridge University Press.

_____ (1993) 'Controlling the arms trade since 1945', in R. D. Burns (ed.) *Encyclopedia of Arms Control and Disarmament, Vol. II*, New York: Charles Scribner's Sons, pp. 1021–39.

Krause, K. and MacDonald, M. K. (1993) 'Regulating arms sales through World War II', in R. D. Burns (ed.) *Encyclopedia of Arms Control and Disarmament, Vol. II*, New York: Charles Scribner's Sons, pp. 707–24.

Kurimoto, E. (1999) *Primitive and Modern Wars*, Tokyo: Iwanami Shoten (in Japanese).

Louis, R. W. (1966) 'Sir Percy Anderson's grand African strategy, 1883-1896', *English Historical Review*, Vol. 81, Issue 319, pp. 292–314.

Matthews, J. (1959) 'Free trade and the Congo Basin Treaties', *South African Journal of Economics*, Vol. 27, Issue 4, pp. 293–300.

McDonald, G. (2002) 'Strengthening controls: small arms measures', in P. Batchelor and K. Krause (eds) *Small Arms Survey 2002:*

Counting the Human Cost, Oxford: Oxford University Press, pp. 234–77.

McDonald G., Hassan S. and Stevenson, C. (2007) 'Back to basics: Transfer controls in global perspective', in E. G. Berman, K. Krause, E. LeBrun and G. McDonald (eds) *Small Arms Survey 2007: Guns and the City*, Cambridge: Cambridge University Press, pp. 117–43.

Miers, S. (1975) *Britain and the Ending of the Slave Trade*, London: Longman.

Muni, S. D. (1988) 'Third World arms control: Role of the non-allied movement', in T. Ohlson (ed.) *Arms Transfer Limitations and Third World Security*, Oxford: Oxford University Press, pp. 191–201.

Nader, L. (1969) 'Up the anthropologist: Perspectives gained from "studying up"', in D. Hyms (ed.) *Reinventing Anthropology*, New York: Pantheon Books, pp. 284–311.

Olabuenaga, P. A. A. and Gramizzi, C. (2015) 'Article 11 diversion', in C. Da Silva and B. Wood (eds) *Weapons and International Law: The Arms Trade Treaty*, Brussel: Larcier, pp. 88–115.

Onozuka, T. (2012) 'How did arms spread easily?', in K. Yokoi and T. Onozuka (eds) *World History of Armament and Arms Transfers: How Did Arms Spread Easily*, Tokyo: Nihon Keizai Hyoronsha, pp. 1–21 (in Japanese).

Ohta, I. (2016) 'Outcomes and prospects on research project on "African Potentials"', *Journal of African Studies (Africa-Kenkyu)*, Vol. 90, pp. 93–5 (in Japanese).

Parker, S. (2016) 'Article 11. diversion', in A. Clapham, S. Casey-Maslen, G. Giacca and S. Parker (eds) *The Arms Trade Treaty: A Commentary*, Oxford: Oxford University Press, pp. 342–65.

Pasha, R. G. (1892) *Seven Years in the Soudan: Being a Record of Explorations, Adventures, and Campaigns Against the Arab Slave Trade*, London: Sampson Low, Marston and Company.

Poitevin, C. (2013) 'European Union initiatives to control small arms and light weapons: Towards a more coordinated approach', *Non-Proliferation Papers*, No. 33 (https://www.files.ethz.ch/isn/175460/EUNPC_no%2033.pdf) (accessed: 5 October 2020).

Shultz, R. H. (1988) *The Soviet Union and Revolutionary Warfare: Principles,*

Practices, and Regional Comparisons, Stanford: Hoover Institution Press.

SIPRI (Stockholm International Peace Research Institute) (1971) *The Arms Trade with the Third World*, Stockholm: Almqvist and Wiksell.

Smith, C. (2008) 'Weapon transfers to non-state armed groups', *Disarmament Forum*, No. 1, pp. 45–51.

Stavrianakis, A., Xinyu, L. and Binxin, Z. (2013) *Arms and the Responsibility to Protect: Western and Chinese Involvement in Libya*, London: Saferworld.

Stone, D. (2000) 'Imperialism and sovereignty: The League of Nations' drive to control the global arms trade', *Journal of Contemporary History*, Vol. 35, No.2, pp. 213–30.

The Office of the United Nations High Commissioner for Human Rights (2014) *Arms Trade Treaty: UN Human Rights Experts Urge All States to Ratify It and Consider Disarmament* (Geneva, 23 December 2014),

(http://www.ohchr.org/EN/NewsEvents/Pages/DisplayNews.aspx?NewsID=15455&LangID=E#sthash.0tgl2RfZ.dpuf) (accessed: 5 October 2020).

Wulf, H. (1991) 'United Nations deliberations on the arms trade', in I. Anthony (ed.) *Arms Export Regulations*, Oxford: Oxford University Press, pp. 228–37.

Yihdego, Z. (2007) *The Arms Trade and International Law*, Oxford: Hart Publishing.

ARCHIVES
LNA (League of Nations Archives), A.13.1925.IX.
TNA (The National Archives, Kew) ADM 1/8699/113.

EU DOCUMENTS
8675/2/98, Rev. 2 (5 June 1998).
1999/34/CFSP (17 December 1998).
2002/589/CFSP (12 July 2002).

OSCE DOCUMENTS
FSC/3/96 (25 November 1993).
FSC.DOC/1/00/Rev.1 (24 November 2000, reissued on 20 June

2012).

FSC.DEC/3/04 (26 May 2004).

FSC.DEC/5/08 (26 May 2008).

UN DOCUMENTS

A/RES/15/1514 (14 December 1960).

A/RES/20/2131 (21 December 1965).

A/RES/25/2625 (24 October 1970).

A/RES/43/75I (7 September 1988).

A/46/301 (9 September 1991).

A/RES/46/36L (9 December 1991).

A/RES/55/255 (31 May 2001).

A/CONF.192/15 (20 July 2001).

S/RES/1373 (28 September 2001).

S/RES/1390 (16 January 2002).

S/RES/1540 (28 April 2004).

A/RES/59/90 (3 December 2004).

A/RES/60/77 (8 December 2005).

A/Conf. 217/2013/L.3 (27 March 2013).

A/67/L.58 and Add 1(1-2 April 2013).

GA/11354 (2 April 2013).

Chapter 3

Competing Local Knowledges of an Indigenous Plant: The Social Construction of Legitimate Rooibos Use in Post-Apartheid South Africa

Toshihiro Abe

1. Introduction

While the international market has long recognised wine as a leading South African agriproduct, rooibos has recently emerged as a unique and beneficial plant among other agriproducts in a global context.

The plant's uniqueness may be primarily attributed to the specificities of its vegetation. The cultivation of the rooibos plant (*Aspalathus linearis*) is concentrated in the Cederberg region, which is located around 250–300 km north of Cape Town and is characterised by rainfall of between 200 and 450 mm per annum, temperatures that can range from 0° C in winter months to 45° C in summer, a height above sea level in excess of 450 m, winter rainfall, deep, well-drained sandy soils (for taproot digging in excess of 3 m), a soil pH below 7 and its location in the fynbos (fine bush) biome (Hayes 2000: 3–4; SARC 2018:5). While these environmental conditions have been scientifically maintained, attempts to cultivate rooibos in other regions within and outside South Africa have all met with failure (Van den Berg 2012) for reasons that remain unclear.

Rooibos is currently widely acknowledged as a caffeine-free herbal tea that offers a healthy alternative to green tea, black tea and coffee for everyday consumption. Rooibos's appeal also derives from its potential benefits, which have yet to be proven, though embryonic studies and anecdotal episodes point toward its efficacy in several areas, including reduction of cholesterol levels, antidiabetic properties through regulation of blood sugar and anti-ageing properties, including reduction of wrinkles.[1] Moreover, by virtue of its contents that include 'copper, iron, protein, potassium, calcium,

69

fluoride, zinc, manganese, alpha-hydroxyl (great for the skin) and magnesium, (…) it has anti-viral, anti-spasmodic and anti-allergic properties'.[2] Medical research has recently investigated rooibos's antioxidant properties, which may have a direct positive impact on athletes' performances and indirect positive anti-ageing effects (Ajuwon, Marnewick and Davids 2015; Canda, Oguntibeju and Marnewick 2014).

However, the limited geographical range of rooibos growth and cultivation have impeded the availability of attractive rooibos products in a rapidly growing market – similar to natural marine resources – given the global demand for health-promoting herbal tea (Figures 1 to 3). The total export volume increased to 7,176 tons in 2007 from 1,023 tons in 1998 and 1,827 tons in 1999; however, the export volumes in 2015 and 2016 were 6,561 tons and 6,038 tons, respectively, attesting to the significant limitations that inhibit its production (Department of Agriculture, Forestry and Fisheries 2016:13; SARC 2018: 10).

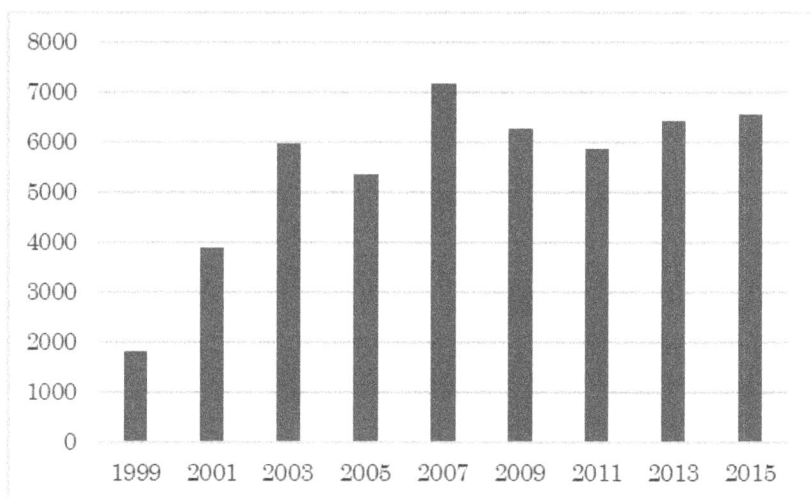

Figure 1. Total export volumes of rooibos tea from South Africa per year (tons)

Source: Department of Agriculture, Forestry and Fisheries (2016: 13)

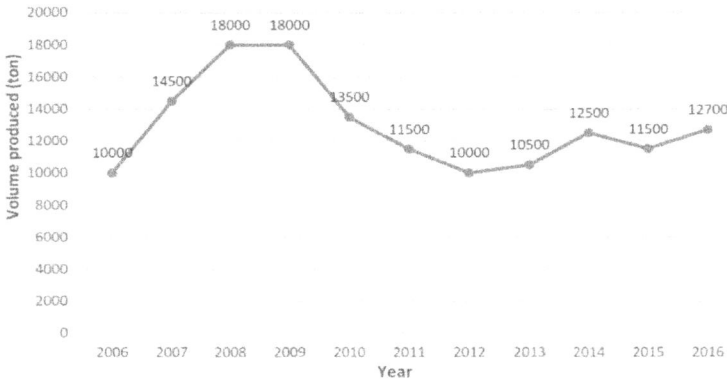

Figure 2. Recent rooibos production

Source: SARC (2017: 8)

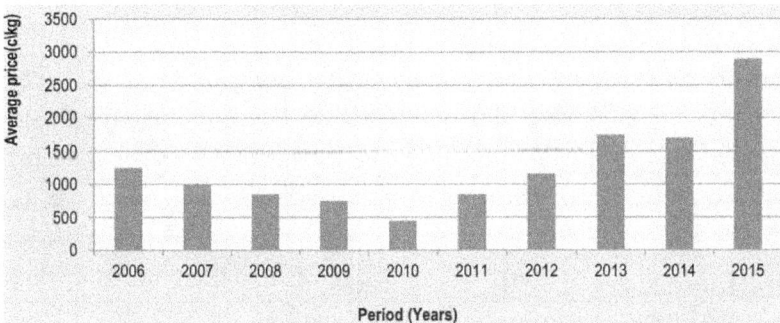

Figure 3. Rooibos tea average producer prices in South Africa

Source: Department of Agriculture, Forestry and Fisheries (2016: 7)

Increasing demand on the limited production capacity not only from regular international customers, such as Germany, the Netherlands, Japan, the UK and the US but also from rising newcomers, including China and Taiwan, have led to the increased value and price of rooibos as a valuable agriproduct, prompting a heated debate around the question of who has the right to benefit from the rooibos trade. Rachel Wynberg highlights the stark disparity between white commercial farmers and their coloured counterparts: the former occupy 93 per cent of the planted area and the latter,

71

'small-scale' farmers operating in harsher land conditions, produce only 2 per cent of the country's rooibos tea yield.[3]

The primary stakeholders in the above contestation comprise: (a) coloured or Khoisan people; and (b) Afrikaners; but (c) black Africans have recently entered this arena of contestation as an institutional custodian, mainly through governmental organisations. To examine these groups briefly, in the context of rooibos cultivation and use: (a) the Khoisan people have long been utilising wild rooibos since before the arrival of European settlers who later obtained knowledge about rooibos usage; and (b) Afrikaners are the social group who established the system of modern rooibos cultivation during the apartheid regime in the 20th century, and this process has been officially recorded. Next, questions about the rights to intellectual property – and the new concept of 'traditional knowledge', which will be discussed below – have emerged, giving rise to further questions about the origins of rooibos tea use and the first acknowledgement of its health benefits. When disputes of this nature arise, evidence for knowledge ownership comes into play. The indigenous people have almost invariably been at a disadvantage compared to European settlers in this aspect due to their culture's reliance on an oral rather than a written tradition; notions of private property, contracts and exclusive ownership were all imported to Africa by European settlers. This has given rise to the complaint that, as a vested interest group, Afrikaners have had the advantage from the outset, supported by rights talk and the mechanisms of the modern justice system.

In the post-apartheid context, the impasse in the rights talk concerning ownership of original knowledge with respect to rooibos use and the associated evidence has opened the debate to the third party, black African bureaucrats. Actors in this latter category promote the idea that rooibos is a national product and that ownership of and benefit from rooibos use should be officially controlled. As such, they argue, a proper institutional procedure for producing and benefiting from rooibos should be established. So far, few coloured or Khoisan and Afrikaner experts have contributed to institutional design on this issue in governmental organisations, perhaps partly reflecting the population balance of the country as a whole (the national population is classified as 79 per cent black, 9 per cent coloured, 9 per cent white and 2.5 per cent Asian (Statistics South Africa 2012)).

This emerging arena of contestation is well recognised in the current context, in which local and global demands intermingle in a complex manner. Sarah Ives focuses on rooibos's characteristics as socially constructed, linking the debate on 'who and what belongs in the rooibos landscape' with socially and politically active agendas (2017: 67). Harvesting, processing, consuming, cultivating or protecting rooibos are thus connected to social experiences, cultural meanings and, recently, identity politics, all of which entail specific rules in the game of meaning making in which stakeholders are engaged. At the same time, these rules contrarily produce new guises for those social experiences, cultural meanings and identity politics in an ongoing discourse of social construction. The series of experiences and meanings attached to rooibos use by several stakeholders are appropriately expressed by the term 'local knowledge' or 'local knowledge*', so that we are required to forge new pathways toward recognising and linking each of these local knowledges (Geertz 1983: 233).

As such, this arena of contestation is different from and more complicated than cases of other agriproducts with colonial backgrounds, such as sugar, cacao and rubber, which socially and politically demarcate the overseas processer/beneficiary and 'exploited' locals, reinforcing the former as a hub for trade networks (Ives 2017: 141). The poor producibility of these colonial agriproducts outside their regions of origin have promoted the reinforcement of this system.

Contestation around various unique aspects of the rooibos plant recently precipitated a landmark event that may be framed in contemporary rights terms. After nine years of negotiation, a benefit-sharing agreement between commercial rooibos firms and Khoisan indigenous organisations was reached in November 2019. This agreement stipulates that 1.5 per cent of the farm gate price from rooibos processors should go to Khoisan organisations through the government's bioprospecting trust fund as an annual traditional knowledge levy. Calculations based on that year's production indicate that the amount may reach 800,000 US dollars annually.[4]

This chapter focuses on the dynamism of politics and discourses in terms of benefit attribution/allocation/sharing of rooibos production in South Africa today. What is the crucial local knowledge that informs the plant's cultivation? To what extent is the rooibos plant currently wild or domesticated? Who should be identified as the legitimate rights holder? What are the possible options in terms of coping with the expanding global market, with specific international needs? The sections that follow begin with the debate surrounding the historical origins of rooibos use in South Africa. Scholars have pursued all written records on local rooibos use; however, the critical point on the origin has long vanished in the indigenous oral history tradition. The next stage, in which rooibos became a cultivated agricultural plant, was characterised by various actors composed of Khoisan or coloureds, Afrikaners and Russian immigrants. After the end of apartheid, with a new stakeholder in the mix – the majority party, the African National Congress (ANC) – local knowledge about rooibos use was replaced in the new arena of contestation by legislative terms and ideas imported from a global context. Rooibos itself has been characterised as a national plant in facing repetitive challenges by foreign enterprises seeking to acquire patent rights. Despite having been placed in such a global framework, a potential function of rooibos indigeneity is the continuation of a unique social cohesion while also giving it a competitive status among domestic stakeholders. Such 'management of diversity' (Gebre, Ohta and Matsuda 2017: 21), with particular mention made of the wild rooibos species, will be finally discussed from a more symbolic perspective, in view of African Potentials.

2. Interaction of Local Knowledges

2-1. Historical Origins of Rooibos Use

While it is widely believed that wild rooibos has long been used by indigenous people in the Cederberg area, the use of rooibos as a tea was first recorded in 1772 by Swedish botanist, Carl Thunberg. His diary, published as *Travels in Europe, Africa and Asia,* tell us that 'the leaves of *Borbonia cordata* are used by the country people to make tea' (Hayes 2000: 1). This seems to indicate that the original knowledge holders in relation to rooibos in the region at that time were the indigenous Khoi and/or San people. Certainly, the Khoi and San peoples inhabited the region in the 18th century. However, a counter-argument to the above notion has also been advanced based on the key terms, *Borbonia cordata* and 'country people'. Some scholars have argued that the former term does not denote rooibos (Gorelik 2017: 5; Le Quellec 2009), while the latter could be interpreted as Dutch settlers rather than Khoisan (Wynberg 2017: 43).

Although a historical record will contain some indicators, these indicators require further indicators to fix their meanings. Scant historical materials cannot match that requirement. In his thorough review of literature from the colonial era, Boris Gorelik concluded that no one described the use of *Aspalathus linearis* as a beverage among indigenous people (Gorelik 2017). Thus, an exploration with the aim of identifying an objective record fades away before the concept of the indigenous people's oral history.

One historical text that takes up the story at the beginning of the 20th century records observations about local rooibos use by Russian Jewish immigrant, Barend Ginsberg, who was descended from the Popoff family who were known as dealers in black tea (Wynberg 2017: 43). Barend Ginsberg's son, Benjamin, observed the local coloured people around Citrusdal using rooibos to make tea. Grandson, Bruce Ginsberg, has noted that, 'In earlier times, the Hottentots would cut the tea with knives and bruise it with wooden mallets against rocks. After mixing water with the bruised product, they left the bruised leaves in cracks in the rocks to sweat and partly ferment under the hot sun, before throwing it out on flat rocks to dry. Once dried, it would be swept together with rough, home-made reed brooms, and placed in bags to be carried down the mountains and sold' (ibid.).

The attempts on the part of the Ginsberg family and a local farmer, Olaf Bergh, to domesticate rooibos cultivation developed considerably when they obtained the cooperation of Dr le Fras Nortier, a medical doctor and agricultural researcher based in Clanwilliam during the 1920s, in seeking a potential cultivating method. Nortier succeeded in his mission and has become known as the father of the rooibos tea industry.[5]

As mentioned above, Barend Ginsberg was Russian Jewish and migrated in the early 1900s. Therefore, this does not support the idea that either the Khoisan or Afrikaners contributed to establishing the modern industrial system of rooibos cultivation, suggesting, rather, a fundamental but indirect influence from coloured people with a crucial but supporting role played by Nortier in Ginsberg's project.

One further critical episode concerning seed collection should also be recounted here. A Khoi woman, Tryntjie Swarts, accidentally uncovered a natural eco-system when working at Nortier's farm, thereby contributing significantly to his research productivity. An interview with Swarts by James van Putten reads as follows:

> When Dr Nortier began planting tea, he needed seeds to be collected. The best way to do this was to lie on one's tummy and use the wetted tip of a match to pick out seeds from the soil. One day, Tryntjie was lying on her stomach and saw an ant collecting seeds. The next day, she told her husband Jan to bring a spade and they discovered heaps of seeds in the ant burrows. (…) But 'wine talks', and one evening, after lots of wine, she spilled the beans to a group of friends, and everyone knew about the 'golden nests' (Wynberg 2017: 43).

Seed collection was a crucial but difficult mission at that time, and local gatherers were paid '£5 per matchbox, which would have been approximately R7,000[6] today' (Gorelik 2017: 38). With this finding, Benjamin was able to expand his business network to neighbouring areas and launch the first rooibos tea company, Eleven O'Clock (Gorelik 2017: 36; Wynberg 2017: 43–4).

These episodes show that, even at the dawn of modern industrialisation in rooibos farming, Khoi, Russian and Afrikaner figures contributed to deepening local knowledge regarding rooibos production. One farmer's comment, in particular: 'There has been no human intervention in the seeds yet' (Ives 2017: 82) reminds us of the significance of the above story when considering the concept of local knowledge in rooibos farming, as it blurs the distinction between knowledge holders with respect to wild rooibos and those with knowledge of cultivated rooibos. Afrikaners may be primarily attributed to the latter position, as we will see in the following section. However, Khoisan people should also be included among the latter.

2-2. Local Knowledge at the Stage of Commercial Farming

2-2-1. The Story of Seed Collection Continues

Further stories of seed collection may also be told. Tryntjie Swarts's discovery, without doubt, contributed to opening the door to the commercial farming of cultivated rooibos. However, the character of rooibos seed, which resists human intervention, has required greater development of low-tech solutions based on long-term careful observation to sustain farming since the time of Nortier's project up to present-day cultivation. The explanation offered below by a farmer in Clanwilliam demonstrates how Afrikaner farmers have deployed their local knowledge, even since entering the stage of industrialisation:

> Now to be able to grow those little plants (seedlets), you need seeds.
> ….
>
> If you come into the plantations in November and early December, you will see hundreds of seeds on the flowers. And then, you may think, 'Oh that is lovely, you harvest the seeds and you have got the seeds for next year's March plant.' Ah… nature doesn't make it easy for farmers. It's totally impossible to harvest those seeds from the plant. But even if you can do it, it won't help you. Because the seeds are still green. You can go and plant green seeds but nothing will grow. They will all just rot and die. So, you have to wait for the seeds to become ripe on the plant. Now, Nature has a second way of making things difficult. At the moment the seed is ripe, the pod splits open like that … and it shoots out the seed. So now, you must find that 3–4-mm seed down there. Nature has a third way of making things difficult. Let's see how I can find the seeds. They are the same colour as sand …
>
> So, two methods are used to collect the seeds. The first method is used by farmers at the very small plantations. … They search for a very specific kind of ant, alumite. They find the ants and follow them to their nests, because the ants collect the seeds and take them into their nests.
> …

But now, that's only half the story, or not even half. ... The plant is so clever. In case you didn't know, plants are far more intelligent than human beings. ... So, what the plant does to protect the seeds is, on that little seed, they grow a tiny little thing that can best be described as an appendix. That little appendix has nothing to do with the seed. That is for the ants. So, the ants collect the seeds, take them into their nests, and they eat only these little appendices. And the real seeds are now perfectly protected on the ground. Clever. But the plants are even more clever. Those seeds will not germinate at the same time, even if the conditions for germination are perfect. The reason is obvious: if they all germinate at once, and there is drought or fire, they will all be killed.[7] ...

But in the bigger farms, the farmers cannot get the seeds from the ants' nests. There are just not enough ants for them. So, the bigger farmers, they must buy these seeds from farmers who plant rooibos, not for tea, but for seeds. Now these farmers don't harvest; they fertilise the plants, stimulate them to produce masses of seeds, but then they face exactly the same problems as outlined above. They cannot harvest the seeds from the plants. ...

What they do?... In December when the plants are in seed, they go into the plantations with ordinary brooms, like those used to sweep the house, and they sweep around the plants. The top 2 to 3 mm of sand is swept into small heaps that are picked up and dumped into bath water. The sand sinks to the bottom of the water, and the seeds float. They skim the seeds, the seeds are placed into a machine that blows them dry, and the air dries the seed. (August 2018, Clanwilliam)

The farmer's humorous words, particularly those underlined, refer to the deployment of local knowledges obtained, not by using modern technology but through engaged observation of natural mechanisms. Afrikaner farmers developed rooibos cultivation throughout the 20th-century apartheid regime, yet, owing to the rooibos plant's unique nature, which continues to maintain a 'wild' status that defies human intervention, they were compelled to pursue their understanding of it in the local environmental context.

As one Afrikaans farmer explained, with regard to the plant's own protective mechanism, 'If there is no fire, only the soft seeds will germinate. The hard seeds need fire, and in fires the hardest seeds still do not germinate. It's nature protecting itself' (Ives 2017: 82). Essentially, the germination mechanisms of the rooibos plant remain beyond the capabilities of human intervention. Even at the stage of cultivation, local knowledge thus appears as merely an outcome of studying a natural system that lies beyond human control.

These episodes call to mind the question of the extent to which the current rooibos plant is deemed to have been domesticated. Logically, a question about the meaning of wildness follows. For instance, why can farmers not collect seeds directly from the rooibos plant? Because the farmer must wait for the rooibos seed to ripen in a pod until the seed bursts out, and immature green seeds artificially extracted from the plant are of no use to the farmers. This knowledge was acquired after efforts at cultivation had begun, but the level of knowledge remains at a similar level to that long used by indigenous people using wild rooibos, with respect to the plant's uncontrollable status.

2-2-2. Knowledge for Sustainable Cultivation

Local knowledge about rooibos farming goes further in dealing with the environmental elements. An Afrikaner farmer indicates the specific condition of the soil, which differs from 'the pH of 7 that typical European plants require' (Ives 2017: 80). If the soil were changed to accommodate other plants, such as grapes, 'the natural bacteria die, and regaining the acidity is next to impossible …. Once they decide to do citrus on the soil, that's it. You can't go back to rooibos' (Ives 2017: 80).

Ives reports similar comments from other Afrikaner farmers, one of whom said that he kept his land natural to protect the endemic species, criticising other farmers, 'particularly those who cultivated citrus' (Ives 2017: 81). It is certain that rooibos growth depends considerably on specific soil conditions, so that protecting the original composition of the soil itself constitutes a form of local knowledge in circumstances where other imported crops and plants are being prepared for cultivation in the indigenous soil. Local (environmental) contexts and conditions have been changing, and the local knowledge that is critical to the rooibos plant's survival must be updated accordingly.

However, the following comment from a coloured farmer compels us to reconsider the concept of indigenous plants' natural status:

> [A] coloured farmer … repeatedly emphasised how natural his farming practices were. … 'When we plant, our tea is wild tea mixed with planted tea, mixed with other natural bushes – because this is nature' (Ives 2017: 92).

3. Configuration of Local Knowledges Regarding Rooibos Use in Post-Apartheid South Africa

3-1. New Frameworks and Vocabularies for Local Knowledges Have Been Imported

As outlined in earlier sections, local knowledges concerning rooibos use have long been the domain of those who cultivate the soil and, although the origins of the plant's use may have been attributed to Khoi and San people in the historical past, during the process of cultivation, not only Khoisan and Afrikaners but also other immigrant experts, such as the Ginsberg family, have been involved as critical actors. If we acknowledge all these actors as significant contributors to the rooibos industry of today, we cannot dismiss the Khoisan people's role nor that of the Afrikaner population. With that said, the present-day rooibos market is almost entirely occupied by white enterprises, and this has provoked new political action, with new terms, regarding the ownership of local knowledges.

In September 2010, the South African San Council sent a letter to the Director-General of Environmental Affairs and claimed rights as the primary knowledge holders regarding rooibos and honeybush tea use (Schroeder et al. 2020; Wynberg 2017: 41). Khoi people were forced to take action to negotiate with the San council toward joint recognition with respect to the traditional rights, and these parties published a memorandum of understanding acknowledging the importance of working together on 'traditional knowledge and associated intellectual property rights, in particular with regard to rooibos and honeybush'.[8]

80

Local knowledge, in its original form regarding the use of rooibos leaves to make tea, was renamed, according to the new framework of bioprospecting, as intellectual property (IP) and traditional knowledge (TK). Indubitably, these are terms that practitioners in the planting fields have never used.

Among these legal terms, certain types of TK can be protected by IP law; however, other types of TK cannot be protected by the IP framework, because IP's foundations lie in individual property rights (Ushenta 2019: 5, 10). The notion of TK stems from cultural knowledge shared and passed on through successive generations across a historical timespan; therefore, TK cannot necessarily be exclusively attributed to a certain homogeneous group as the knowledge holders.

These terms have notably entered the debate in the South African context after the government's ratification of the Nagoya Protocol on Access to Genetic Resources and the Fair and Equitable Sharing of Benefits Arising from their Utilisation to the Convention on Biological Diversity, which falls under the Convention of Biological Diversity (CBD)[9] category. Article 5 of the Nagoya protocol states that the related party (user) who benefits from utilising the concerned genetic resources must follow 'domestic legislation regarding the established rights of these indigenous and local communities over these genetic resources', based on 'mutually agreed terms'. Article 12 of the protocol reiterates the point: 'In implementing their obligations under this Protocol, Parties shall in accordance with domestic law take into consideration indigenous and local communities' customary laws, community protocols and procedures, as applicable, with respect to traditional knowledge associated with genetic resources.'

How are the parties to proceed, then, in the absence of domestic legislation or customary laws? From the usage of specific terms, it is clear that the protocol was first intended to secure the rights of indigenous peoples against the threat of aggressive actors from developed countries, such as pharmaceutical companies or multinational corporations.

In South Africa, partly as a reflection of this trend, the Ministry of Science and Technology published a Protection, Promotion,

Development and Management of Indigenous Knowledge Systems Bill, 2014 (*Government Gazette* 38574, 20 March 2015), which was opened for public comment on 20 March, 2015, in the *Government Gazette*. The bill's stated objectives were 'To provide for the protection, promotion, development and management of indigenous knowledge systems; to provide for the establishment and functions of the National Indigenous Knowledge Systems Office; to provide for the management of rights of indigenous knowledge holders; to provide for the establishment and functions of the Advisory Panel on indigenous knowledge systems; to provide for access and conditions of access to knowledge of indigenous communities; to provide for the registration, accreditation and certification of indigenous knowledge holders and practitioners; to provide for the facilitation and coordination of indigenous knowledge systems-based innovation; and to provide for matters incidental thereto'.

At this stage, local knowledges are subject to examination, official recognition, registration with an appropriate holder and administration not for use outside the regulation. A competition arose between various local knowledges for recognition as legitimate under the imported framework, and the institutionalisation of local knowledges was thus impending.

Furthermore, the Bill of 2014 ostentatiously opened the new game of legal discourses, particularly with regard to the relationship with Intellectual Property Law Amendment Act 2013 (IPLAA) which also deals with the notion of indigenous knowledge under the custody of the Department of Trade and Industry, but with a different approach from that of the IKS Bill.[10] The Bill of 2014 was scrutinised by comments and reviews, and a revised bill was drafted in 2016. Following interdepartmental works on the overlapping matters between the IKS Bill and IPLAA, a redrafted Bill was approved by the National Assembly on 13 September, 2018.[11] The IKS Bill defines the term 'indigenous knowledge' as 'knowledge of a functional nature; knowledge of natural resources; and indigenous cultural expressions', and thus the clause is appropriate to the rooibos issue.

As Ushenta indicates, the IKS Bill has prompted the assertion that indigenous knowledge is a national asset that should be officially protected. However, 'it does not expressly recognise that it is the right of traditional knowledge holders to have their knowledge protected' (Ushenta 2019: 49). Put differently, the term 'local' in relation to local knowledge has now been extended to South African locals, thus belonging to the nation.

3-2. A New Contentious Arena Regarding Local Knowledges

Other elements beyond the South African government's ratification of the Nagoya protocol, which make up the background to the institutionalisation of local knowledge on rooibos use, have emerged in aggressive foreign business strategies over the past two decades.

In 1993, a company named Forever Young, founded by a South African, Annique Theron, filed a trademark application for the term 'rooibos' to the United States Patent and Trademark Office, and it was approved in 1994. The reason for this was that skincare products containing rooibos extract had been well received in the European and US markets.[12] South African Rooibos Limited filed a lawsuit in 1995 against this registration with the support of the South African government and Western Cape Province. After Forever Young passed its patent right to another US company (Burke International) in 2001, the case continued between Rooibos Limited and Burke International until 2005, followed by a settlement in which both parties voluntarily withdrew their trademark registrations for exclusive global rights to the term 'rooibos'.

Again, in 2013, a French company, Compagnie de Trucy, attempted to obtain a trademark patent in France with the name 'rooibos'. This time, South African authorities took action against this move through EU channels and opened a new pathway for debates of this nature with the introduction of the term geographical indication (GI), which is distinct from a trademark and certifies a product by the name of its place of production (as, for example, champagne, port and sherry).[13] In 2014, the South African Ministry of Trade and Industry successfully ended the French company's operation by registering GI status in the economic partnership agreement between southern African nations and the European Union.[14]

Given the global trend in attempting to acquire exclusive rights and benefits from local products based on local knowledges, the local government cannot but promote any sort of institutional and legislative mechanism aimed at controlling, managing or maintaining products that rely on local knowledges. However, experts in such legal and political fields are often removed from the pragmatic arena of local knowledge. In the case of rooibos, the new party overseeing such institutional management is composed of politicians and bureaucrats affiliated to the ruling ANC party, which is dominated by a black African majority. At first glance, this does not appear to have any particular bearing, yet, the following statistics reveal the political influence:

> The demographics of the rooibos-growing region are dramatically different from the rest of the country. It is classified as 80 per cent colored, 15 per cent white, 5 per cent black and less than 1 per cent Asian. The national population is classified as 79 per cent black, 9 per cent colored, 9 per cent white and 2.5 per cent Asian (Coombe, Ives and Huizenga 2014: 226).

This drastic difference may have constituted one of the reasons for the heated debates in public comments on the IKS Bills of 2014 and 2016, in the form of questions about the role and mandate of the National Indigenous Knowledge Systems Office (NIKSO). NIKSO would be in charge of comprehensive tasks around IKS legislation. The tasks would include functioning as a registration office for tasks such as accreditation and certification of indigenous knowledge applicants. It is further expected to function as a consultancy capable of assisting indigenous communities that require help in promoting businesses or as a platform for exploring innovation.[15] It is clear that NIKSO would be the dominant player in the game surrounding the legitimacy of local knowledges, prompting criticism of the vague grounds on which NIKSO wields its power. This is actually the point that the South African Rooibos Council emphasised most strongly in the public hearing on the Bill at the Department of Science and Technology.[16] Predictably, rights issues would inevitably lead to conflict regarding legitimate rights holders.

Nevertheless, NIKSO was criticised as not having been based on established mechanisms for dispute resolution (SARC 2018;[17] Ushenta 2019: 19–20). Rather, without a concrete base for dispute resolution, the concept of benefit-sharing among conflicting parties has emerged as one of NIKSO's tasks. A more controversial mandate is that NIKSO should be the official custodian of the concerned product if the conflicting parties fail to reach a mutual agreement (Protection, Promotion, Development and Management of Indigenous Knowledge Systems Bill, 2016 (*Government Gazette* 39910, 8 April 2016)), a clause that should be regarded with suspicion by both Afrikaner businesses and Khoisan organisations: 'In a situation where no community has come forward to claim indigenous knowledge, the Bill stated that NIKSO would act as custodian. The concern was how funds were accrued from such ownership and benefits approved. No provision was made as to how decisions would be made by communities. It was unclear whether a consensus or majority was required for decisions … if it [the Bill] was passed as is a lot of power would be in the hands of NIKSO …' (Submission by the South African Rooibos Council).[18]

As such, the rooibos industry has continuously reiterated its stance that it does not admit the legitimate status of the Khoisan people's local knowledge and has stayed away from the negotiation table until concern arose around whether the industry would be granted the licence to launch a rooibos business. The benefit-sharing agreement of March 2019 was reached among the following actors: the Department of Environmental Affairs, the South African Rooibos Council (i.e. the rooibos industry), the South African San Council and the National Khoi and San Council (i.e. traditional knowledge holders).

At this stage, local knowledges on rooibos use cannot be used by their original holders without permission from the official licence provider, regardless of whether the knowledge derives from a Khoisan or an Afrikaner source. Put differently, local knowledge is placed in an abstract sphere in which the term is defined and identified with other legal terms but not with the rooibos product itself, indirectly referring to the national framework for its belonging.

Possible outcomes of this political deal, as Wynberg observes, include new conflicting agendas regarding future legitimate knowledge holders among the indigenous people:

> Questions of how exactly benefits will be shared at a local level remain unresolved, and could result in conflicts. … Although small-scale rooibos producer communities of the Cederberg and Suid Bokkeveld are nominally included in the agreement as part of the Khoi people, this assumes that such communities identify with contemporary Khoi political structures. These coloured farmers are typically mixed-race descendants of European settlers, former slaves, and Khoi and San people, who do not easily identify as 'indigenous'. However, this could change. As one farmer remarked: 'The [rooibos] agreement means that people are asking themselves who is Khoisan. Everyone now wants to be recognised as Khoisan.'[19]

Yet one Khoisan activist explains that this point is not essential[20]: First, Khoisan beneficiaries would not be limited to those somehow having a 'pure' indigenous pedigree – many descendants have already mixed with people from other roots, and under the UN Declaration on Indigeneity even a sixteenth of DNA markers qualifies someone for indigenous status. Second, the money produced from the benefit-sharing agreement is likely to chiefly be invested in providing sustainable options for Khoisan autonomous rooibos production, including by establishing think tanks, educating young scholars in botanic studies and agriculture and providing autonomous farms. Khoisan people who have long directly engaged in rooibos farms or associated businesses will be those primarily dealt with, but benefit sharing itself will not simply equate to redistribution of money to individual stakeholders. Accordingly, an increase in the number of persons who claim Khoisan descent is not a matter of serious concern, even if some claim a pseudoidentity.

4. Concluding Remarks: Images of Local Knowledge in a Global Market

In earlier sections, we began with the basic local knowledge that allowed humans to recognise rooibos as having beneficial properties and to use it to make tea via a fermentation process, followed by another type of local knowledge whereby humans could arrange and maintain environmental conditions conducive to rooibos cultivation. Related technologies in business and politics, aimed at enlarging the rooibos market, developed during the apartheid regime, which left the specific social relationship between the Afrikaner community and the Khoisan people.[21] However, the end of the apartheid regime, including the ANC's political power with a black African majority, opened up a new framework that allowed the government to deal with the unique plant. Rooibos was then given a national status that entails the following two changes in a global context: first, rooibos was positioned as a beneficial genetic resource, according to an international convention, which requires the concerned government to take care of the original users' rights; and second, international companies attempted to gain patent rights to rooibos in the international arena so that the South African government as well as business groups needed to protect their rights against these international rivals. The South African situation is also unique in comparison with the use of beneficial plants in other countries with respect to the stakeholders' relationships with one another: the substantial holder groups of local knowledges may comprise two groups – Khoisan and Afrikaner – and the new custodians – the governmental organisations composed mainly of black Africans – have emerged with their own political agenda. These stakeholders constitute the triad that has its roots in the apartheid past – two major conflicting parties, Afrikaner and black African, with Khoisan, or coloured, between them. This triadic structure clearly differs from a structure in which the locals are obliged to resist biopiracy or improper usage of local resources by entities from foreign developed countries, which might be a presuppositional understanding of the indigenous knowledge (rights) concept as it is understood in the Nagoya protocol. As outlined above, the unique triad witnessed in South Africa has resulted in contentious discourses on legitimate rule with respect to local knowledges: Which local knowledge stakeholder – Khoisan or Afrikaner – should be judged more original in terms of holding or inheriting indigenous knowledge according to the global norm? In this era of global aggressive competition, should rooibos be institutionally protected because of its national role in both its symbolic and economic forms? To what extent can a government body with a black African majority manage this issue as an institutional custodian?

However, globalisation, which is involved in the rooibos industry, has generated a different trend to the institutional and normal discourse about legitimate rights holders. Global markets have deployed a different game with local knowledge stakeholders, with the focus on idealistic images or fantasies about local knowledge rather than on the local knowledge itself. A glance at the shelves of herbal teas in supermarkets allows the consumer to identify various rooibos products by their packaging: some products are neatly wrapped and use simple logos and colours, which perhaps emphasise the product's naturalness or organic status, but other examples attempt to emphasise their country of origin more robustly. Such products include on their packaging wild animals, such as elephants and lions, which are never found in the dry fynbos area suitable for rooibos cultivation, acacia trees in savanna landscapes, Zulu women with Zulu beads, neither of which bear any geographic relation to the rooibos plant, and indigenous people's huts, but those of Bantu-speaking ethnic groups and not of the Khoisan. These packages are appealing, as 'they are from Africa's natural environment', but their points of appeal are wholly false and misleading in their indication of the tea's origin, because the Cederberg region is not home to Zulu people with Zulu beads, acacia trees, lions, zebras, elephants or Bantu-speaking people's huts.

Ives (2017: 191) reported an interview with an individual in charge of marketing at a rooibos company:

> We looked at our competitors … Foreigners loved the animals, but locally, the [animals alone] don't move us. We wanted to give the brand a stronger presence on the shelf. So, we went with animals with a haiku. It's African and Asian. The Haikus are an Asian connotation. The box is white, simple and pure.

Using wild animals that inhabit the savanna might be understood critically as promoting primitivism and orientalistic exoticism in

88

relation to African products. More modestly, we can also say that wild animals are evocative of nature's mysteries, which continue to defy science even in this era of technology. This may reflect the peculiar vegetation mechanisms of rooibos, which has defied attempts at cultivation in areas other than Cederberg, and its mysterious benefits for the human body. A scientific explanation of rooibos's efficacy is first derived from its antioxidant properties, attributed to its flavonoid content, but the mechanisms by which these flavonoids work in rooibos have yet to be revealed. The following statement is typical of rooibos advertising: 'Rooibos Tea: The Miracle Drink That Boosts Your Health … the antioxidants present in Rooibos tea slow down the human aging process and boost the strength of the immune system, resulting in a more energetic, healthier and younger self'.[22] Some may justify the use of signs, such as animals in savanna landscapes and Zulu culture, based on rooibos's status as a national symbol of South African uniqueness, claiming that its assets should not be restricted/attributed to any specific social group. (Although this explanation might invite a further criticism: 'Then, why is no visual sign associated specifically with the Khoisan people included in the design?').

According to Piya Chatterjee, the history of tea consumption may be summed up as 'the mappings of exoticism, the continuous struggles over symbol and sign, and the cultural cartographies of conquest' (Chatterjee 2001: 21), accompanying with a remarkable orientalistic image such as the East India pavilion at the Chicago World's Fair of 1893 which served tea in a setting with 'a lofty gate surmounted by four minarets… profoundly ornamented in an elaborate arabesque design…. Khidmatgars [servants] dressed in red and gold uniforms completed the effect of an oriental magnificence' (Chatterjee 2001: 93). Lipton competed with the strategy by using other oriental images such as 'elephants, striding horses, turbaned natives' at the same exhibition (Chatterjee 2001: 94). Such tendency has not changed in an era of Internet-based marketing. Paige West acknowledges consumers' fantasies and desires to connect 'ecologically noble savages and pure, guileless economic primitiveness' through buying a cup of coffee (West 2012: 233), which coincide with the consumers' relative superiority in modern social and cultural hierarchies (West 2012: 23). Ives adopts this critical stance in analysing the social environment in which the rooibos industry is currently maintained: '… how the rooibos industry uses images of primitivity to sell the product, while it simultaneously masks the structural relations that contribute to regional poverty' (Ives 2017: 22). Her criticism further proceeds to the point where even fair-trade business models are not blameless with respect to this hypocrisy: 'Tea consumers in the United States and Europe can fantasize about preserving a wild "African Bush" or draw comfort from the idea that their purchases help "Third World" laborers earn livelihoods or maintain a particular way of life. For some consumers, the ethics of consumption center on a self-fashioning that removes them from global inequality or complicity in environmental destruction' (Ives 2017: 3).

Marketing methods that use images evoking the primitive and uncultivated to promote sales may also promote a negative disparity or distance between producers and consumers. In this regard, a local farmer's lament – 'We need consumer education. Rooibos of origin. Estates like wine. Name by region, description, and so on' – should be recognised to be a practical path to go for local producers (Ives 2017: 193).

However, this perception of enlightenment does not guarantee the consumers' active learning, as international consumers are not always motivated to understand the backgrounds and politics associated with exotic products. An appreciation that is overly critical on a moralistic basis may reduce the product's appeal, as exemplified by the international response to so-called 'blood diamonds'. Moreover, many consumers in a global market simply do not care about justification or logical criticism regarding the use of misleading images as advertising strategies. This dynamic between international consumers and local producers is not unlike sightseeing. A basic principle of sightseeing is that tourists experience an external world temporarily in circumstances wherein they can enjoy, or at least, tolerate local culture. Few tourists desiring to spend their holiday in nature also want bed bugs, dangerous bacteria and extreme climates, which are inevitable realities of time spent in nature. Rather, they bring their own impressions, fantasies and pre-acquired knowledges to their holiday destinations. Locations in which these images and fantasies can be subsumed and digested are popular with tourists. Surely, these staged relationships between consumers (tourists) and locals are open to criticism, in view of the potential creation of unhealthy distances between them, sometimes informed by distorted stereotypes.

Nonetheless, it is still possible to manage such situations more strategically. General analyses of people's perceptions of the everyday world reveal that human recognition is characterised by continuous arbitrary meaning making, the projection of expectations and fantasies onto any objects within view and repetitive use and remedy of stereotypes. This situation keenly reflects Kirumira's argument on the concept of indigeneity in the contemporary African context, where the concept is 'used to negotiate with social, philosophical, cultural, and environmental issues' (Kirumira 2017: 388), and where we need to interrogate 'almost alternative discourses of/on what indigeneity has come to mean in particular places and at key moments' (ibid.).

People view the world through various frames and diverse meanings, and enjoy the consumption of goods through images and fantasies as opposed to knowledge of their function. The rooibos image, which may not be entirely accurate in terms of the exact knowledge and understanding of local producers, opens up a new pathway for the construction of meaning. Key to this is the fact that the Khoisan people are the original knowledge holders of rooibos usage. This may be maximised to stimulate the fantasies and imaginations of global consumers who may expect mysterious benefits in rooibos and imagine the indigenous people's long history of survival as supported by rooibos consumption.

Tea made from wild rooibos may offer a potential means of coping with both global consumers' preferences for a particular image of rooibos and the experiences and environments of small-scale Khoisan farmers. Although more than 90 per cent of cultivated rooibos production in the current market is centred on large companies owned by white business circles, coloured or Khoisan people in remote areas have long harvested wild(er) rooibos. The wild rooibos family, which can be used for tea, has four main types, namely, rooibos (red bush), vaalbos (grey bush), swartbos (black bush) and rooibruin (red brown). Rooibos (red bush) is further classified into the Cederberg and Nortier (Rockland) types (Hayes 2000: 3; Erickson 2003). The latter was specifically selected by authorities during the apartheid regime, and this has continued on present-day large business farms: 'Consumers preferred the taste and colour associated with rooi tea, thus the Control Board discouraged producers from cultivating tea other than rooi tea. By 1965 all tea produced was rooi tea' (Hayes 2000: 3). However, a scholarly study has recently suggested that the wild forms of rooibos 'might be used to improve characteristics, such as yield and disease resistance, of the cultivated form' (Erickson 2003). Wild rooibos and its components may yield greater health benefits than the cultivated species. Regarding the current global demand for rooibos in light of its purported health benefits, the character of wild rooibos appears to increase its attractiveness, and small-scale farmers in peripheral areas have retained these wild species.

> The variety developed by Nortier (the so-called mak tee, or cultivated tea) is more erect than the semi-prostate wild rooibos. It lives from five to fifteen years and cannot survive fires. Uncultivated tea is more robust and produces crop for longer. Reportedly, rooibos can be harvested from some wild plants for fifty years or more (Gorelik 2017: 38).

Wild rooibos has also been examined in terms of its adaptability in the face of future – or, ongoing – climate change. For example, wild rooibos prefers and thrives with less precipitation than cultivated rooibos and, thus, the possible adaptation of an earlier rooibos type to warming conditions may be inferred (Lötter and Maitre 2014: 1213–4).

Wild rooibos in such contexts would be treated as premium rooibos, superior to cultivated rooibos, and would continue to satisfy the needs of global consumers who desire evocative images and stories. Few consumers will undertake a pilgrimage to the area of rooibos production. Accordingly, there may be scope for strategic action on the part of indigenous people to deploy an elaborated image of indigeneity that aligns well with, and indeed complements, the geographical indication (GI) certification trend. Competing local knowledges about rooibos use in post-apartheid South Africa thus generate a multi-layered dynamism of discourse on indigeneity, comprising the concepts of indigenous plant, indigenous ethnic group and indigenous knowledge systems in the context of global politics. In the words of Edward Kirumira, as '[i]ndigeneity becomes a dynamic, socially constructed and re-constructed African worldview' (Kirumira 2017: 393), competing discourses on the origins of, and crucial contributions to, current rooibos use demonstrate how rooibos indigeneity functions to create a social assemblage in a pluralistic society.

Endonotes

[1] https://www.medicalnewstoday.com/articles/323637.php#7-potential-health-benefits (accessed: 20 December 2019).

[2] http://www.sarooibos.co.za (accessed: 4 January 2020).

[3] Rachel Wynberg, 'San and Khoi claim benefits from rooibos' (1 Nov 2019). https://mg.co.za/article/2019-11-01-00-san-and-khoi-claim-benefits-from-rooibos (accessed: 3 January 2020).

Wynberg recognises the significance of the agreement among ethnic groups in terms of benefit-sharing compared to other plant cases in South Africa. She compares hoodia – which is used for its anti-obesity properties – pelargonium, buchu and kanna to rooibos, noting, however, that these plants promise 'nothing in the order of that anticipated from rooibos'.

[4] Rachel Wynberg, 'San and Khoi claim benefits from rooibos' (1 Nov 2019). https://mg.co.za/article/2019-11-01-00-san-and-khoi-claim-benefits-from-rooibos (accessed: 3 January 2020);

Brian Browdie, 'South Africa's Khoisan community will finally get a share of the commercialisation of rooibos' (6 Nov 2019) https://qz.com/africa/1742670/south-africas-khoisan-to-get-a-share-rooibos-tea-commerce/ (accessed: 20 December 2019).

[5] https://www.s2a3.org.za/bio/Biograph_final.php?serial=2046 (accessed: 23 December 2019).

[6] Approximately 500 US dollars as of January 2020.

[7] However, the method of using fire to cause tough rooibos seeds to

germinate may be rooted in local practices, of which the original knowledge holders are obscure: 'To stimulate sprouting of rooibos bushes and meet the increased demand for tea, farmers and harvesters regularly burnt the land where the plant occurred, often immediately after, gathering in the crop. To a lesser extent, this method is still employed by Coloured communities and cooperatives who harvest wild rooibos. The practice could have evolved from indigenous techniques. Isaac Schapera reported that the north-western tribes of the San burnt veld at the end of the dry season so that edible plants could germinate better when the rains began' (Gorelik 2017: 37).

[8] San and Khoi Memorandum of Association signed on 18 July 2013.

[9] A UN conference called the Earth Summit in Rio de Janeiro in 1992 introduced the notion of traditional knowledge of indigenous and local communities and, thus, embodying it. 'Although the CBD does not create guaranteed rights for traditional communities, it is thought to be one of the most significant international instruments with regard to the protection of traditional knowledge, as it was the first international instrument to give recognition to traditional knowledge and call for its protection' (Ushenta 2019: 25).

[10] In the IP Amendment Act (*Government Gazette*, 10 December, 2013), indigenous cultural expressions or knowledge are referred to as 'phonetic or verbal expressions' such as stories and poetry; 'musical and sound expressions' such as songs; 'expressions by actions' such as dances; 'tangible expressions' such as handicrafts and architecture. Although the phrase 'including, but not limited to' appears just before the examples given above, it is clear that the clause includes no specific focus on the rooibos or honeybush matters raised by the Khoisan people following the government's ratification of the Nagoya Protocol in 2010.

[11] https://pmg.org.za/committee-meeting/26232/; Ushenta (2019: 10).

[12] See WIPO HP:
https://www.wipo.int/ipadvantage/en/details.jsp?id=2691.

[13] 'Tensions between EU and South Africa brewing over Rooibos' (24 April 2013)
http://www.ictsd.org/bridges-news/bridges-africa/news/tensions-between-eu-and-south-africa-brewing-over-rooibos.

[14] 'Rooibos protected in EU trade pact' *Business Report* (21 July 2014)
https://www.iol.co.za/business-report/international/rooibos-

protected-in-eu-trade-pact-1723219.

'Geographic name protection has also been given to South African wines from several regions, like Robertson, in the same manner that the French industry protects its Bordeaux and Champagne trademarks.

In addition, the volume of local wine that can be exported to Europe tariff-free every year has been increased from 47 million litres to 110 million litres in terms of the trade deal.'

[15] New TK Bill – South Africa, https://afro-ip.blogspot.com/2016/04/new-tk-bill-south-africa.html.

[16] Protection, Promotion, Development and Management of Indigenous Knowledge Systems Bill: public hearings day 2, Department of Science and Technology (25 January 2017), Chairperson: Ms L Maseko (ANC), https://pmg.org.za/committee-meeting/23881/.

[17] https://pmg.org.za/committee-meeting/23881/.

[18] https://pmg.org.za/committee-meeting/23881/.

[19] Rachel Wynberg, 'San and Khoi claim benefits from rooibos' (1 Nov 2019). https://mg.co.za/article/2019-11-01-00-san-and-khoi-claim-benefits-from-rooibos.

[20] Interviewed by author, February 2020, Cape Town.

[21] 'Most coloured residents did not have access to land. Today, commercial farmers—who are almost exclusively white—oversee the cultivation of approximately 93 percent of rooibos, while small-scale coloured farmers, unable to access significant amounts of land, cultivate less than 7 percent (Sandra Kruger and Associates 2009)' in (Ives 2017: 6).

[22] https://savvytokyo.com/rooibos-tea-miracle-drink-boosts-health/.

Acknowledgement

This work was supported by JSPS KAKENHI Grant Number JP16H06318.

References

Ajuwon, O. R., Marnewick, J. L., and Davids, L. M. (2015) 'Rooibos

(*Aspalathus linearis*) and its Major Flavonoids — Potential Against Oxidative Stress-Induced Conditions', in S. J. T. Gowder (ed.) *Basic Principles and Clinical Significance of Oxidative Stress*, Rijeka: InteckOpen
(https://www.intechopen.com/books/basic-principles-and-clinical-significance-of-oxidative-stress/rooibos-aspalathus-linearis-and-its-major-flavonoids-potential-against-oxidative-stress-induced-cond) (accessed: 23 December 2020)

Canda, B. D., Oguntibeju, O. O. and Marnewick, J. L. (2014) 'Effects of Consumption of Rooibos (*Aspalathus linearis*) and a Rooibos-Derived Commercial Supplement on Hepatic Tissue Injury by *tert*-Butyl Hydroperoxide in Wistar Rats', *Oxidative Medicine and Cellular Longevity*, Vol. 2014 (online).
(http://dx.doi.org/10.1155/2014/716832)
(accessed: 23 December 2020)

Chatterjee, P. (2001) *A Time for Tea: Women, Labor and Post/Colonial Politics on an Indian Plantation*, Durham: Duke University Press.

Coombe, R. J., Ives, S. and Huizenga, D. (2014) 'The Social Imaginary of GIS in Contested Environments: Politicised Heritage and the Racialised Landscapes of South African Rooibos Tea', in Matthew David and Deborah Halbert (eds), *Sage Handbook on Intellectual Property*, Thousand Oaks: Sage Publications, pp. 224–37.

Department of Agriculture, Forestry and Fisheries (2016) 'A profile of the South African Rooibos Market Value Chain 2016', (https://www.nda.agric.za/doaDev/sideMenu/Marketing/Annual%20Publications/Commodity%20Profiles/field%20crops/Rooibos%20Tea%20Market%20Value%20Chain%20Profile%202020 16.pdf) (accessed: 23 December 2019).

Erickson, L. (2003) 'Rooibos Tea: Research into Antioxidant and Antimutagenic Properties', *Herbal Gram*, 59 pp. 34–45.

Gebre, Y., Ohta, I. and Matsuda, M. (2017) 'Introduction: Achieving peace and coexistence through African Potentials', in Y. Gebre, I. Ohta and M. Mtasuda (eds) *African Virtues in the Pursuit of Conviviality: Exploring Local Solutions in Light of Global Prescriptions*, Bamenda: Langaa RPCIG, pp. 3–37.

Geertz, C. (1983) *Local Knowledge: Further Essays in Interpretive Anthropology*, New York: Basic Books.

Gorelik, B. (2017) Rooibos: An Ethnographic Perspective: A study of the origins and nature of the traditional knowledge associated with the *Aspalathus linearis*, Pniel: Rooibos Council, (https://sarooibos.co.za/wp/wp-content/uploads/2018/10/20180723-SARC-format-TK-Paper-SU-1.pdf) (accessed: 22 December 2019).

Hayes, P. B. (2000) 'Enhancing the Competitiveness of the Rooibos Industry', MPhil thesis, University of Stellenbosch.

Ives, S. (2017) *Steeped in Heritage: The Racial Politics of South African Rooibos Tea*, Durham: Duke University Press.

Kirumira, E. (2017) 'Revisiting indigeneity: African Potentials as a discourse for sustainable development in Africa', in Y. Gebre, I. Ohta and M. Mtasuda (eds), *African Virtues in the Pursuit of Conviviality: Exploring Local Solutions in Light of Global Prescriptions*, Bamenda: Langaa RPCIG, pp. 379–97.

Le Quellec, J. L. (2009) 'Revisiting the image of "bushmen tea"', *IFAS Research Newsletter*, No. 10, pp. 7–9 (HAL Archives, Lesedi, Johannesburg).

Lötter, D. and Maitre, D. (2014) 'Modelling the distribution of *Aspalathus linearis* (Rooibos tea): Implications of climate change for livelihoods dependent on both cultivation and harvesting from the wild', *Ecology and Evolution*, Vol. 4, Issue 8, pp. 1209–21.

SARC (South African Rooibos Council) (2017) *Rooibos Industry Fact Sheet 2017*, (http://sarooibos.co.za/wp/wp-content/uploads/2017/11/SARC-2017-Fact-Sheet.pdf) (accessed: 3 January 2020).

———— (2018) *Rooibos Industry Fact Sheet 2018*, (https://sarooibos.co.za/wp/wp-content/uploads/2018/08/SARC-2018-Fact-Sheet-1.pdf) (accessed: 3 January 2020).

Schroeder, D., Chennells, R., Louw, C., Snyders, L. and Hodges, T. (2020) 'The rooibos benefit sharing agreement—breaking new ground with respect, honesty, fairness, and care', *Cambridge Quarterly of Healthcare Ethics*, Vol. 29, Issue 2, pp. 285–301.

Statistics South Africa (2012) *Census 2011 Statistical Release*, (https://www.statssa.gov.za/publications/P03014/P030142011.pdf) (accessed: 3 January 2020).

Ushenta, N. (2019) 'A comparative assessment of South Africa's proposed legislation to protect traditional knowledge', LLM thesis, Faculty of Law, University of Pretoria.

Van den Berg, J. (2012) 'Farmers must proactively manage crops to protect rooibos industry', *Bizcommunity*, 23 April 2012 (https://www.bizcommunity.com/PDF/PDF.aspx?l=196&c=11&ct=1&ci=74122) (accessed: 11 November 2020).

West, P. (2012) *From Modern Production to Imagined Primitive: The Social World of Coffee from Papua New Guinea*, Durham: Duke University Press.

Wynberg, R. (2017) 'Making sense of access and benefit sharing in the rooibos industry: Towards a holistic, just and sustainable framing', *South African Journal of Botany*, Vol. 110, pp. 39–51.

Chapter 4

The Working Collapsed State as a Resilient Reaction in the Contemporary World: The Case of Somalia

Mitsugi Endo

1. Introduction

In African political studies, 'a significant proportion of the literature has depicted a continent in which formal institutions do not perform as intended; rather, official rules are described as being weak and fragile, rendered vulnerable to executive manipulation by the salience of corrupt personal networks and ethnic politics' (Cheeseman (ed.) 2018). In *Africa Works*, Chabal and Daloz (1999) wrote, '[t]he state in sub-Saharan Africa has not been institutionalized – in that it has not become structurally differentiated from society – so that its formal structure ill-manages to conceal the patrimonial and particularistic nature of power. … But what we want to stress here, in contrast to most interpretations, is that there are powerfully instrumental reasons for the informalization of politics' (1999: 1–2). More generally, the state in Africa has been recognised as 'the product of a historically rooted set of informal institutions' (Bayart 2009).

Somalia lost its central government in 1991 but, since then, a number of efforts have been made to reconstruct some form of centralised state for the purpose of restoring order. However, despite the establishment of the Federal Government of Somalia (FGS) in the capital city of Mogadishu in 2012, the political fragmentation and fragility of south-central Somalia have continued, partly because of the activities of Al-Shabaab. Moreover, for nearly a decade (between 2008 and 2016), despite external institution-building and state-building efforts, Somalia topped the list of countries in the Fragile States Index (former Failed States Index). Somalia is therefore perceived in the contemporary world as a perfect case of a collapsed state and another graveyard of foreign aid.

This chapter describes how a collapsed state can continue to exist (while not necessarily functioning), using Somalia as a representative example. In the literature on Somalia, Ken Menkhaus, a specialist on Somalia, defined 'functional failed states' as those 'with weak institutions but with a durable social compact and other critical features that allow for basic security, economic activity, and peace, along the lines of what Somaliland in the north has enjoyed for nearly two decades' (2014: 155). He referred to both Somaliland and Puntland as functional failed states in the sense that 'they have maintained some degree of public order and stability and have seen economic recovery in their area of control' (2014: 164), unlike the 'dysfunctional failed state' that has existed in south-central Somalia since 2004, where even a modest capacity to exercise authority over territory or to deliver basic security and social services is still lacking. Therefore, the concept of functioning' implies that an administration is effective in governance, at least to some extent, and that a functional failed state is thus a transient stage for Somalia as it extricates itself from its long-standing crisis (ibid.: 171). The discussion is based on a distinction between a working collapsed state and a functional failed state. The distinction between 'working' and 'functioning' in the context of Somalia was made by Hills, in an analysis of police development, although the two terms seem to be interchangeable in that 'Somalia ... may be an exceptionally weak and insecure state, but it offers an arena in which police officers and institutions can—and do—function' (2014: 106).

In this chapter, the concept of 'working' is the same as that used by Chabal and Daloz (1999) in the context of sub-Saharan Africa; that is, in the sense of a non-institutionalised informality of politics. In addition, the interface of a collapsed state with international or external aid is examined with respect to 'extraversion' as defined by Bayart (2000).[1]

This chapter is structured as follows. First, the term 'collapsed state' is conceptualised within the framework of sovereignty, including that of Somalia. Second, the realities of the collapsed state as it exists in Somalia are specifically considered. Third, the workings of a collapsed state are assessed based on an anecdote that appeared in a UN Monitoring Report (UNSC 2010a). This is followed by an analysis of the working collapsed state according to the concept of 'interdependence sovereignty', as presented in Krasner (1999), and through the strategy of extraversion. The chapter then concludes with a dynamic model of a contemporary international system.

2. Conceptualising the Collapsed State

One of the earliest critiques developed by Hagmann and Hoehne against the understanding of state failure was the lack of critical relevancy of the state convergence thesis, which 'leads to the biased notion that the modern state as it has developed in Europe and North America over recent centuries is "accomplished", "mature", and "stable", while the state in other regions of the world is "undeveloped", "pre-modern" and "fragile"' (Hagmann and Hoehne 2009: 45). In the state convergence thesis,

> 'the state' becomes a reified idea, a 'thing', which is a priori assumed and taken for granted. As a result, media reports and academic debates tend to overlook the often violent and unforeseen processes which, historically, have accompanied the formation of states (ibid.).

Therefore, the debate around state failure quickly culminates in recommendations on how to strengthen or repair fragile or collapsed African states in the name of state building. What is unique in the argument of Hagmann and Hoehne is that 'rather than equating the erosion of legal-rational domination (as embodied by the nation-state) to anarchy and social anomy', the authors call for a more differentiated approach to statehood that renders intelligible variegated trajectories of political authority within and beyond the nation state. In this sense, as Lund (2006) argued, political authority in Africa and elsewhere often manifests itself in the form of twilight institutions that transcend conventional dichotomies between state and non-state, formal and informal or public and private. Thus, state formation in Africa and particularly in Somalia is perceived as an ongoing, incomplete process. Accordingly, state failure is not necessarily a problem, but a new condition in which the resilience of society enables it to function in the absence of government, by

101

pursuing new public or 'regulatory authority' (Roitman 2001).

Against this background argument, in this chapter, the concept of a collapsed state is used as defined below, and not as the much more common but relatively vague term 'failed state', because the former can be seen along a spectrum of different types of states, ranging from the collapsed state to the more conventional (ideal) sovereign state.

Rotberg explains a collapsed state as follows:

> A *collapsed* state is a rare and extreme version of a failed state. Political goods are obtained through private or ad hoc means. Security is equated with the rule of the strong. A collapsed state exhibits a vacuum of authority. It is a mere geographical expression, a black hole into which a failed polity has fallen. There is dark energy, but the forces of entropy have overwhelmed the radiance that hitherto provided some semblance of order and other vital political goods to inhabitants (no longer the citizens) embraced by language or ethnic affinities or borders ... When those collapses occurred, substate actors took over, as they always do when the prime polity disappeared. Those warlords, or substate actors, gained control over regions and subregions within what had been a nation-state, built up their own local security apparatus and mechanism, sanctioned markets and other trading arrangements, and even established an attenuated form of international relations ... Despite the parceling out of the collapsed state into warlord fiefdoms, there still is a prevalence of disorder, anomic behavior, and the kinds of anarchic mentality and entrepreneurial endeavors ... that are compatible with an external network of terror (Rotberg [ed.] 2004: 9–10).

This explanation more or less describes the situation of Somalia since 1991. However, it seems to be derived from empirical observation, whereas in this chapter a simpler definition of a collapsed state is provided, such that it is placed in the context of contemporary international relations. This requires a consideration of the concept of sovereignty as developed by Krasner within a theory of international relations (2004: 87). Krasner ascribed three elements to conventional sovereignty: international legal sovereignty, Westphalian/Vatellian sovereignty and domestic sovereignty. The basic rule of international legal sovereignty is to recognise juridically independent territorial entities, and in Westphalian/Vatellian sovereignty it implies refraining from interventions in the internal affairs of other states. Domestic sovereignty does not involve a norm or a rule but, instead, refers to the nature of domestic authority structures and the extent to which they are able to control activities within a state's boundaries. In the ideal sovereign state system, international legal sovereignty, Westphalian/Vatellian sovereignty and domestic sovereignty are mutually supportive.

However, it is unfortunately true that 'one of the most striking aspects of the contemporary world is the extent to which domestic sovereignty has faltered so badly in states that still enjoy international legal, and sometimes even Westphalian/Vatellian, sovereignty' (Krasner 2004: 88). This is in fact the situation in Somalia, and Krasner touches on this point by noting that 'Somalia, for instance, is still an internationally recognized entity, even though it has barely any national institutions; and external actors have not, in recent years, tried to do much about Somalia's domestic sovereignty, or the lack thereof' (Krasner 2004: 88).

In this chapter, Krasner's three dimensions of sovereignty are used to define the state as comprising political entities enjoying international legal and Westphalian/Vatellian sovereignty, while government can be defined as made up of entities that give rise to domestic sovereignty. These definitions of state and government allow non-state and non-government to be defined as well. Thus, a non-state does not enjoy international legal or Westphalian/Vatellian sovereignty, and non-government refers to entities lacking domestic sovereignty or domestic authority structures. The typologies derived from these definitions of state and government are compared in Table 1.

According to this typology, a collapsed state is still a type of state but without a responsible central government in the international context. Therefore, the concept of a collapsed state exists only with respect to externally or internationally defined sovereignty. In other words, a collapsed state is an extreme case of a quasi-state that is based on very limited, negative sovereignty (Jackson 1990). Nonetheless, a collapsed state is still a legally recognised state, although collapse or failure conflates the absence of a central government with the assumption of anarchy. The problem is then that a collapsed state is not expected to accomplish the control of its territory as required by it internationally.

Table 1. Typology of political entities based on the concepts of state and government

	State	Non-state
Government	(Ideal) sovereign state (nation state)	De facto state or non (un) -recognised state
Non-government	(Complete) collapsed state	Non-state actors (including private companies)

3. Somalia as a Collapsed State

Before Somalia became a collapsed state, it was ruled by Mohamed Siad Barre. His corrupt administration survived on Cold-War-fuelled foreign aid and divide-and-rule tactics among the country's clans, which generated deep animosities between them. In the 1980s, after its defeat in the Ogaden War against neighbouring Ethiopia, Somalia became a failed state. Following a drastic reduction in Western aid, especially from the United States, after 1989 further state failure was inevitable. A full-scale civil war erupted in 1991, causing the total collapse of the Siad Barre regime and of Somalia as a state, as defined in the previous section. Neither the Somali people nor the international community have since been able to configure and install a stable, effective and legitimate central government in Mogadishu, despite several peace-making efforts.

However, as argued in the recent literature on Somalia, the absence of a central government does not necessarily mean a total absence of governance or the development of anarchy. Other social and local institutions have filled the vacuum left by the absence of central authority in the regions and form the backbone of governance. One of the most influential social structures embedded in Somali society is the clan. Local conflict resolution mechanisms based on *xeer* (Somali customary law) are backed and managed by clan elders, who take responsibility for maintaining law and order to some extent. This local mechanism has supported the emergence of relatively stable regions, such as Somaliland (Issaq), which declared independence in 1991 and established more or less Western-style democratic governance, and Puntland (Harti), which formed a 'government' in 1998 but did not declare independence, claiming instead to be a federal state in a future Somalia. Thus, in these and other areas local governance structures are strong enough for people to transact with confidence, as evidenced by the relative success of trust-based money-transfer companies in Somalia. In terms of economic activities, Menkhaus observed,

> [i]n Somalia, some war entrepreneurs who made small fortunes out of the civil war in 1991–92 began diversifying into quasi-legitimate business and fixed investments – plantations, real estate, remittance and telecommunications companies. This shift 'from warlord to landlord' was pivotal for the rise of a business community in Somalia, which helped support rather than undermine local systems of law and order (Menkhaus 2010: 180).

Consequently, even in the absence of a central government (Le Sage 2005), varying combinations of Somali militia-faction leaders, businessmen, clan elders and community leaders have worked with Somali religious leaders from within their sub-clans to improve local security conditions, by relying on Islam, the other pillar of Somali social structure. After the war, Somalia's then new Islamic *shari'a* courts played three key roles: first, they organised a militia to apprehend criminals; second, they made legal decisions in both civil and criminal cases; and, third, they assumed responsibility for the incarceration of convicted prisoners. Therefore, in political terms, without central government, Somalia was able to establish patchy governance, albeit with structures that were not well qualified to meet the international standards of responsible territorial control.

Table 2. Key development indicators before and after statelessness

	1985—1990	2000—2005	Welfare change
GDP per capita (PPP constant $)	836	600	?
Life expectancy (years)	46.0	48.5	improved
One-year-olds fully immunised against measles (%)	30	40	improved
One-year-olds fully immunised against TB (%)	31	50	improved
Physicians (per 100,000)	152	115	improved
Infants with low birth weight (%)	3.4	4.0	improved
Infant mortality rate (per 1,000)	16.0	0.3	improved
Maternal mortality rate (per 100,000)	1,600	1,100	improved
Population with access to water (%)	29	29	same
Population with access to sanitation (%)	18	26	improved
Population with access to at least one health facility (%)	28.0	54.8	improved
Extreme poverty (% < $1 per day)	60.0	43.2	improved
Radios (per 1,000)	4.0	98.5	improved
Telephones (per 1,000)	1.9	14.9	improved
TVs (per 1,000)	1.2	3.7	improved
Fatality due to measles	8,000	5,598	improved
Adult literacy rate (%)	24.0	19.2	worse
Combined school enrolment (%)	12.9	7.5	worse

Source: Leeson (2007: 697, Table 1)

Furthermore, a collapsed state does not necessarily mean a complete lack of services, as demonstrated for Somalia by the data in

Table 2 (Leeson 2007).

Rather, in a collapsed state an equilibrium is created that does not lead to but actively prevents the establishment of a central state, because '[b]usinesspeople and others who have adapted to a context of state failure can be very reluctant to embrace efforts to reintroduce state authority into their lives and in the process create new uncertainties and risks. This is especially true when their previous experience of the state was negatively imaged – when the government was predatory and oppressive' as in the case of Somalia under the rule of Siad Barre (Menkhaus 2010: 178). Following the collapse of the Barre regime, many Somali businessmen engaged prodigiously in income-generating activities such that, while the general populace in major urban areas has been impoverished by conflicts between warlords, some businessmen have prospered from the removal of state controls on their endeavours (Leonard and Samantar 2011). In economic terms, the situation of Somalia can therefore be understood as an extreme *laissez-faire* environment, or ultimate liberalism.

As a result, the experience of Somalia has been interpreted in a variety of ways. An analysis by Hagmann and Hoehne (2009) of [sub-]national political orders in Somali-inhabited territories demonstrated that state formation has evolved in contradiction to the state convergence thesis, a Western model of state formation that was accordingly criticised by those authors. However, while the Somali political order defies Western models of the state in many respects, state collapse has imposed serious social costs with regard to citizenship, national identity and sovereignty. Furthermore, the absence of a functioning central government in southern Somalia and the non-recognition of Somaliland have had negative repercussions on both the lives and the security of Somalis. Leonard and Samantar (2011) observed that the basic idea of (modern) states, which recognise one another and are presumed to control the territories they nominally occupy and to act on their behalf, does not fit the reality of collapsed states and sets up a barrier to the reconstruction of political order within them by alternative governance systems. The phenomenon of a collapsed state can therefore be viewed as a very new challenge to the modern international system itself.

4. How Does a Collapsed State Work?

The discussion in this section draws on an anecdote that appeared in a UN Monitoring Report (UNSC 2010a) examining the role of businesspeople, including those engaged in criminal activities, as actors primarily concerned with economic, rather than political or military gain (Ahmed 2014/2015: 93).

The case is that of the Adaani family, one of the three largest contractors for the World Food Programme (WFP) in Somalia. The family has long been a financier of armed groups and in the 2000s was a close ally of the Hizbul Islam leader (UNSC 2010a: 7). In theory, access to WFP contracts is subject to open tender and competitive bidding, including in the absence of effective formal government. In practice, however, the system offers little or no scope for genuine competition (ibid.: 61). According to the report,

> for more than 12 years, delivery of WFP food aid has been dominated by three individuals and their family members or close associates: Abukar Omar Adaani, Abdulqadir Mohamed Nur 'Enow' and Mohamed Deylaaf. In 2009, these three individuals secured 80 per cent of WFP delivery contracts as part of the WFP transportation budget of approximately $200 million. On account of their contracts with WFP, these three men have become some of the wealthiest and most influential individuals in Somalia (ibid.).

Of further note,

> in addition to providing services to WFP, those contractors have also long exercised de facto control over two of southern Somalia's most strategic and lucrative ports: Eel Ma'aan, to the north of Mogadishu, in which Enow and Adaani are partners; and Marka, to the south of Mogadishu, which Deylaaf operated for over a decade. In both a literal and figurative sense, these three individuals have long been 'gatekeepers' of WFP food aid to Somalia (ibid.: 63).

However, gatekeeping was not the only role undertaken by these businesspeople, as they were also heavily involved in diverting food aid obtained through the WFP, as follows:

Abdulqadir Nur 'Enow' is Chairman and CEO of Deeqa Construction and Water Well Drilling Co Ltd in Kenya and Somalia. It is incorporated in the United States as Deeqa Enterprise LLC, based in Annandale, Virginia, and it is incorporated in the United Arab Emirates as SAMDEQ General Trading Company LLC.122. Enow's wife, Khadija Ossoble Ali, is a registered agent for Deeqa Co. She is also the President of an international non-governmental organization in Mogadishu named SAACID (ibid.: 63).

While Deeqa operates as a transporter for WFP across much of south-central Somalia, SAACID regularly acts as an implementing partner for WFP in Mogadishu, and the Middle Shabelle and Lower Shabelle regions—including some of the densest concentrations of internally displaced persons. Since WFP relies upon the signature of an implementing partner as verification of a delivery by a transporter, the verification by SAACID of food aid deliveries by Deeqa involves an apparent conflict of interest and a potential loophole in a very limited mechanism of accountability. It may also offer considerable potential for large-scale diversion (ibid.).

Among these businesspeople, Abukar Omar Adaani,

is a businessman from the Warsengeli branch of the Abgaal sub-clan of the Hawiye, and a principal partner in the Eel Ma'aan port. With his three sons (Abdulqadir Haji Abukar Adaani, Ali Haji Abukar Adaani and Abdullahi Haji Abukar Adaani) and his brother (Mohamud Omar Adaani), he operates a number of trading and import/export companies, as well as other concerns in Somalia, Kenya and the United Arab Emirates. These include the Ramadan Hotel in northern Mogadishu, the Ramadan Trading Company involved in the sugar trade through Kismaayo and, most prominently, one of the main WFP contracting firms, Swift Traders Ltd. He also maintains direct or indirect interests in other WFP contracting firms bidding for the same tenders, including Banadir General Services (part of the Banadir group of companies through which Adaani and Enow in partnership managed Eel Ma'aan port) and Banadir Gate East Africa General Trading Company (a spin-off from the Banadir group) (ibid.: 64).

In addition, Abukar Omar Adaani was 'a principal financier of the Union of Islamic Courts in the lead-up to its June 2006 takeover of Mogadishu, in which the Eel Ma'aan militia served as the core fighting force of UIC (Union of Islamic Courts)' (ibid.: 65). For Adaani, this investment seems to have been 'both ideologically motivated as well as a financial gamble in which he hoped to reap the benefits of a UIC takeover of the country' (ibid.). However, when Ethiopian troops invaded Somalia, reaching Mogadishu on 29 December 2006, 'Adaani's gambit failed and Adaani emerged as a patron of opposition forces in northern Mogadishu' (ibid.) against the Transitional Federal Government (TFG), which was supported by Ethiopia.

When Sheikh Sharif became President of a reconstituted TFG, in January 2009, after the Djibouti Process initiated by the UN, 'Adaani sought to reclaim his earlier investment in UIC and political support of Sharif, either through influence in the formation of the Cabinet and the running of the government or through compensation that he reportedly valued at $50 million. President Sharif refused both' (ibid.).

For some time, there was severe tension between Sheikh Sharif and Adaani, whose intention of 'reopening Eel Ma'aan port at the beginning of 2009 with the support of WFP, which favoured the improvement of Eel Ma'aan ostensibly as a contingency plan in case Mogadishu port was closed' (ibid.). In addition, the Eel Ma'aan area was controlled by a combination of Al-Shabaab and Hizbul Islam forces, which remained with Adaani's tacit approval.

Although this is an anecdote that describes one aspect of the state of affairs in Somalia, it illustrates a unique dimension of the working collapsed state. Due to the limited function and capabilities of the TFG during its existence in Somalia, commercial and humanitarian transactions became dominated by businesspeople like Adaani in southern Somalia. For the WFP, in its efforts to provide humanitarian assistance, the gates (ports) to humanitarian spaces such as refugee camps were not in the hands of government but in those of businesspeople, such that contracts with them were inevitable. However, if the beneficiaries of those arrangements were proscribed as terrorists, the 'informal taxation and diversion of aid that was tolerated by donors and aid agencies for years as the "price of doing business" in Somalia therefore became illegal' (Bradbury 2010: 13). Thus, in the context of globalisation, even if there are no or limited effective governmental institutions, an alternative mechanism may fill the gap but it will never bring stability and may even create additional turbulence. In the case of the WFP, this alternative mechanism forced it to suspend assistance in south-central Somalia. In UN Security Council Resolution 1916, issued in March 2010, the UNSC 'condemns politicization, misuse, and misappropriation of humanitarian assistance by armed groups and calls upon Member States and the United Nations to take all feasible steps to mitigate these aforementioned practices in Somalia' (UNSC 2010b: 2).

5. Analytical Perspective on the Working Collapsed State

One of the unique conceptualisations developed by Krasner (1999) and subsequently integrated into that of domestic sovereignty, described above (2004), was 'interdependence sovereignty', which refers to the ability of public authorities to control transborder movements. This concept is very useful for analysing the activities of the Adaani family. Krasner set interdependence sovereignty within the context of the dimensions of sovereignty (authority and control):

> Authority involves a mutually recognized right for an actor to engage in specific kinds of activities. If authority is effective, force or compulsion would never have to be exercised. Authority would be conterminous with control. But control can be achieved simply through the use of brute force with no mutual recognition of authority. In practice, the boundary between control and authority can be hazy. A loss of control over a period of time could lead to a loss of authority. The effective exercise of control, or the acceptance of a rule for purely instrumental reasons, could generate new systems of authority … Interdependence sovereignty exclusively refers to control: can a state control movements across its own borders? (Krasner 1999: 10).

111

Therefore, with the loss of interdependence sovereignty (control over transborder flows), domestic sovereignty, in the sense of domestic control and, therefore, the domestic authority of the state, would almost certainly be lost as well. The activities of the Adaani family conferred 'interdependence sovereignty' on behalf of the TFG. As a result, sovereignty was in part effectively utilised and controlled by non-state actors, who eventually increased their authority by monopolising transborder transactions.

In fact, the phenomenon described above and its analysis have also been applied to understand contemporary international relations 'from below', as pointed out by the influential Africanist Christopher Clapham,

> [A] conception of international relations as consisting essentially in interactions *between* states, needs to be supplemented and in some degree displaced by a picture of the international system as a political arena driven by the struggle for control over the flow of resources across state boundaries. In this process, in which states collaborate every bit as much as they compete with one another, such control is needed for them to maintain themselves in both material and ideological terms. The epitome of sovereign statehood is not the diplomat but the customs officer. States need to extract revenue from the passage of goods across their frontiers, and devise mechanisms such as national currencies to assist them in the process. The evasion of control through smuggling undermines both the economic basis and the political structure of the state. But smuggling in a broader sense may encompass a wide range of intangible as well as material goods. In the case of food, 'smuggled' by relief agencies into territory controlled by insurgent movements, the inability of the state to regulate international resource flows strikes directly at its capacity for political control (Clapham 1996: 272).

The partial manipulation of sovereignty is therefore very much an everyday practice of international systems around Africa. A similar phenomenon was observed by Roitman (2001) in an assessment of the Chad Basin,

> [t]his does not mean, however, that the failings of state regulatory

authority – which are by no means unique to the African continent – are indicative of a loss of sovereignty. State power and sovereignty are not equivalent, and lapses in the former do not indicate the displacement of the latter. Likewise, manifestations of competing sources of wealth and authority … are not sovereign simply because they exercise authoritative power over specific domains (Roitman 2001: 249).

6. State Building as Extraversion in Somalia

In the case of Somalia, '[b]usinesspeople and others who have adapted to a context of state failure can be very reluctant to embrace efforts to reintroduce state authority into their lives and in the process create new uncertainties and risks. This is especially true when their previous experience of the state was negative – when the government was predatory and oppressive' (Menkhaus 2010: 178). Consequently, 'risk aversion is a powerful factor in the reluctance of some business and civic interests to throw their full support behind state-rebuilding efforts, even though the potential pay-off would be large' (ibid.). Menkhaus refers to this situation as 'governance without government', which is more or less similar to the concept of a working collapsed state as presented in this chapter.

Related to this observation of a continuing failure of state-building efforts, Hagmann (2016: 10) noted that 'Bayart's concept of extraversion is particularly insightful for understanding not only Somalia's relations with the external world but also the frequent failures of successive stabilization attempts and their impacts on local and national political settlements'. Africanists are well aware that one of the key dimensions of extraversion is that 'Africa had never been disconnected from the world but that, on the contrary, its ruling elites had accustomed themselves to make their dependence on the colonial metropoles and donors both productive and advantageous' (Bayart 2000: 241), in a view of history over the *longue durée*. This includes the manipulation of transborder transactions. 'Consequently, strategies of extraversion—the conversion of dependence into resources and authority—occur not only in a bilateral fashion but all along the different links in this network' (Hagmann 2016: 26).

Hagmann applied the concept of extraversion to describe 'the processes by which international interventions are locally embedded via the strategic use that actors make of them' (ibid.: 13), in reference to the state-building effort of Somalia. In accordance with the concept of interdependence sovereignty, Hagmann described Somalia as 'a noticeably transnational space ... which is marked by a multiplicity of state and non-state actors who exert *de facto* sovereignty' (ibid.: 12).

Referring to the collapsed state since 1991, Hagmann noted that, 'because of this longstanding history of resource inflows, Somali political and economic elites have employed numerous strategies of extraversion centred on the appropriation of external rents and resources. The constant inflow of resources as part of stabilization and statebuilding interventions has generated an incentive structure that motivates elites to fashion their rhetoric and actions in response to it' (2016: 25). While Hagmann applied the concept of extraversion to the more recent phase of Somali politics, i.e. since the establishment of the TFG and even the FGS, it is also an appropriate description of the food transactions between the WFP and businesspeople like the Adaani family, whose resources and money management allowed them to become a powerful political force as well.

Appropriation is at the centre of extraversion activity, as it 'garners authority and resources from dominant outside powers' (ibid.: 51). In this context, the political leaders of Somalia embraced the state, as defined above in terms of external recognition, when they formed a series of transitional governments beginning in 2000. There are many examples of appropriation, as illustrated above by the diversion of aid, and it poses a serious problem for humanitarian agencies. Even more serious is that 'Somalis have actively appropriated the humanitarian, development and diplomatic rhetoric, paradigms and blueprints that have accompanied consecutive external stabilization attempts' (ibid.: 52). This has resulted in a very intimate connection between internationalised attempts at stabilisation and local appropriation, one that can account for failed state-centred state-building in south-central Somalia. As accurately summarised by Menkhaus, 'political elites in newly declared governments have devoted most of their energies toward securing foreign aid in the name of state-building' (2011: 11).

Therefore, 'the extraversion strategies pursued by political figures, who were part of the transitional and now of federal governments, are not a surprise. They are the logical consequence of the commodification that had occurred in their formative stages, during the peace and reconciliation conferences that created them' (Hagmann 2016: 53). Hagmann also cited the issue of clans, appropriated by Somali political leaders, by observing that clan identity has been used as a parameter for power sharing, such as in the 4.5 Formula (ibid.: 56),

> [c]onsequently, the politicized use and abuse of the idea of clan in post-1991 Somalia is not merely the result of local tradition or culture, as primordialists suggest, but has been co-produced by extraversion under conditions of external stabilization (Hagmann 2016: 55).

By considering the extraversion strategy in Somalia, Hagmann concluded that 'under external state-centric stabilization, local elites convert financial and social capital into social relations that are beneficial for them' (ibid.: 59).

Thus, extraversion, especially appropriation, provides the basis for the working of a collapsed state within a contemporary international system in which different groups of people seek to ensure their own survival.

7. Concluding Remarks

Figure 1 presents several of the dynamic dimensions of the matrix described in Table 1. In focusing on the working collapsed state, this chapter has analysed, in the main, the dynamics of 'direction for state' and the 'denial of state-building' and their relationship to the concept of the collapsed state (right-lower part of the figure). Here, the state has been utilised for a variety of purposes, such as transborder transactions and resource mobilisation, to ensure the survival of Somali elites.

As detailed in Figure 1, the presumed goal of state-building is to integrate the divided dimensions of sovereignty (domestic and interdependence) into a government and, thus, to achieve, ultimately, an ideal sovereign state. However, as detailed in this chapter, in Somalia there have been a variety of actions that, by appropriating these efforts, have prevented effective institutionalisation and thus territorial administration. These activities to achieve state convergence are a good example of a collapsed state that works in a contemporary international system, albeit in a very cynical manner. This example nonetheless demonstrates the resilience of Somali society in the contemporary world.

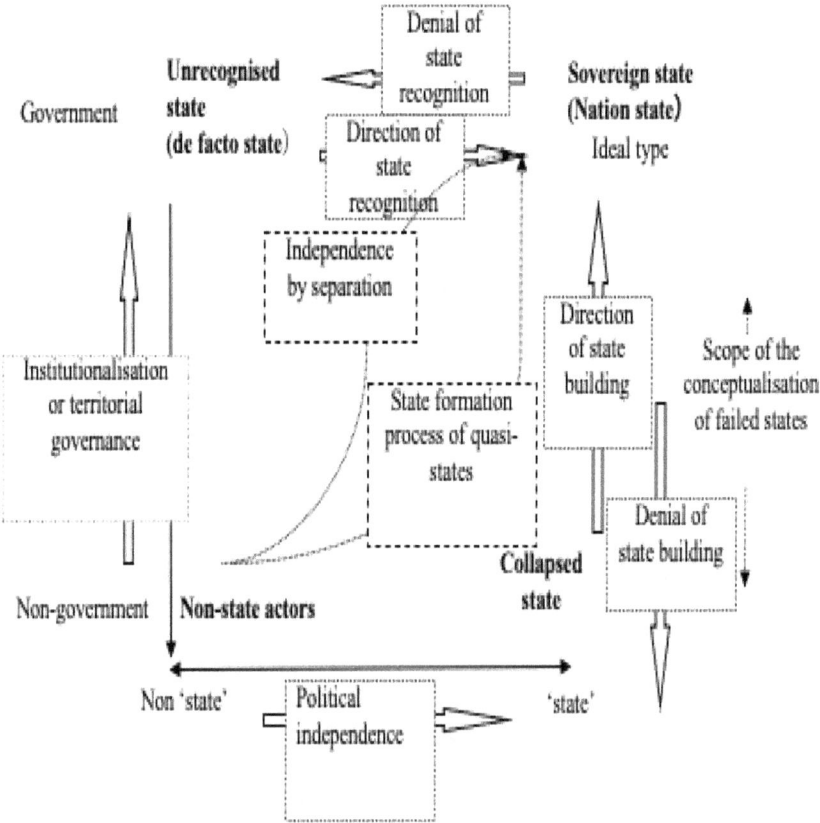

Figure 1. The types of actors and states in the contemporary world and the dynamics of state formation and state-building

Endnotes

[1] The idea of extraversion in the context of Somalia was developed and analysed by Hagmann (2016) to some extent, as discussed in the later part of this chapter.

Acknowledgement

This work was supported by JSPS KAKENHI Grant Number JP16H06318.

References

Ahmed, A. (2014/2015) 'The security bazaar: Business interests and islamist power in civil war Somalia', *International Security*, Vol. 39, No. 3, pp. 89–117.

Bayart, J.-F. (2000) 'Africa in the World: A history of extraversion', *African Affairs*, Vol. 99, No. 395, pp. 217–67.

_____ (2009) *The State in Africa: The Politics of the Belly*, 2nd edition, London: Polity.

Bradbury, M. (2010) *State-Building, Counterterrorism, and Licensing Humanitarianism in Somalia*, Feinstein International Center Briefing Paper, Boston: Feinstein International Center, Tufts University.

Chabal, P. and Daloz, J.-P. (1999) *Africa Works: Disorder as Political Instrument*, London: James Currey.

Cheeseman, N. (ed.) (2018) *Institutions and Democracy in Africa: How the Rules of the Game Shape Political Developments*, Cambridge: Cambridge University Press.

Clapham, C. (1996) *Africa and the International System: The Politics of State Survival*, Cambridge: Cambridge University Press.

Hagmann, T. (2016) *Stabilization, Extraversion and Political Settlements in Somalia*, Nairobi: Rift Valley Institute.

Hagmann, T. and Hoehne, M. V. (2009) 'Failures of the state failure debate: Evidence from the Somali territories', *Journal of International Development*, Vol. 21, pp. 42–57.

Hills, A. (2014) 'Somalia works: Police development as state building', *African Affairs*, Vol. 113, No. 459, pp. 88–107.

Jackson, R. H. (1990) *Quasi-States: Sovereignty, International Relations and the Third World*, Cambridge: Cambridge University Press.

Krasner, S. (1999) *Sovereignty: Organized Hypocrisy*, Princeton: Princeton University Press.

_____ (2004) 'Sharing sovereignty: New institutions for collapsed and failing states', *International Security*, Vol. 29, No. 2, pp. 85–120.

Le Sage, A. (2005) *Stateless Justice in Somalia: Formal and Informal Rule of Law Initiatives*, Geneva: Centre for Humanitarian Dialogue.

Leeson, Peter (2007) 'Better off statelessness: Somalia before and after government collapse', *Journal of Comparative Economics*, Vol. 35, Issue 4, pp.669–710.

Leonard, D. K. and Samantar, M. S. (2011) 'What does the Somali experience teach us about the social contract and the state', *Development and Change*, Vol. 42, Issue 2, pp. 559–84.

Lund, C. (2006) 'Twilight institutions: Public authority and local politics in Africa', *Development and Change*, Vol. 37, No. 4, pp. 685–705.

Menkhaus, K. (2010) 'State failure and ungoverned space', in M. Berdal and A. Wennmann (eds) *Ending Wars, Consolidating Peace: Economic Perspectives*, London: Routledge, pp. 171–88.

_____ (2011) *Somalia and the Horn of Africa, Background Case Study, World Development Report 2011*, Washington DC: World Bank.

_____ (2014) 'State failure, state-building, and prospects for a "functional failed state" in Somalia', *The Annals of the American Academy*, Vol. 656, pp. 154–72.

Roitman, J. (2001) 'New sovereigns?: Regulatory authority in the Chad Basin', in T. M. Callaghy, R. Kassimir and R. Latham (eds) *Intervention and Transnationalism in Africa: Global-Local Networks of Power*, Cambridge: Cambridge University Press, pp. 240–63.

Rotberg, R. I. (ed.) (2004) *When States Fail: Causes and Consequences*, Princeton: Princeton University Press.

UNSC (United Nations, Security Council) (2010a) *Report of the Monitoring Group on Somalia Pursuant to Security Council Resolution 1853 (2008)*, New York: United Nations.

_____ (2010b) *Security Council Extends Mandate of Group Monitoring*

Weapons Bans in Somalia, Eritrea, Unanimously Adopting Resolution 1916 (2009), United Nations Security Council SC/9888, 19 March 2010.

Chapter 5

When African Potentials Fail to Work: The Background to Recent Land Conflicts in Africa

Shinichi Takeuchi

1. Introduction

The importance of the 'African Potentials' concept cannot be overstated. Despite stereotypical images of conflict, violence and disorder, African societies have their own methods of conflict resolution as well as reconciliation and peace building, and researchers have recognised this during their fieldwork in Africa. African societies undoubtedly have remarkable capacities with respect to achieving peaceful coexistence through their salient features, including their interface function, aspiration for pluralism, collective agency and networking, dynamism and flexibility, resilience and tolerance, and innovativeness and creative expression (Gebre, Ohta and Matsuda 2017).

On the basis of this understanding, this chapter examines the reasons for, and backgrounds to, land conflicts that have recently proliferated in rural Africa and considers why 'African Potentials' has recently encountered difficulties with regard to land conflicts. The purpose of this chapter was not to deny or downplay the concept of 'African Potentials' but to contribute to its elaboration. No society is without conflict, and African societies have naturally witnessed numerous land conflicts, which are among the more common types of conflict worldwide. Nonetheless, recent features of land conflicts in Africa have prompted serious reflection.

While conflict over land can be found everywhere, it may result in large-scale violence with devastating consequences if the mechanisms of conflict resolution fail to work. There is a broad consensus that tension over land in rural Africa has mounted in recent years. Owing to several factors, including population increase, a global land rush and strong demand from urban dwellers, the continent has recently witnessed fierce competition for land. In fact, some land conflicts, together with other factors – including, particularly, the absence of effective state governance –, have created considerable insecurity in some areas, such as the eastern provinces of the Democratic Republic of the Congo and the central and northern part of Mali (Autesserre 2010; Mitra 2017). Aside from these rather extreme cases, land conflicts with considerable violence have broken out throughout rural Africa.

The increase in serious land conflict in rural areas indicates the rise of tension over customary land, which accounts for a significant proportion of rural Africa (Alden-Wily 2008; Boone 2014).[1] Importantly, however, it has been observed that management of customary land is characterised by such features as negotiability, flexibility and ambiguity (Berry 1993). These saliencies, reflecting the society's inclusiveness and egalitarian tendencies, considerably overlap with those of 'African Potentials'. The question that must be asked here is: Why are conflicts over land currently proliferating in rural Africa? Especially in a context in which rural Africa is composed, overwhelmingly, of customary land.

Shedding light on the ongoing rapid changes in rural Africa by focusing on structural and institutional factors, this chapter argues that the reduced availability of customary land has intensified competition over land among community members. The argument begins by illustrating the nature of customary tenure in Africa and tracing the evolution of policy interventions up to the 1980s, when scholars were generally in agreement regarding the merits of customary land tenure. Then, to outline the background to the mounting tension over customary land, two structural factors – population growth and increasing demand for customary land – and one institutional factor – the land law reform – will be analysed in detail. The final section examines concrete cases of land conflict to clarify their features and elucidate how these structural and institutional factors have contributed to the eruption of violence. The structural factors have heightened pressure on the land while the institutional factor has facilitated the legalisation and officialisation of customary land tenure, thus promoting land tenure security for specific actors while ruling it out for others. We conclude that recent rural changes may be attributed to the fact that Africa's rural communities have increasingly lost control over the land.

2. Flexibility and Negotiability in the African Land Tenure System

Regarding the use and transfer of customary land in Africa, scholars have often emphasised its flexible, negotiable and ambiguous nature. Customary land has hitherto covered a significant part of the continent, and areas with private property rights remain limited with the exception of a small number of former settler colonies.[2] Under customary tenure, individuals' rights over land are curtailed in comparison with private property rights because ownership of customary lands is considered to lie not with individuals but with local communities. Individuals have users' rights, which are usually contingent on social relations, as the rights are granted only to members of communities that have ownership of the land. Transfer rights are usually restricted: community members can inherit community land within families as long as it is used by themselves but selling and purchasing are tightly restricted. While these features are evident across the continent, customary land tenure is rather flexible, and it is not relevant to understand it as a fixed regulation. Admittedly, customary land tenure was institutionalised under colonial rule (Chanock 1991). However, it has always included some leeway or negotiability for supporting community members in managing the difficulties they face in life (Berry 1993; Moore 1998).

Although customary land tenure has often been described as 'communal tenure', the term is misleading. Despite the common understanding that formal ownership of land belongs to communities, customary land is substantially managed by a nuclear family, and each individual has robust user rights that are inheritable. In this sense, it shares many features with family land. However, importantly, customary tenure reflects the hierarchical relationships that exist both within and between social groups (Bruce 1988), thereby constituting a multi-layered structure of various rights. In short, it is characterised by its social embeddedness. Therefore, the use and the transfer of customary land, which is heavily dependent on social relations, often require a series of complex negotiations among stakeholders. Unlike land with private property rights, the value of customary land is not measurable with a market price. The fact that many individuals have a say in its uses and transactions makes various rights related to the customary land flexible, negotiable and ambiguous.

A long and heated debate has surrounded the possibility of agricultural development on customary land. Arguments stressing the necessity of introducing private land rights to promote agricultural production arose during the colonial period, and several settlement programmes were implemented for this purpose in some colonies, including British East Africa (Kenya) and Belgian Congo.[3] In Kenya, while the settlement programme was mainly aimed at quelling resistance against the colonial government rather than at enhancing agricultural development *per se*, the independent government took over the programme and continued to provide parcels with private property rights for farmers. Although the World Bank, which has consistently advocated for the introduction of private land rights, praised the Kenyan policy in its report (World Bank 1975: 71), scholars have been highly critical of its outcomes and have revealed that such policies have exacerbated land conflicts (Coldham 1978, 1979; Shipton 1988; Haugerud 1989).

The critical assessments and disastrous results of programmes transforming customary tenure into 'modernised' tenure strengthened the 'conviction that the glosses of customary and communal tenure have caused more trouble than not' (Peters 2002: 51). Since the 1980s, scholars have broadly agreed that customary land tenure has worked efficiently and effectively and met the needs of small-scale farmers in Africa. Even World Bank scholars have recognised the merits of flexible land use in customary tenure and stated that 'as long as there is effective governance, communal tenure systems can constitute a low-cost way of providing tenure security' (Deininger and Binswanger 2001: 419). In other words, the flexibility and negotiability of customary land tenure have been widely recognised as factors that contribute to tenure security and are considered compatible with a market economy and agricultural growth.

3. Population Growth and Strong Demand for Land

No reliable data on land conflict trends are available. Owing to its broad range and varying degrees, it is almost impossible to collect accurate data on land conflict. Conflicts over land occur between neighbours, between farmers and herders, and between communities and governments or private companies attempting to expropriate parcels. It is difficult to enumerate all land conflicts: they are not necessarily brought before the courts; they may or may not be accompanied by violence; they are not always widely reported; they may be expressed together with other grievances. Although attempts to compile a database on related topics are undoubtedly valuable, they are hardly usable for time series and/or cross-country analyses.[4]

Despite the lack of accurate data, a consensus that land conflicts are increasing and even intensifying in Africa prevails (Anseeuw and Alden (eds) 2010; Boone 2014). Violent land conflicts have been widely reported recently, as will be discussed further below. In addition, structural factors exacerbating tension over land have recently been conspicuous. First, Africa's population is rapidly growing, as Table 1 clearly shows. While the population density exceeded 100 persons per square kilometre in only five small countries (Burundi, Comoros, Mauritius, Rwanda and Seychelles) in 1960, this had increased to 16 countries in 2018. Population pressure on the land has undoubtedly increased remarkably. Despite the widely accepted argument (Hyden 1980, Herbst 2000), Africa can no longer be considered a land-abundant/labour-scarce continent.

Second, demand for land in rural Africa has risen sharply. This is not only a consequence of population growth. Economic liberalisation policies, implemented since the 1980s and the subsequent hyper-globalisation, have contributed significantly to the increase in demand. Against the backdrop of rapid economic growth in emergent economies, liberalisation policies have attracted massive direct investments in agricultural, mining and forestry sectors in Africa since the 2000s. It culminated in the food crisis in 2008, as foreign and national capitals competed to acquire African lands for the purpose of procuring agricultural products for food and biofuel, and timber and mineral resources.

Table 1.   Evolution of population density in Africa

Population Density	1960*	1970**	1980**	1990**	2000**	2018**
More than 100 persons /km²	Burundi, Comoros, Mauritius, Rwanda, Seychelles	Sao Tome and Principe	Nigeria, Malawi	Cabo Verde, Gambia, Uganda	Ghana, Togo	Benin, Sierra Leone
50-99 persons /km²	Cabo Verde, Malawi, Nigeria, Sao Tome and Principe	Gambia, Togo, Uganda	Egypt, Ghana, Lesotho, Morocco, Sierra Leone, Tunisia	Benin, Cote d'Ivoire, Eswatini, Ethiopia, Kenya, Senegal	Burkina Faso, Guinea-Bissau, Tanzania	Cameroon, Guinea, Liberia

Source: World Bank, *World Development Indicators.*

Note: * Names of countries whose population density exceeded 100 persons per km² or was between 50 and 99 persons km² in 1960. ** Names of countries whose population density newly exceeded 100 persons per km² or was between 50 and 99 persons per km² in each year. The table indicates that, for instance, Uganda's population density was less than 50 persons per km² in 1960, exceeded 50 between 1961 and 1970, and exceeded 100 between 1981 and 1990.

The magnitude of recent land deals in Africa has been enormous. Table 2, compiled based on the Land Matrix data,[5] indicates that the size of land under deal exceeds a quarter of the total size of arable land (27 per cent). In six countries, namely Gabon, Liberia, Madagascar, Republic of the Congo, Sao Tome et Principe and Sierra Leone, the size of land under deal is larger than that of arable land.[6] Considering that the Land Matrix began collecting data only in 2000, the table shows that land in rural Africa has come under deal with surprising speed during the last two decades.

Table 2. Size of land under commercial deals

	No. of deals	Size of deals (1,000 ha, domestic)	Size of deals (1,000 ha, transnational)	Total size of deals (a) (1,000 ha)	Arable lands (b) (1,000 ha)	a/b (%)
Algeria	5	30	76	106	7,462	1.4
Angola	40	123	549	672	4,900	13.7
Benin	12	105	255	360	2,700	13.3
Botswana	6	0	28	28	260	10.9
Burkina Faso	20	27	878	906	6,000	15.1
Burundi	1	0	0	0	1,200	0.0
Cameroon	58	904	2,089	2,994	6,200	48.3
Central African Republic	9	0	1,414	1,414	1,800	78.6
Chad	3	0	21	21	5,200	0.4
Cote d'Ivoire	29	0	477	477	3,500	13.6
DR Congo	91	2,734	8,092	10,827	12,500	86.6
Egypt	16	155	178	333	2,866	11.6
Eritrea	2	0	3	3	690	0.5
Ethiopia	151	542	1,806	2,348	15,721	14.9
Gabon	16	300	2,564	2,864	325	881.2
Gambia	3	0	230	230	440	52.3
Ghana	101	83	1,305	1,388	4,700	29.5
Guinea	15	0	2,257	2,257	3,100	72.8
Guinea Bissau	2	0	3	3	300	1.0
Kenya	76	297	770	1,068	5,800	18.4
Lesotho	3	0	0	0	219	0.1
Liberia	63	1,495	1,713	3,208	500	641.6
Libya	2	0	40	40	1,720	2.3
Madagascar	76	214	3,994	4,208	3,000	140.3
Malawi	28	83	176	258	3,600	7.2

Mali	49	520	510	1,030	6,411	16.1
Mauritania	11	7	114	121	400	30.3
Mauritius	2	3	1	4	75	4.7
Morocco	10	4	719	722	7,497	9.6
Mozambique	187	371	4,579	4,951	5,650	87.6
Namibia	28	10	54	64	800	8.0
Niger	9	280	182	462	16,800	2.7
Nigeria	92	696	462	1,158	34,000	3.4
Republic of the Congo	18	0	2,333	2,333	550	424.2
Rwanda	16	10	38	48	1,152	4.2
Sao Tome et Principe	1	0	5	5	4	122.9
Senegal	44	44	635	680	3,200	21.2
Sierra Leone	54	383	1,924	2,308	1,584	145.7
South Africa	22	347	168	515	12,000	4.3
South Sudan	26	307	4,172	4,479	19,823	46.7
Sudan	47	480	4,298	4,778		
Swaziland	12	0	51	51	175	28.9
Tanzania	128	448	992	1,440	13,500	10.7
Togo	1	0	1	1	2,650	0.0
Tunisia	7	0	3	3	2,570	0.1
Uganda	65	156	1,008	1,164	6,900	16.9
Zambia	97	132	1,344	1,476	3,800	38.8
Zimbabwe	29	107	415	522	4,000	13.0
Total	1,783	11,400	52,926	64,326	238,243	27.0
		18%	82%	100%		

Source: Tabulated by the author using data from Land Matrix (accessed on 16 May 2020) and FAOSTAT (accessed on 18 May 2020).

Note: No data on arable land were available for Sudan or South Sudan. Data were available only for former Sudan. Therefore, Land Matrix data for the two countries were combined to calculate the ratio to arable land.

The table also indicates that African land has been targeted not only by foreign but also by national capitals. As to the Land Matrix data, the deal scopes in Table 2 are distinguished according to whether they are domestic or transnational. Although the size occupied by domestic actors is much smaller (18 per cent) than that occupied by transnational actors (82 per cent), it illustrates that both local and national actors have scrambled for lands in Africa. The fact that the number of domestic actors (495 cases) accounts for 28 per cent of the total number of recorded deals (1,783 cases) means that their average deal size is smaller than that of transnational actors. As the Land Matrix data only cover land deals larger than 200 hectare, it is highly likely that innumerable smaller land deals have been carried out by domestic actors.

These data show that African rural societies have changed drastically in recent years. Despite the marked tendency toward urbanisation, 60 per cent of the population in sub-Saharan Africa currently live in rural areas.[7] The remarkable speed of population growth indicates that African rural areas have seen a significant increase in inhabitants. It should additionally be noted that customary land has been specifically targeted in large-scale land deals. In the global land rush, of which sub-Saharan Africa has been the central focus (Sassen 2013), government-driven large-scale leasing has occurred (Alden-Wily 2011). Pursuing neo-liberal economic policies, African governments have competed for attracting foreign direct investment (FDI). Consequently, a huge swathe of African land has been handed over to foreign investors in particular (Deininger and Byerlee 2011). In this process, the most affected areas have not been cultivated lands and settlements but unfarmed commons, including rangeland and forest. The governments have intentionally directed private investors to these areas, as their ownership has belonged to the state in the eyes of the law, and they have been considered '"unowned, vacant, idle and available", precisely because they are unfarmed' (Alden-Wily 2011: 736). Even if these unfarmed areas are not directly used by inhabitants, they have been indispensable for members of related communities. The reduced availability of customary land, therefore, has seriously affected people's lives in rural Africa.

4. Land Law Reforms

Regarding the recent increased tension over land in Africa, the role of land law reforms implemented since the 1990s has been crucial. During this period, in parallel with a proliferation of large-scale land deals, more than 30 African countries introduced new policies and laws on land. Despite small differences in these policies and laws, it is evident that the institutional reforms have generally aimed at transforming customary land to facilitate privatisation (Martín, Darias and Fernández 2019: 597). Consequently, along with policies adopted by African governments for the promotion of FDI as well as the worldwide economic boom in the period, institutional reform has contributed significantly to the transfer of customary lands for the sake of large-scale land deals.

Why have many African countries launched the land law reform for facilitating privatisation since the 1990s? As we have seen above, there had been a broad consensus among academia that the customary land tenure in Africa could provide tenure security for small farmers. However, African countries as well as donors have been generally eager to implement the tenure reform. So far, the results have been mixed. Whereas new land laws and policies have unanimously set the objective of strengthening tenure security, large-scale land deals have simultaneously deprived farmers and herders of a huge swathe of customary lands. How can we explain this ironic development?

First, motivations for land tenure reform clearly differed among stakeholders. When academia argued that customary land could provide tenure security, it was referring to tenure security for indigenous small-scale land users including farmers and herders. The basic premise of this argument was 'the desirability of owner-operated family farms' (Deininger and Binswanger 2001: 407). The preference for a developmental strategy prioritising small farmers has been so far well accepted among scholars. However, such a strategy has not necessarily been chosen by policy makers. In fact, policy debates on agriculture in Africa in the 1990s have centred on its low productivity, which led to a serious economic crisis in the 1980s (Peters 2002: 51). It was argued in this context that customary land provided only ambiguous rights for users, thereby reducing farmers' incentives to invest in their lands and resulting in low agricultural productivity (Feder and Noronha 1987). Although this logic for the promotion of private property had already been seen in the colonial period, it was enthusiastically accepted among policy makers in the 1990s. As a result, African countries have generally implemented policies aimed at the formalisation (legalisation) of land rights (Ubink 2009) and the promotion of FDI at the same time. Even in countries such as Ethiopia, which in the 1990s adopted a pro-poor agricultural policy prioritising small farmers, policy priorities have shifted drastically during the 2000s to promote market economies and attract FDI (Lefort 2012).

Promoting market economies and prioritising FDI have been common policies supported by donors and African governments, and their close relationship was epitomised in the New Alliance for Food Security and Nutrition (hereafter New Alliance) launched in 2012. The New Alliance, a policy framework adopted at the G8 summit, has been repeatedly criticised for its prioritisation of private companies over small farmers. Since the 1990s, African governments have generally promoted foreign investments in the agricultural sector in line with the donors' stance.[8] Consequently, the institutional reform carried out in the same period has, in many cases, resulted in strengthening the land tenure security for investors (private companies) rather than for smallholders.[9]

Another powerful motivation for the land law reform involved the opportunity to gain political dominance. Land is a politically sensitive issue: implementation of a new land policy may destabilise the existing political order, but it may also build a patronage network. In fact, in some countries, the provision of land titles was utilised to mobilise support for the incumbent government. Rwanda was just such a case: following victory in the civil war, the former rebels – the Rwandan Patriotic Front (RPF) – established a government and implemented a series of radical interventionist policies over land. The 'land sharing' policy, which was mainly operated around 1996–97, is representative. It aimed to secure the land for Tutsi returnees, who had returned en masse after the civil war, to the detriment of Hutu inhabitants, who were ordered to give up half of their land properties for the returnees (Bruce 2009; Takeuchi and Marara 2014). Later, as a result of the enactment of a new land law in 2005, Rwanda launched the land registration programme and had finished delivering the land certificate throughout the territory by 2013. Obviously, one of the key motivations for this rapid implementation was to formalise the land rights given through the 'land sharing' to Tutsi returnees, who have long been the core supporters of the current ruling party, the RPF.

The situation was similar in Ethiopia. In the country, where the dominant Ethiopian Peoples' Revolutionary Democratic Front (EPRDF) seized political power in 1991, the land registration programme was accelerated following the election in 2005, which was marked by the rise of the opposition party. The motivation to deliver the land certificate hastily was interpreted as a desire to 'win back the support of the rural population and to undermine the chance of the opposition' (Dessalegn 2009: 68). In both Rwanda and Ethiopia, land reforms were conducted using a top-down approach and the interests of the state – namely, the ruling parties – were prioritised. As a consequence of the delivery of land certificates to the nationals, the ruling parties' power base and the state's capability to exercise control over land have been strengthened (Takeuchi and Marara 2014; Ayano 2018).

As these examples show, the promotion of tenure security for small farmers has not necessarily been the key motivation behind the land tenure reforms that African countries have launched since the 1990s. Although these reforms emphasised the importance of ensuring land tenure security and of legalising land rights, those whose tenure security has been ensured and whose land rights have (not) been recognised following the reform should be carefully scrutinised. The effects of a land tenure reform may differ substantially depending on whose land tenure security has been protected, and the formalisation of land rights may trigger the exclusion of other land users. Land law reform may clarify one party's land rights but may deprive another of their rights (Ubink 2009).[10]

5. Reasons for Land Conflicts

Land conflicts arise for different reasons. In the context of recent rapid population increases and intensified demand for land, land acquisition by outsiders to the rural community has provoked several conflicts. Over the last two decades, customary land in rural Africa has been targeted by outsiders, including foreign and national private companies, governments and local elites. Particularly, in parallel with the economic growth of emerging countries such as China, massive investments have been made in the fields of agriculture, mining and forestry, occupying huge swathes of land, as Table 2 shows. These large-scale land deals, often criticised as 'land grabbing', have inevitably provoked several conflicts in the rural community.[11]

Another important factor in land acquisition that may cause conflicts is the return of refugees following civil war. In countries such as Rwanda and Burundi, large numbers of protracted refugees, having lived abroad for several decades, returned following the end of the civil wars in the 1990s and the 2000s, respectively. In both countries, the return of refugees en masse has given rise to land conflicts, characterised by ethnic tension between returnees and occupants of the land (Takeuchi and Marara 2014; Ndayirukiye and Takeuchi 2014). In Rwanda, the above-mentioned 'land sharing' caused numerous disputes, though the Hutus' discontent over expropriated land was entirely suppressed by the government, who gave top priority to ensuring Tutsi returnees' land tenure security. In Burundi, after the massive outflow of the Hutus in the southern regions as a result of the large-scale violence in 1972, the Tutsi-led government encouraged the movement of people in other regions to come and occupy the vacant lands, causing many Tutsis from land-scarce regions to migrate and settle there. The return of the Hutu refugees began following the conclusion of the peace agreement and the establishment of the power-sharing government in the 2000s, thereby generating tension between returnees and the occupants of their lands.

In accounting for land conflicts, emphasising the difference between community members and outsiders is not always appropriate. Historically, African rural communities have accepted and co-existed with outsiders, and the distinction between the two is often nebulous. Nevertheless, such distinctions and oppositions can be created and exacerbated by political and socio-economic factors. On the one hand, a significant political shock such as armed conflict can trigger serious land conflicts in the peace process (Unruh 2003), because destabilisation of the existing political order may lead to new claims for properties through a weakening of the political power that underpinned the former property regime (Boone 2018). On the other hand, profound socio-economic impacts on a community would have similar effects. In fact, high pressure on customary lands has provoked numerous land conflicts among community members. Recently, tension has been mounting among those who have co-existed for long periods.

Conflicts between farmers and herders are typical cases. Currently, several serious armed conflicts in Africa have been connected to local antagonism between communities who engage in different land-use activities, mainly farming and herding.[12] In the devastating conflicts in central Mali, northern Burkina Faso and central Nigeria, the ethnic groups dependent on herding activities, such as the Fulani and Tuareg, have been involved in conflicts with neighbouring farmers, such as the Dogon, Bambara, Mossi and Tiv (Moritz 2010; Olaniyan, Francis and Uzodike 2015; Akerjiir 2018). In the protracted conflict in the eastern region of the Democratic Republic of the Congo, the pastoralist Banyamulenge have been central actors in the battle (Verweijen and Vlassenroot 2015).

It should be emphasised that these different communities have long co-existed and benefited from the complementarity of their socio-economic activities. For instance, herders profited from farmers' permission to graze cattle in the fields after harvest, while farmers were also able to raise cattle by entrusting them to herders. Such mutually advantageous relationships are still alive, even today, in many places in Africa (Bukari, Papa and Jürgen 2018). Recently, however, the increasing scarcity of available lands for agriculture and livestock raising has generated rising tension between land users. In addition, inter-communal violence has escalated through the politicisation and militarisation of conflicts provoked by external actors.[13]

134

In particular, increased land scarcity has exacerbated tension over land use among members of the rural societies concerned. Several studies have highlighted increasing tension within local communities. In Ghana, where urbanisation has elevated land values in semi-urban areas, conflicts have frequently broken out between chiefs and their subjects because the former leased communal land without considering the welfare of the community (Ubink 2007). Another example of intra-community conflict in Ghana has illuminated the fact that chiefs often preferred to make transactions involving local resources with outsiders because they could gain revenues, whereas they could not obtain such benefits from their subjects who have innate and legitimate rights to use the resources (Amanor 2009).

Although outright confrontation between the local community and investors may have declined recently due to international and national guidelines and regulations on agricultural investment,[14] large-scale land deals have certainly intensified the existing tension and conflict between community members. A study on a large-scale sugarcane project in Sierra Leone illustrates this (Bottazzi, Goguen and Rist 2016). As the project was funded by international public funding agencies, the company – a consortium between a Swiss-based transnational petroleum company and the government of Sierra Leone – was obliged to comply with the main international regulations on agricultural investment and made considerable efforts to establish 'free, prior and informed consent'. As a result, the company concluded an agreement with the government, three chiefdom councils and the heads of the land-owning families concerning leases of a total of 54,000 hectare and promised to provide compensation and payments for local communities. However, the agreement has intensified conflicts among their members precisely because of such payments, which have been monopolised by a few members, namely elders from among the patrilineal descendants of the village founder. By contrast, youths, females, matrilineal descendants of the village founder and immigrants were excluded from the distribution of such payments.

African customary tenure has been characterised by its multi-layered rights over land. Simply put, a small number of people from the highest ranks of the community – typically kings, paramount chiefs or descendants of the village founder – have rights over the administration of their territory and have the authority to allocate land. All community members have rights for land use. In theory, community outsiders, such as immigrants, are entitled to land-use rights as long as they become clients of the rights holders and pay them some symbolic tributes. In other words, an outsider can be a community member and obtain legitimate customary land rights through integration into a hierarchical social relationship in the community (Bruce 1988). The above-mentioned conflict in Sierra Leone arose from the interpretation that the rights to administer customary land should be considered 'ownership' or 'property rights' in statutory law. Naturally, the interpretation, which benefited only a few high-ranking members of the community and entirely excluded other people, ignited and exacerbated the frustration of socially marginalised groups.[15] Similar land conflict patterns are evident across Africa, as people are increasingly motivated to accumulate as much land as possible in the context of reducing the availability of customary land (Peters and Kambewa 2007).

6. Conclusion

Recent rural changes in Africa have made the resolution of land conflict increasingly difficult. Whereas conflicts in customary land were formerly handled through various negotiations among local community members, such a space for negotiation has steadily diminished. This chapter has demonstrated the important structural and institutional factors behind recent rural changes that restrict the availability of customary land. Owing to several factors, including population growth and the considerable demand for land, the availability of common lands in rural Africa has rapidly diminished. Institutional change has accelerated this process. In the context of the liberalisation policy attracting active investments in rural lands, land law reform has facilitated ownership of vast swathes of customary land under statutory law. Although the transformation of customary rights into official ownership under statutory law has strengthened the tenure security of certificate holders, it may have excluded other rights holders who formerly depended on the same area. The formalisation of customary land rights has undoubtedly diminished the negotiability of their competition and confrontation.

Whereas recent rural changes are multifaceted, the most critical of these relates to the nature of the rural community. Owing to the factors mentioned above, rural communities in Africa have markedly lost control over land, although the extent to which they have lost control varies significantly from one country (and region) to another. The African rural community began to lose its autonomy during the colonial period, while nevertheless retaining its control over land. The colonial authority strengthened the power of traditional chiefs by institutionalising them under indirect rule and prevented the commercialisation of customary land to ensure the chiefs' power base (Meek 1968; Chanock 1991). The paramount importance of customary land tenure was also maintained by the newly independent countries. Consequently, customary land has accounted for an overwhelming part of rural Africa, ensuring that land tenure remains flexible, negotiable and ambiguous.

Recently, due to structural and institutional changes, the availability of customary land has diminished rapidly, affecting the behaviours of inside actors in rural communities. Clearly, this has sensitised people to the economic benefits: the above-mentioned Ghanaian chiefs' leasing of communal land to outsiders despite the opposition of community members exemplifies this. In north-eastern Zambia, farmers have rushed to register customary land for their private use (Oyama 2017). These acts are likely to provoke tension over land among community members and result in the further weakening of customary land tenure (Peters 2013). In this context, rural communities are likely to have lost their autonomy from the state while their members are likely to have lost their sense of belonging, although some have successfully become enriched at the individual level. In parallel with the reduced availability of customary land, rural communities will certainly be deprived of the power and legitimacy required to ensure land rights for their members, and outside authorities, such as bureaucrats, politicians, private companies, political parties and the state, will play increasingly decisive roles in the community's land affairs.

The mutually affected processes between the limited availability of customary land and changes in the nature of the rural community have transformed the pattern of land conflict. Today, land rights in rural Africa are becoming increasingly less ambiguous, inclusive and negotiable. In addition to the contraction of cultivated areas, current rural changes include transformation in the land rights system. The combination of the two has provoked frequent conflicts over land. In this context, their resolution through negotiation has become increasingly difficult.

The situation is complex, as a return to customary land tenure is neither possible nor desirable (Peters 2002). As discussed above, social inequity, inequality and insecurity have already been prevalent with respect to customary land tenure. Several countries formally recognise the role of the chief in land governance and, in fact, chiefs generally gain the people's respect. Nevertheless, we cannot assume that they are always benevolent protectors of the community. Considering that land management is essential to the governance of rural communities, the state has to play an instrumental role to promote social justice there. Serious efforts are required for the creation and successful functioning of a system that involves stakeholders, including the state, chiefs and community members, and to establish a mechanism for equitable land governance. It is in this process that the power for good of African Potentials is truly required.

Endnotes

[1] Alden-Wily estimated that the customary domain covered more than three quarters of the total land area in sub-Saharan Africa (Alden-Wily 2011: 735).

[2] According to Boone (2014: 23), although the average percentage of the land registered under private title was considered to be less than ten per cent, it was exceptionally high only in five Southern African countries, namely South Africa (72 per cent), Namibia (44 per cent), Lesotho (44 per cent), Zimbabwe (41 per cent or 33 per cent) and Swaziland (27 per cent),

obviously due to the legacy of European settlers' land acquisition.

3 In Kenya, the British colonial government launched the so-called Swynnerton Plan in 1954, promoting private properties for African farmers. The policy providing private land rights for farmers was inherited by the independent Kenyan government. Belgian Congo had implemented a similar policy called *paysannat* since the 1930s (Staner 1955). Providing a parcel of land, the policy was aimed at fostering small farmers using modern techniques, but was abandoned after independence.

4 The Robert Strauss Center for International Security and Law has built a Social Conflict Analysis Database, which includes time series data on tension over 'food, water, subsistence' and 'environmental degradation' in Africa (Salehyan et al. 2012). A UNEP report also provides important information about conflicts over natural resources (Schwartz and Singh 1999). However, these data are either insufficient or misleading with respect to identifying the historical trends in conflict over land.

5 Retrieved from Land Matrix Data (https://landmatrix.org/data/) on 16 May 2020.

6 As these countries have important areas of tropical forests, which is not included in arable land in FAO's definition, the extremely high ratio of the size of lands under deal may show that large areas of tropical forest have been put under deal for logging and other purposes.

7 In 2018, the rural population in sub-Saharan Africa accounted for 59.8 per cent of the total (data from the *World Development Indicators*). Although its tendency to decrease is clear, as it was 81.9 per cent in 1970, the proportion of the rural population is still significant in Africa compared with other regions in the world.

8 The New Alliance has worked closely with the African Union Commission.

9 In this process, the ideological influence of De Soto (2000) has often been pointed out. See Manji (2006) for detail.

10 World Bank researchers revealed that systematic land registration and the issue of certificates in Rwanda improved land access for women in legalised marriages, though they had contrary effects for women whose marriages were not legalised (Ali, Deininger and Goldstein 2014).

11 For land conflicts with foreign companies, see Fahey (2014), Geenen and Hönke (2014), Sjögren (2014) and Cowaloosur (2014). Claessens, Mudinga and Ansoms (2014) and Bisoka and Ansoms (2014) deal with land

acquisition by local elites.

[12] Famers and herders are not dichotomous categories, as pastoralists may also cultivate and agriculturalists may also have livestock. However, differences in their subsistence activities, together with other cultural aspects, can lead to the construction of different identities.

[13] In Sahel regions, the threats of radical Islamists connected to Al Qaida and the Islamic State have often provoked excessive violence from the security forces against the Fulani community that has been accused of supporting radical Islamists (International Crisis Group 2019). In the conflict of the Eastern DRC, the Banyamulenge have been always accused by neighbours of real or imaginary links with Rwanda's government. Although the connection has been rather complex and the Banyamulenge have never been monolithic in terms of their relations with Rwanda, a part of the group did indeed work with the Rwandan government during the civil war to dominate huge areas of the Eastern DRC (Reyntjens 2009).

[14] As a representative example, see FAO (2012). See also Seufert (2013).

[15] Problems caused by the elders' domination in Sierra Leonian rural societies have already been identified as a root cause of the civil war in the 1990s (Peters and Richards 2011).

Acknowledgement

This work was supported by JSPS KAKENHI Grant Numbers JP16H06318, JP16KT0046, JP18H03439, and JP19KK0031.

References

Akerjiir, A. S. (2018) 'Increasing farmer-herder conflict in Nigeria: An assessment of the clashes between the Fulani herdsmen and indigenous farmers in Ukpabi-Nimbo community Enugu State', Master of Arts thesis in International Development Studies, Wageningen University.

Alden-Wily, L. (2008) 'Custom and commonage in Africa rethinking the orthodoxies', *Land Use Policy*, Vol. 25, Issue. 1, pp. 43–52.

_____ (2011) 'The law is to blame: The vulnerable status of

common property rights in Sub-Saharan Africa', *Development and Change,* Vol. 42, Issue. 3, pp. 733–57.

Ali, D. A., Deininger, K. and Goldstein, M. (2014) 'Environmental and gender impacts of land tenure regularization in Africa: Pilot evidence from Rwanda', *Journal of Development Economics,* Vol. 110, pp. 262–75.

Amanor, K. S. (2009) 'Tree plantations, agricultural commodification, and land tenure security in Ghana', in J. M. Ubink, A. J. Hoekema and W. J. Assies (eds) *Legalising Land Rights: Local Practices, State Responses and Tenure Security in Africa, Asia and Latin America,* Leiden: Leiden University Press, pp. 133–61.

Anseeuw, W. and Alden, C. (eds) (2010) *The Struggle over Land in Africa: Conflicts, Politics and Change.* Cape Town: HSRC Press.

Autesserre, S. (2010) *The Trouble with the Congo: Local Violence and the Failure of International Peacebuilding,* Cambridge: Cambridge University Press.

Ayano, M. F. (2018) 'Rural land registration in Ethiopia: Myths and realities', *Law and Society Review,* Vo. 52, No. 4, pp. 1060–97.

Berry, S. (1993) *No Condition is Permanent: The Social Dynamics of Agrarian Change in Sub-Sharan Africa,* Madison: The University of Wisconsin Press.

Bisoka, A. N. and Ansoms, A. (2014) 'Land grabbing and power relations in Burundi: Practical norms and real governance', in A. Ansoms and T. Hilhorst (eds) *Losing Your Land: Dispossession in the Great Lakes,* Suffolk: James Currey, pp. 125–40.

Boone, C. (2014) *Property and Political Order in Africa: Land Rights and the Structure of Politics,* Cambridge: Cambridge University Press.

———— (2018) 'Shifting vision of property under competing political regimes: Changing uses of Cote d'Ivoire's 1998 land law', *Journal of Modern African Studies,* Vol. 56, No. 2. pp. 189–216.

Bottazzi, P., Goguen, A. and Rist, S. (2016) 'Conflicts of customary land tenure in rural Africa: Is large-scale land acquisition a driver of "institutional innovation"?', *The Journal of Peasant Studies,* Vol. 43, No. 5, pp. 971–88.

Bruce, J. W. (1988) 'A perspective on indigenous land tenure: Systems and land concentration', in R. E. Downs and S. P. Reyna (eds) *Land and Society in Contemporary Africa,* Hanover: University of New

England Press, pp. 23–52.

_____ (2009) 'International standards, improvisation and the role of international humanitarian organizations in the return of land in post-conflict Rwanda', in S. Pantuliano (ed.) *Uncharted Territory: Land, Conflict and Humanitarian Action*, Rugby: Practical Action Publishing, pp. 109–31.

Bukari, K. N., Papa, S. and Jürgen, S. (2018) 'Cooperation and co-existence between farmers and herders in the Midst of violent farmer-herder conflicts in Ghana', *African Studies Review*, Vol. 61, No. 2, pp. 78–102.

Chanock, M. (1991) 'Paradigms, policies and property: A review of the customary law of land tenure', in K. Mann and R. Roberts (eds), *Law in Colonial Africa*, Portzmouth: Heinemann, pp. 61–84.

Claessens, K., Mudinga, E. and Ansoms, A. (2014) 'Competition over soil and subsoil: Land grabbing by local elites in South Kivu, DRC', in A. Ansoms and T. Hilhorst (eds) *Losing Your Land: Dispossession in the Great Lakes*, Suffolk: James Currey, pp. 82–102.

Coldham, S. (1978) 'The effect of registration upon customary land rights in Kenya', *Journal of African Law*, Vol. 22, No. 2, pp, 91–111.

_____ (1979) 'Land-tenure reform in Kenya: The limits of law', *The Journal of Modern African Studies*, Vol. 17, No. 4, pp. 615–27.

Cowaloosur, H. (2014) 'Land grab in new garb: Chinese special economic zones in Africa: The case of Mauritius', *African Identities*, Vol. 12, No. 1, pp. 94–109.

De Soto, H. (2000) *The Mystery of Capital: Why Capitalism Triumphs in the West and Fails Everywhere Else*, London: Black Swan.

Deininger, K. and Byerlee, D. (2011) *Rising Global Interest in Farmland: Can It Yield Sustainable and Equitable Benefits?*, Washington DC: World Bank.

Deininger, K. and Binswanger, H. (2001) 'The evolution of the World Bank's land policy', in A. de Janvry, G. Gordillo, P. Jean-Philippe and E. Sadoulet (eds) *Access to Land, Rural Poverty, and Public Action*, Oxford: Oxford University Press, pp. 406–40.

Dessalegn, R. (2009) 'Land rights and tenure security: Rural land registration in Ethiopia', in J. M. Ubink, A. J. Hoekema and W. J. Assies (eds) *Legality Land Rights: Local Practices, State Responses and Tenure Security in Africa, Asia and Latin America*, Leiden: Leiden

University Press, pp. 59–95.

Fahey, D. (2014) 'This land is my land: Land grabbing in Ituri (DRC)', in A. Ansoms and T. Hilhorst (eds) *Losing Your Land: Dispossession in the Great Lakes*, Suffolk: James Currey, pp. 36–57.

FAO (Food and Agriculture Organization of the United Nations) (2012) *Voluntary Guidelines on the Responsible Governance of Tenure of Land, Fisheries and Forests in the Context of National Food Security*, Rome: FAO.

Feder, G. and Noronha, R. (1987) 'Land rights systems and agricultural development in Sub-Saharan Africa', *World Bank Research Observer*, Vol. 2, No. 2, pp. 143–69.

Gebre, Y., Ohta, I. and Matsuda, M. (2017) 'Introduction: Achieving peace and coexistence through African Potentials', in Y. Gebre, I. Ohta and M. Matsuda (eds) *African Virtues in the Pursuit of Conviviality: Exploring Local Solutions in Light of Global Prescriptions*, Bamenda: Langaa RPCIG, pp. 3–37.

Geenen, S. and Hönke, H. (2014) 'Land grabbing by mining companies: Local contentions and state reconfiguration in South Kivu (DRC)', in A. Ansoms and T. Hilhorst (eds) *Losing Your Land: Dispossession in the Great Lakes*, Suffolk: James Currey, pp. 58–81.

Haugerud, A. (1989) 'Land tenure and agrarian change in Kenya', *Africa*, Vol. 59, No. 1, pp. 61–90.

Herbst, J. (2000) *States and Power in Africa: Comparative Lessons in Authority and Control*, Princeton: Princeton University Press.

Hyden, G. (1980) *Beyond Ujamaa in Tanzania: Underdevelopment and an Uncaptured Peasantry*, London: Heinemann.

International Crisis Group (2019) *Speaking with the "Bad Guys": Toward Dialogue with Central Mali's Jihadists*, Africa Report No. 276, Brussel: International Crisis Group.

Lefort, R. (2012) 'Free market economy, 'developmental state' and party-state hegemony in Ethiopia: The case of the "model farmers"', *Journal of Modern African Studies*, Vol. 50, No. 4, pp. 681–706.

Manji, A. (2006) *The Politics of Land Reform in Africa: From Communal Tenure to Free Markets*, London: Zed Books.

Martín, V. O. M., Darias, L. M. J. and Fernández, C. S. M. (2019) 'Agrarian reforms in Africa 1980-2016: Solution or evolution of the agrarian question?', *Africa*, Vol. 89, No. 3, pp. 586–607.

Meek, C. K. (1968) *Land Law and Custom in the Colonies (Second Edition)*, London: Frank Cass.

Mitra, S. (2017) 'Mali's fertile grounds for conflict: Climate change and resource stress', Clingendael Institute (https://www.jstor.org/stable/resrep17352) (accessed: 23 September 2020).

Moore, S. F. (1998) 'Changing African land tenure: Reflections on the incapacities of the state', *European Journal of Development Research*, Vol. 10, No. 2, pp. 33–49.

Moritz, M. (2010) 'Understanding herder-farmer conflicts in West Africa: Outline of processual approach', *Human Organization*, Vol. 69, No. 2, pp. 138–48.

Ndayirukiye, S. and Takeuchi, S. (2014) 'Dealing with land problems in post-conflict Burundi', in S, Takeuchi (ed.) *Confronting Land and Property Problems for Peace*, Oxon: Routledge, pp. 109–31.

Olaniyan, A., Francis, M. and Uzodike, N. O. (2015) 'The cattle are "Ghanaians" but the herders are strangers: Farmer-herder conflicts, expulsion policy, and pastoralist question in Agogo, Ghana', *African Studies Quarterly*, Vol. 15, No. 2, pp. 53–67.

Oyama, S. (2017) 'National land policy and chief's land administration in customary land in Zambia', in S. Takeuchi. (ed.) *In Land and Power in Africa: Understanding Drastic Rural Changes in the Age of Land Reform*, Chiba: Institute of Developing Economies, pp. 71–105 (in Japanese).

Peters, K. and Richards, P. (2011) 'Rebellion and agrarian tensions in Sierra Leone', *Journal of Agrarian Change*, Vol. 11, No. 3, pp. 377–95.

Peters, P. E. (2002) 'The limits of negotiability: Security, equity and class formation in Africa's land systems', in K. Juul and C. Lund (eds) *Negotiating Property in Africa*, Portsmouth: Heinemann, pp. 45–66.

_____ (2013) 'Conflicts over land and threats to customary tenure in Africa', *African Affairs*, Vol. 112, No. 449, pp. 543–62.

Peters, P. E. and Kambewa, D. (2007) 'Whose security? Deepening social conflict over "customary" land in the shadow of land tenure reform in Malawi', *Journal of Modern African Studies,* Vol. 45, No. 3, pp. 447–72.

Reyntjens, F. (2009) *The Great African War: Congo and Regional Geopolitics, 1996-2006,* Cambridge: Cambridge University Press.

Sassen, S. (2013) 'Land grabs today: Feeding the disassembling of national territory', *Globalizations,* Vol. 10, No. 1, pp. 25–46.

Salehyan, I., Hendrix, C. S., Hamner, J., Case, C., Linebarger, C., Stull, E. and Williams, J. (2012) 'Social conflict in Africa: A new database', *International Interactions,* Vol. 38, No. 4, pp. 503–11.

Schwartz, D. and Singh, A. (1999) *Environmental Conditions, Resources, and Conflicts: An Introductory Overview and Data Collection.* Nairobi: United Nations Environmental Programme.

Seufert, P. (2013) 'The FAO voluntary guidelines on the responsible governance of tenure of land, fisheries and forests', *Globalizations,* Vol. 10, No. 1, pp. 181–6.

Shipton, P. (1988) 'The Kenyan land tenure reform: Misunderstanding in the public creation of private property', in R. E. Downs and P. Reyna (eds) *Land and Society in Contemporary Africa,* Hanover: University Press of New England, pp. 91–135.

Sjögren, A. (2014) 'Scrambling for the promised land: Land acquisitions and the politics of representation in post-war Acholi, northern Uganda', *African Identities,* Vol. 12, No. 1, pp. 62–75.

Stancr, P. (1955) 'Les paysannats indigènes du Congo belge et du Ruanda-Urundi', *Bulletin agricole du Congo belge,* Vol. 46, Issue 3, pp. 467–558.

Takeuchi, S. and Marara, J. (2014) 'Land tenure security in post-conflict Rwanda', in S. Takeuchi (ed.) *Confronting Land and Property Problems for Peace,* Oxon: Routledge, pp. 86–108.

Ubink, J. M. (2007) 'Tenure security: Wishful policy thinking or reality? A case from peri-urban Ghana', *Journal of African Law,* Vol. 51, No. 2, pp. 215–48.

———— (2009) 'Legalising land rights in Africa, Asia and Latin America: An introduction', in J. M. Ubink, A. J. Hoekema and W. J. Assies (eds) *Legalizing Land Rights: Local Practices, State Responses and Tenure Security in Africa, Asia and Latin America,* Leiden: Leiden University Pres, pp. 7–31.

Unruh, J. D. (2003) 'Land tenure and legal pluralism in the peace process', *Peace & Change*, Vol. 28, No. 3, pp. 352–77.

Verweijen, J. and Vlassenroot, K. (2015) 'Armed mobilization and the nexus of territory, identity, and authority: The contested territorial aspirations of the Banyamulenge in DR Congo', *Journal of Contemporary African Studies*, Vol. 33, No. 2, pp. 191–212.

World Bank (1975) *Land Reform: Sector Policy Paper*, Washington DC: World Bank.

Chapter 6

'Peace from Below' as an African Potential: Wars and Peace in South Sudan

Eisei Kurimoto

1. Wunlit Dinka–Nuer Peace and Reconciliation Conference (1999) and 'Peace from Below'

In an essay published in 2000, I emphasised the importance of 'Peace from Below' in contrast to 'Peace from Above' in the context of South Sudan's[1] peacebuilding efforts. Peace from below is local, indigenous and endogenous, whereas peace from above is external, transplanted to and imposed on the countries at war (Kurimoto 2000; see also 2011, 2014). The direct stimulus for my writing that essay was the Wunlit Dinka–Nuer[2] West Bank Peace and Reconciliation Conference, which met for nine days from the end of February 1999, deep inside war-torn South Sudan. Some 1,500 people participated, representing different Dinka and Western Nuer sections, together with observers and facilitators from abroad. Before 1999, very few had heard of Wunlit, a small Dinka village in the north-eastern Bhar al-Ghazal region, near the border with the Upper Nile region,[3] where the conference was held. After 1999, it became a symbol of local and indigenous peace making and peacebuilding, or 'People-to-People Peace' initiatives (Bradbury et al 2006: 31–61; LeRiche and Arnold 2012: 236–7). Participants were reported to have finally agreed to make peace and reconcile. It seemed to me an extremely remarkable and encouraging event.

The civil war in Sudan broke out in 1983, when the Sudan People's Liberation Movement/Sudan People's Liberation Army (SPLM/SPLA)[4] was formed and launched a war of liberation against the Sudanese government in Khartoum. By 1999 and 2000, the civil war in Sudan had lasted for 16 or 17 years and had imposed devastating effects on the people. It is said to have claimed about two

147

million lives and displaced hundreds of thousands. Although efforts toward peace mediations had been made by international agencies and actors, none had been successful, and it seemed that the war would continue without end.

Moreover, the war expanded and became extremely complicated (Kurimoto 1996: 114–53; Johnson, D. 2016: chaps. 7-9). It started in the 1980s when the Khartoum government organised various 'tribal' militias[5] as a counter-insurgency measure to fight the SPLA. It became more pronounced after the SPLM/A split into two major factions in August 1991. One faction was led by John Garang, the founder of SPLM/A, who is ethnically a Twic Dinka, and the other by Riek Machar, who is ethnically a Dok Nuer. They started to fight each other, and Riek's faction eventually established an alliance with the Khartoum government, whom it was supposed to fight.[6] Begun allegedly as a war of liberation against the oppressive regime in Khartoum, the conflict increasingly assumed an aspect of fratricide, with South Sudanese attacking and killing one another, combatants and non-combatants alike (Nyaba 2000). Relations with neighbouring countries were also reflected in the war. For instance, the Lord's Resistance Army (LRA), supported by the Khartoum government, operated in Central and Eastern Equatoria, fighting the SPLA. Later, the Uganda Peoples' Defence Forces set up bases inside South Sudan to mop up the LRA. Another factor contributing to this complexity was the dissemination of small arms and light weapons. Many civilians or villagers were armed with automatic rifles and other modern weapons,[7] and the boundary between combatants and non-combatants was blurred. In a sense, society as a whole was militarised. This was a major factor in the escalation of violent incidents in inter- and intra-ethnic conflicts. The fratricide became ethnicised, and the Dinka and Nuer emerged as the main protagonists. Among the Nuer themselves, different wars were also ongoing (Johnson, D. 2016: chap. 8).

As an anthropologist who had started fieldwork in South Sudan in 1978 (Kurimoto 1996) and had maintained connections with people there, it was very painful for me to see the situation, and sometimes I felt hopeless. This was the situation that the people, gathered at Wunlit in late February 1999, had to deal with.

The Dinka and Nuer peoples[8] are neighbours, and they have close historical and cultural connections. Linguistically, they both speak Western Nilotic languages, and they share a lot of basic vocabulary. In the area where the Wunlit Conference was held, which is in the borderland between the Bahr al-Ghazal and Upper Nile regions, they share territories that are used for cattle grazing and fishing during the dry season. On the one hand, they have been enemies, attacking each other (Evans-Pritchard 1940). On the other, they also have a history of co-existence. They share many 'cross-cutting ties' (Schlee 1989, 1997) through intermarriages, friendship and trade. That mode of co-existence was greatly weakened during the Sudanese civil war because people in general, that is, non-combatants or civilians, became deeply divided as friends or enemies. Furthermore, the dividing lines were always subject to change, shifting over time; today's friend could be an enemy tomorrow.

In Unity State of the Upper Nile region, where the majority of inhabitants are Nuer and whose representatives participated in the Wunlit Conference, the war situation became particularly chaotic in the 1990s (Johnson, D. 2016: 121–26). This was a strategically critical location for the government in Khartoum, as oil field development schemes were going on with massive Chinese support.[9] To secure the oil fields, the government exploited the rivalries among Nuer leaders, even among those who had been allied with the government. This is the background against which I felt that the Wunlit Conference was a highly remarkable achievement, although at the time, information available on the internet was still very limited, and I could not learn the details.[10] Fortunately, I had a chance to meet Rev. Dr William O. Lowrey, an American Presbyterian pastor, in 1999 in Kyoto.[11] Rev. Lowrey was one of the organisers of the Wunlit Conference and was well informed about the situation. Rev. Lowrey told me the details and supplied me with documents from the conference. Then, in February and March 2000, I met with several senior members of the SPLM/A and church personnel in Nairobi, and they unanimously spoke highly of the achievements of the Wunlit Conference. I also learned that this sort of peace making, called 'people-to-people peace' or a 'grassroots peace process', is principally supported by church organisations. The New Sudan Council of Churches (NSCC) was particularly instrumental in such initiatives. The NSCC is an ecumenical organisation of all Christian denominations working in New Sudan (a SPLM/A term referring to the liberated territories, in contrast to 'Old Sudan', which refers to the territories under the control of Khartoum). The parallel organisation in Old Sudan is the Sudan Council of Churches (SCC); the NSCC and SCC are, of course, in close contact.

In South Sudan, there are three major churches: Catholic, Anglican (Episcopal) and Presbyterian. In South Sudan, where there are no other 'national' organisations, as far as 'civil society' is concerned, Christian churches and church-based organisations are virtually the only viable civil organisations that can be trusted by the people, irrespective of their ethnic and regional differences[12] and their affiliation with different armies. Thus, a church may provide a rare space where 'enemies' can sit together. The active involvement of churches and church-based organisations in humanitarian assistance during the war, along with the clergy's open and vocal criticism of both the government and SPLM/A and their calls for peace, contributed to the trust granted to churches during the war. Their international connections are, of course, one of their strengths.

At the time, the success of the Wunlit Conference seemed to be both amazing and fascinating. I could easily imagine, as an anthropological fieldworker who is familiar with rural areas of South Sudan, how extremely difficult it was to organise such a big conference, not only in a war zone but also in the middle of nowhere, where there was no permanent road or lodging. Even to secure enough food and water for the participants must have been difficult. Apart from these logistical issues, even more striking is that those who had raided and killed each other for years could sit together, talking openly for days about the grievances and suffering inflicted by the other, and finally reach an agreement. Another fascinating point for me was that 'traditional' authorities and rituals that are meaningful for both the Dinka and Nuer peoples were activated and intentionally used. These included the Dinka 'master of the fishing spear' (*bany bith*), the Nuer 'earth priest' (*kwar muon*),[13] the sacrifice of a white bull and communal feasts.

Another remarkable facet of the Wunlit Conference was that, as became clear over time, peaceful relations between the two parties were truly achieved and held. 'The local impact of Wunlit on the West Bank was immediate. Inter-group violence between those who participated in Wunlit ceased. To demonstrate this, Nuer participants walked home across Dinka territory. Abducted women, children and cattle were returned to their families or a bride price was negotiated to legitimise unions between abductors and abductees' (Bradbury et al. 2006: 47). This is exceptional because, as we shall see later, although many grassroots peace and reconciliation conferences were organised during the war, not many were successful. Many agreements on peace and reconciliation were never observed or were soon breached, and resolutions were never implemented. This is why the case of Wunlit is worth examination.

It is clear that people were tired of the prolonged conflict, hostilities and instability that made their lives very difficult. Above all, peace and reconciliation were crucial for the reconstitution of normal life and livelihood that can only be achieved through inter-ethnic co-existence by way of free movement, trade and sharing of natural resources for pastoralism and fishing.

The Wunlit Conference could not have been realised without support from the SPLM/A-Mainstream. Its leadership decided to support the event not simply because of goodwill but also because they thought that the conference would be a good opportunity to win back the trust of the Western Nuer, the majority of whom had become enemies after the 1991 split. The outcome was as the SPLM/A-Mainstream wished (Johnson, D. 2016: 125). In the conference, this group was represented by Salva Kiir Mayardid, the deputy commander-in-chief of the SPLA and deputy chairman of the SPLM (who is now the President of the Republic of South Sudan). On the first day of the conference, he concluded the opening with a moving speech.[14]

This Conference is being conducted in the midst of the great loss of elemental blood by both Dinka and Nuer people. I'll therefore not waste time but start by urging all participants to take this opportunity to reflect deeply on the terrible losses we have suffered, Dinka and Nuer, at each other's hands, as well as through the fratricide within our ethnic groups.

Let us use this Conference to reach conclusions and recommendations so that there shall be no more losses between Dinka and Nuer.

This Conference is not based on dreams but on reality. It has sprung from the grass roots. It was not concocted in some foreign capital and brought to you in a package. It is you who made this Conference. It is you who are making peace. It is you who are making this effort on the ground. This is the basis of my confidence in the success of the Conference.

It is significant that Salva Kiir clearly distinguished between peace from below that 'has sprung from the grass roots' and peace from above that is 'concocted in some foreign capital and brought to you in a package' and applauded the former. It is a great irony, however, that 14 years later, he betrayed his own words, 'There shall be no more losses between Dinka and Nuer.' In December 2013, he allowed a large-scale massacre of Nuer citizens in Juba by presidential Dinka militias. This event was to become the starting point of a new civil war in a new country, the Republic of South Sudan.

2. 'People-to-People Peace' during Sudan's Civil War (1983–2005)

The Wunlit Dinka–Nuer Peace and Reconciliation Conference did not emerge from nowhere. It had a pre-history as the culmination of processes that had started some years ago under the banner of 'People-to-People Peace', and the NSCC played a major role in conceiving and implementing it (New Sudan Council of Churches 2004; Bradbury et al. 2006).

South Sudan has been a huge experimental field for peace making and peacebuilding for the past three decades. I have already discussed the complex nature of Sudan's civil war (1983–2005). A variety of wars were fought at different levels and in different places, devastating all of South Sudan, and people had become deeply divided between friends and enemies. Therefore, it is not surprising that many concerned people, both South Sudanese and foreigners, thought that something should be done. It is very significant that during the latter half of the civil war period, a number of people-to-people peace or grassroots peace process programmes were carried out. Some conferences were held in Kenya and Uganda, but the majority occurred inside South Sudan. According to *Local Peace Processes in Sudan: A Baseline Study,* a report by the Rift Valley Institute that is based on research commissioned by the UK Department for International Development, 108 local peace conferences, aimed at resolving local conflicts in South Sudan, had been held by the end of 2004. Then, in 2005, another 15 were held. They were held in different locations and included a variety of South Sudanese ethnic groups and sub-groups[15] (Bradbury et al. 2006; Kurimoto 2014: 38–9). This report is comprehensive and is extremely useful and suggestive when one considers the possibilities and limits of peace from below.

One of the early, and one of the largest, of these events was the Akobo Peace Conference of 1994 (Lowrey 1997; Braubury et al. 2006: 38–40). This was an intra-Nuer peace and reconciliation conference between the Lou Nuer and Eastern Jikany Nuer, who had been attacking and killing each other extensively for about two years. The starting point of the deadly conflict was absurdly simple, a quarrel over fish caught by some Lou Nuer men in Jikany territory. Three Lou men were killed, and mutual revenge attacks, one after another, followed. The vicious cycle escalated. As shown later, within a short period of time, more than 1,300 people were killed and about 75,000 cattle raided. The government in Khartoum supplied arms to both sides to destabilise the area for its own benefit. The area was under the control of the SPLM/A-Nasir[16] faction, which could not resolve the conflict. Instead of resolving it, its soldiers joined relatives on both sides of the conflict. When Riek Machar, the leader of the SPLM/A-Nasir, visited Akobo in May 1994, he was challenged by furious Nuer women. They threatened that if he did not intervene, they would join with their men to escalate the conflict. This was the root of the Akobo Peace Conference. It was a large event in terms of the number of participants, with almost 500 official delegates representing all Nuer sections, 10 neighbouring ethnic groups and 1,500 observers. Many of the observers were the Eastern Jikany and Lou Nuer themselves, but members of international organisations and NGOs were also included. It was a very long conference as well; the whole process took 45 days and concluded in the middle of

September 1994. Traditional authorities of Nuer society, that is, 'earth priests' (or 'leopard skin priests/chiefs', *kuar muon*) and prophets (*gok* or *gwan kuoth*)[17] played a key role in mediation and authorised agreements, a practice carried forward to the Wunlit Conference.

The Akobo conference was coordinated by Rev. Dr William Lowrey and Dr Michael Wal Duany, both of whom also played prominent roles in the Wunlit Conference. Dr Duany, who was born in Akobo, is a veteran politician and a scholar who is respected both by the Lou and Jikany. A unique element of this conference was that they 'counted the cost', listing in detail all the lives and property lost since the beginning of 1993. The counting took time and started about three months before the conference began. The results of the count were as follows:

Persons killed		Cattle raided
Jikany.	857	24,428
Lou	482	50,817

In addition to the above, the Jikany suffered 3,000 homes burnt, 50 canoes destroyed and 1,300 tons of grain destroyed. The values were calculated according to Nuer customary law, using 'cattle equivalency': 1 killed person = 50 cows, 1 burnt home = 1 cow and 1 canoe = 3 cows. In sum, the total losses on both sides, calculated in terms of cattle equivalency, were Jikany 75,848 and Lou 74,917 (Lowrey 1997: 137–8). Additionally, about 150,000 people were reportedly displaced. First, it is clear that this sort of inter-communal conflict can be extremely destructive and can cause enormous damage. Second, the amount of damage was nearly equal on both sides, about 75 to 76 thousand units, when the cost is expressed in terms of cattle equivalency. This calculation resulted in agreement that compensation should not be paid by each side to the other.

The Akobo Conference is remarkable in many ways. It was very well planned and coordinated. It exemplified the usefulness and effectiveness of traditional authorities. Women's active participation was noteworthy. Most significantly, the warring parties stayed together for weeks discussing the suffering and grievances inflicted by the other party and listening to what the others said. They finally reached an agreement that hostilities would cease and mutual relations would return to normal. These achievements explain why the Akobo Conference became a model for later ones, including the Wunlit Conference.

Many of the resolutions, however, were not implemented, particularly those requiring full and genuine support from the SPLM/A-Nasir. These included the restoration of the traditional system of justice under the chiefs, the creation of special courts to handle violations of the peace agreement and the creation of special police units to implement the agreement. These were not realised due to the administrative weakness of Riek Machar's faction. It is doubtful whether Riek himself had a serious commitment to the conference or to achieving genuine reconciliation and peace; even if he did, he lacked the capacity to carry it out. In fact, at the time, Riek's power base was being eroded, and it continued to be so (Johnson, D. 2016: 117–21; Nyaba 2000: 123, 142). This failure suggests the necessity of joining the peace-from-below with the peace-from-above approach. In this case, the 'above' refers to governmental agencies of any sort, including those of a guerrilla movement, that administer the area.

3. Limits of Peace from Below: The Case of Eastern Equatoria

From 15 to 19 December 2003, I had an opportunity to attend the East Bank Equatoria Grassroots Peacebuilding Conference held in Lokichokio in north-western Kenya. It was the concluding session of the three years of the Pax Christi Netherlands-sponsored programmes in the SPLM/A-controlled areas of East Bank Equatoria, which included training for 'peace contact persons' and 'peace mobilisers' at the local level and a media capacities-enhancement programme. About 130 people participated, representing civil society and SPLM civil administration in five counties. Then, for about two weeks from 22 December 2003 to 5 January 2004, I toured various places in SPLM/A-controlled areas in Eastern Equatoria. The mission was to evaluate the results of local peace programmes sponsored by Pax Christi. I visited Kapoeta,

Ikotos and Chukudum, and the Kimatong centre (Kurimoto 2004). This trip provided me with invaluable opportunities to witness grassroots peacebuilding programmes on the ground and a precious chance to go back to the area where I had conducted fieldwork after two decades and meet some old friends.[18]

The focal point of peace and reconciliation programmes in the SPLM/A-controlled Eastern Equatoria was the Kidepo Valley. The Kidepo River originates in the highlands of north-eastern Uganda and runs northwards. The valley is about 25 km wide and more than 120 km long; on the east side are the Didinga Mountains and Buya Hills and on the west are the Lopit and Dongotona Mountains. The Buya (Boya, Narim or Longarim), Didinga and Toposa live in the eastern part of the valley, and the Lopit, Tenet, Lotuho (Latuka), Logir and Lango in the west. Permanent villages are located at the foot or on the slopes of the mountains and hills. The vast plains are uninhabited, and all of these groups set up cattle camps there during the dry season; cattle raiding parties roam across the valley.

Below is a list of 19 inter- and intra-ethnic cattle raids between 2002 and 2004. This information was gathered during my research tour (Kurimoto 2004: 47–8). I do not claim that it is comprehensive, but it adequately illustrates the general situation. I intentionally made the list simple, knowing the danger and inappropriateness of saying, for example, 'Buya raided Toposa'. To be exact, it should be, 'A group of armed Buya men from X village raided Y Toposa cattle camp of A village of B section'.

2002

Feb.	Toposa (Paringa section) raided Buya: 260 cattle taken; later collected and returned to Buya by SPLA.
June	Buya raided Toposa (Riwoto section): 200 cattle taken.
Nov.	Logir raided Didinga (Monita village): 113 cattle taken, one Didinga died.

2003

April	(Kidepo Peace and Reconciliation Conference)
	Logir (Lodwara village) raided Buya: one Logir died, SPLA collected 117 cattle. Logir raided Didinga (Monita village): 348

156

	cattle taken. Buya raided Logir (Lodwara village): 103 cattle taken.
June	Didinga (Kikilai village) raided Logir (Ramola village): 15 cattle taken; later collected by SPLA and returned to the owner.
	Logir raided Didinga (Betelado village): about 60 cattle taken, one Didinga died.
Aug.	Toposa raided Didinga (Lotuke area): many cattle taken.
Sep.	Buya raided Toposa (Machi section).
Oct.	Didinga raided Logir (Ramula village): 30 cattle taken, one Logir died.
Nov.	Didinga raided Toposa.
	Toposa raided Buya.
Dec.	Didinga (Monita village) raided Logir (Mogina village): 270 cattle taken.
	Logir (Lodwara and Ramula villages) raided Didinga: 1,504 cattle taken, one Didinga died.

2004

Jan.	Logir raided a cattle camp of Buya: two Logir and two Buya died.
	Logir together with men from Loguruny and Iloli (Lotuho villages) attacked the cattle camp of Buya: 25 Logir and two Buya died.
	Hiyala villages (Lotuho) raided a cattle camp of Lobira village (Lotuho): three Lobira died; raided cattle were collected and returned by the SPLM civil authorities.
	Men from Haforere village raided Ilieu: three Ilieu died (intra-Lotuho).

When we consider the assailants' ethnicity, seven of 19 were Logir, including one interesting case in which Logir men jointly carried out a raid with Lotuho men: four Didinga, three Toposa, three Buya and two Lotuho. Logir men were particularly active in carrying out raids. Only the Lotuho raid cattle among themselves, i.e., between villages. Generally speaking, ethnic groups raid each other, and there is a clear pattern of retaliation, with a raid followed by a counter raid as revenge. This is one part of a longer history of vicious cycles of violence.

In four cases, the SPLM/A confiscated the raided cattle and

returned them to the owners.[19] Although this happened in only four cases of 19, it is significant as evidence that at least some sort of administration was being established to maintain law and order in the liberated areas.[20]

It is notable, as will be discussed below, that Logir men twice carried out raids soon after the Kidepo Valley Peace and Reconciliation Conference in April 2003, looting a large number of cattle; one raid was against Buya, and the other against Didinga. In retaliation, both the Buya and Didinga raided the Logir.

Compared to the bloody conflicts in Jonglei state, which will be discussed in the next section, the number of casualties in these cattle raids was very low, and some took place without a death. This would illustrate that the focus of armed conflicts in the area is not to kill enemies but to raid cattle. Seen from this perspective, the incident of January 2004 in which 25 Logir men and two Buya died is an exception. The raid happened immediately after I left the area, and I heard that the Buya men of the targeted cattle camp were able obtain information in advance, so they laid an ambush; this explains the large number of deaths on the Logir side.

The Kidepo Valley Peace and Reconciliation Conference, held on 14 and 15 April 2003, was meant to resolve this chronic conflict realised through cattle raiding. It was the biggest peace and reconciliation conference ever held in Eastern Equatoria. It was held in the bush of the valley and attended by several hundred people. Representatives from ethnic groups along the valley, as well as church and civil organisations, were there. The SPLM/A sent a high-level delegation. The conference was mainly funded by the 'Sudan Peace Fund'[21] and supported by other international NGOs, including Pax Christi Netherlands (Kurimoto 2004: 13).

Irrespective of the size and high-level representatives, it is apparent that the conference was a failure. I met no one who said that the conference was successful. Everyone I talked to or interviewed complained about very poor coordination and organisation. The food was insufficient and was inequitably distributed. Some vividly remember what happened to the T-shirts specially prepared for the conference. When the organisers failed to distribute them to the participants, people rushed to the place where they were kept and simply took them in a rowdy tussle. The episode illustrates that even a small item like a T-shirt can be a cause for quarrelling. Moreover, the conference was very short, only two days, compared to others of a similar sort. It ended without reaching any meaningful agreements. The fact that only a few days after the conference, there were two cattle raids by Logir men against Buya and Didinga cattle camps is seen by many as clear evidence of its failure (Kurimoto 2004).

During the trip, I had a chance to talk to Logir chiefs in Ikotos. They said that although the Logir were made up of three sections, only one was represented at the Kidepo Conference and that men from one of the other two sections carried out the two raids after the conference. The chiefs said that those raids were clearly an expression of dissatisfaction with the way the conference had been coordinated and organised.

This was an important lesson: unless carefully managed, a conference for peace and reconciliation can be a cause for new conflict. In particular, the issue of representation is critical. All sections and sectors of the communities concerned need to be fairly represented in a grassroots peace and reconciliation conference. This is not an easy job. Sufficient time is necessary for the coordination of a conference, and it should be done by those who know the communities very well.

The Buya, together with the Logir, are notorious in Eastern Equatoria as natural-born cattle raiders. I intentionally visited their centre, Kimatong, to listen to their voices. In Kimatong, Cdr. Peter Longole[22] kindly organised a meeting for me with chiefs and elders. He had known me and knew what I wanted to ask. They were extremely bitter about the general marginalisation of the Buya, the underdevelopment of the area, the accusations against them and the attitudes of outsiders including workers from international organisations. A government[23] chief said the following (Kurimoto 2004: 18):

> We are very glad to hear from you about the Kidepo Peace Conference. We were threatened during the conference. In the conference, every tribe was asking to speak. Every tribe was saying that

the Buya are a bad people. Even our brothers, the Lopit, Lotuho, and Logir, were saying the same thing. But when we raised our hands, we were not given a chance to talk. We thanked God that only God knows whether we are a good or a bad people. We are equal … Although they say we are a bad people, we remain in peace. We did nothing bad. During that time, our cattle were stolen. Who did it? I am not saying that the Buya are a good people and the Toposa are a bad people. In every tribe there are some bad people. At the same time, all people are good.

We are suffering because, first, we are few. Second, we have no educated people. Third, we do not have 'fathers'. Other tribes have got something from this new government (the SPLM/A). When you come here, what do you see? Do you find any organisation among those here that is assisting us? Among the Toposa, if you go to Narus, you find development there. If you go to Chukudum, you find development there. If you go to Ikotos, you find development there. … From this new government, we have received nothing. We also want our area to develop like any other area. … Until when should we remain like this? Which government will bring development for us?

He described the general predicament his people faced. His speech was very logical and convincing, requiring no explanation. It reminds us of the importance of considering subtle power relationships among the marginalised peoples in South Sudan. In the general situation of marginalisation, there are those who are more marginalised and those less marginalised. This is significant when we think about inter-ethnic conflict and its resolution.

An elderly chief who knew the British period was very critical of me, seeing me as a representative of white men.[24] He went on to compare the British era with present times.

Are you a government official or someone organising something? When we see a white man like you, we think you are somebody from the government or somebody who understands. Sometimes, you may become a cheater. About the Kidepo Peace Conference, we thought that it would be the final peace that we make. Then we were cheated. Now you are here. … Maybe you are a jobless person. You may go to an NGO to collect money. You are coming here to cheat us. You may not be coming here for actual peace (applause). Maybe people come here searching for salaries. Are you really bringing peace for us?

During the British rule, only one person was in charge of all the tribes, Toposa, Didinga, and Buya. Only one person was controlling the people. Today, we have many Commanders and so on. What is wrong? Are we not willing to control? Have we really decided to do something? … If the war is still going on, leave us. Because it is war that brings confusion. Let the war end first. And then we come to peace.

His speech clearly expresses his deep distrust of those expatriates ('white men') working for international organisations who occasionally come to visit them, claiming that they bring either development or peace, and it was also apparent that his view was shared by others.

Concerning the story that law and order used to be well maintained during the British time, I was told by others that the 'one person' he mentioned was a British captain who had been a district commissioner. He commanded a small force of local policemen. Now, there are many SPLA Commanders with their heavily armed forces, yet there is no law and order. This seemed to be a very revealing commentary. After the CPA, the bizarre situation escalated further, as the SPLA quickly promoted a large number of junior officers to senior ranks, creating a situation wherein there were too many majors, lieutenant-colonels, colonels and brigadiers, and the insecurity continued.

A common comment I heard from many elders was that not all men participate in cattle raiding and that many of those active in raiding are young ex-soldiers. Some complained to me that these men no longer listen to the elders. 'Those young guys are out of our control. When we try to persuade them, they become angry and even point their guns at us,' they said. During the civil war, many young men joined the SPLA and other armies. Their experience as combatants may well have included raiding and looting. This is an aspect of the 'culture of the gun' or the 'culture of violence', and it exemplifies how society has been militarised. When a society is highly militarised, there is a pressing need to demilitarise it, which cannot be achieved simply by taking guns away. This, I would like to suggest, should also be considered in any process of local grassroots peacebuilding.

The cases from Eastern Equatoria demonstrate that grassroots peacebuilding is not as straightforward as one may assume. As a matter of fact, having a peace and reconciliation conference alone does not solve the problem. Such a conference should be a result of long-term and deep engagements with the people concerned, which requires well planned coordination with different stakeholders, representing all the communities. More importantly, a peace and reconciliation conference, even a successful one, is not an end in itself. Rather, it marks the start of a new process that requires monitoring to see how the agreements will be observed and the resolutions implemented.

In Kimatong, to my surprise, I met a group of Lotuho men from Lobira village. They came to settle the case of cattle stolen by Buya men. The case had already been settled by Buya civil authorities, chiefs and elders, and several head of cattle had been returned to the owners. Lobira men were waiting for the remaining cattle to be collected. They looked quite relaxed, walking around without carrying weapons, and were well received by Buya hosts. It struck me that although the Lotuho and Buya have accused each other as if they were deadly enemies, they still maintain cross-cutting ties and means of conflict resolution. It is those aspects that need to be brought to light and be revitalised and utilised in grassroots peacebuilding programmes. It should be also noted, however, that it is exactly because of their ties with Buya that some Lobira are often accused of being collaborators and traitors by other Lotuho.

Unfortunately, the situation of insecurity in Eastern Equatoria did not change after the CPA (2005) (Schomerus 2008) or even after independence in 2011. In one of the worst incidents, which occurred in May 2007, 54 Didinga civilians, most of them women and children, were killed by some 500 armed Toposa men in Lauro (Ngauro). Moreover, 400 goats and 400 head of cattle were also looted. Lauro is located to the east of the Kidepo valley in the northern periphery of the Didinga Mountains. The assailants were armed not only with automatic rifles but also with machine guns, rocket launchers, mortars and so on; some wore military uniforms. They were almost like an army battalion, although no connection to an existing army is known. This is a new type of violent inter-communal conflict in Eastern Equatoria. It was not a simple cattle raid. The scale of killing women and children was unprecedented, which makes us suspicious that simply killing Didinga, perhaps to displace them from the area, was one purpose of the raid. Some have said that the issue at stake was not cattle but land for grazing and gold panning[25] (Schomerus 2008: 37–9).[26]

Insecurity and violence still continue in today's Eastern Equatoria. I would like to mention a single case among many that is familiar to me. At the end of March 2019, a meeting was held in Lohiri village, of the Lotuho, to settle cases of killings and goat thefts between the Lotuho and Pachidi village,[27] of the Pari. Lohiri is in Torit County and Pachidi is in Lafon County; the two County Commissioners were there. Soon after the meeting started, a group of armed Lotuho men suddenly appeared on the scene and started shooting randomly at the delegation from Pachidi. Twenty people died on the spot; 17 of them were from Pachidi, and three were Lotuho, including a chief of Lohila, the next Lotuho village of the Lohiri. It is notable that the incident happened in the presence of two commissioners. Even more shocking was that it was a unilateral attack against those who came to attend an official peace-making conference. Victims did not expect at all that they might be attacked. The Lohiri incident was covered only by Sudanese/South Sudanese media[28] and, although the state governor visited the place, deployed police and army forces and set up an investigation committee, no suspect has been brought to court as of October 2020, and no compensation has been paid. This clearly illustrates the status quo of inter-communal conflicts in Eastern Equatoria today.[29] The peace-from-below approach is still very much necessary, and it should be coordinated by the state government with peace from above.

4. Failure of Peace from Above between 2005 and 2013

Sudan's Civil War finally ended in January 2005, when the Comprehensive Peace Agreement (CPA) was signed. During the six-year transitional period that followed, as the Government of

Southern Sudan (GOSS) was established by the SPLM with the SPLA as its official army, Southern Sudan as a polity enjoyed a special autonomous status. The six-year interim period was supposed to be a time for the consolidation of peace, establishment of administrative and legislative structures, and creation of a judicial system. Generally speaking, it was meant as period for rehabilitation, reconstruction and peacebuilding.

The UN deployed the United Nation Mission in Sudan (UNMISS),[30] a main component of which was up to 10,000 military personnel. Its primary task was to assist with the implementation of the CPA. UN agencies and many international NGOs launched a variety of programmes. The GOSS itself had a considerable budget, thanks to oil revenue, so it was capable, in principle, of implementing programmes.[31] The task ahead seemed enormous; it would start from zero, as the country had been devastated during the 22 years of civil war. Even before the war, South Sudan was one of the least developed regions in Africa, with extremely poor infrastructure and an inadequate and ineffective system of government. Therefore, to be honest, there was little physical structure to be 'reconstructed' and 'rehabilitated'.

There were, of course, some visible developments during the period before the new civil war. Juba, the capital city, expanded and developed quite rapidly, with new buildings, offices, shops and restaurants. As for local governments, state level administrative and legislative buildings were constructed,[32] and some at the county level. Many people, especially soldiers, were employed by the GOSS and local governments. In a sense, what the GOSS could provide to the South Sudanese were salaries for government employees. These salaries were quite good in the beginning. However, as the value of the new national currency, the Sudanese Pound, dropped because of inflation, they became less and less realistic, and payment was often delayed by months.[33]

The people of South Sudan who had survived the war and paid an extremely high price had high hopes for the future under the SPLM-led GOSS with the support of the UN and the international community. The GOSS failed, however, to deliver much-needed basic services in such fields as education, health, water, roads and food production, especially in rural areas.[34] People's hopes were not realised. This pattern of betrayal was to be repeated again after the independence of South Sudan in 2011.[35]

A referendum was carried out in January 2011 as an exercise of the right to self-determination that was stipulated in the CPA. I participated as a member of a monitoring team dispatched by the Japanese government. It was a choice between unity and separation. An overwhelming majority voted for the separation from Sudan, and South Sudan became an independent sovereign state on 9 July 2011.

At the time of independence, the people of South Sudan again had high hopes for the future, just as in 2005. The atmosphere of jubilation was already present during the referendum. Massive support by the UN and the international community continued. A new UN peace-keeping mission, the United Nation Mission in South Sudan (UNMISS), was deployed.[36] Few expected that the hopes and dreams of the people would be betrayed so soon.

It is true that tensions were growing as the rivalries among the SPLM ruling elite surfaced during the approach of the 2015 general elections. But it was a political issue, not a military one. In fact, I was in Juba at the beginning of December 2013 to attend the Forum of the African Potentials programme, together with friends and colleagues. The Forum had been organised by me, and South Sudanese high-ranking politicians and church people, experts from international NGOs and UN officials participated. No one expected, I am sure, that a new war would break out within a week. Ironically enough, the theme of the forum was peacebuilding.[37]

However, a new civil war did erupt in December 2013. On the night of 15 December 2013, shooting started among the Presidential Guards in the capital city of Juba. On the following day, President Kiir Salva Kiir appeared on national TV in a combat uniform and announced a coup attempt by former Vice President Riek Machar. In the meantime, mass killing of Nuer citizens continued for some days in Juba. The massacre was jointly prosecuted by SPLA soldiers loyal to the President and Dinka militia men recruited from the President's home region. [38] SPLA Nuer commanders in the Greater Upper Nile region, hearing of the incident in Juba, started a rebellion, killing Dinka soldiers and citizens as revenge for what happened in

165

Juba. Within days, the fighting developed into a full-scale civil war and the SPLM as the ruling party and the SPLA as the national army broke into two groups: those who supported the President and those who supported the former Vice President. This division overlapped, to a great extent, with the Dinka–Nuer ethnic division. Thus, the new-born state of South Sudan collapsed only two years and five months after its birth. This new civil war continued for years, although from the perspective of most South Sudanese, it was a senseless war (Young 2019; De Waal 2014; Nyaba 2014).

The civil war was primarily fought between Riek Machar's SPLM/A faction, which will be called 'the SPLM/A-IO' ('IO' stands for 'in opposition'), and the main faction loyal to President Kiir, sometimes called 'SPLM/A-in-Juba'. A peace agreement was reached in August 2015, and in April 2016, a transitional government of national unity was established, only to be dismantled in July of that year. The civil war resumed. As during Sudan's civil war, many armed groups were formed apart from the two SPLAs, and wars continued until the 'Revitalised Agreement on the Resolution of the Conflict in the Republic of South Sudan' (R-ARCSS) was signed in September 2018. The implementation of the agreement was postponed three times and, finally, in February 2020, a new transitional government of national unity was formed. As of October 2020, the R-ARCSS has been only partially implemented. Millions of refugees and internally displaced people are yet to be repatriated.

I consider the peacebuilding programmes conducted by the GOSS, UN agencies and international community, i.e., peace from above in general, during the CPA period (2005–11) and post-independence period up to 2013, to be failures for two reasons. First, although peace between the two Sudans has generally held, except for the period when the danger of a total military confrontation arose between the SPLA and the Sudan Armed Forces (SAF) in the disputed region of Abyei between 2007 and 2008, the situation of insecurity and violence has continued in much of South Sudan. In some areas, especially in Jonglei state of the Upper Nile region, it has become worse. Not merely inter-communal conflict but also wars between the SPLA and different armies have broken out. The most destructive and spectacular incidents happened during December

2011 and January 2012, when the Lou Nuer 'White Army'[39] mobilised 6,000 to 8,000 armed men and attacked Murle villages, killing more than 3,000 people. Neither the UNMISS nor the SPLA could deter the attack or protect the civilians (ICG 2009, 2014; Thomas 2015: chaps 6–8; Johnson, H. 2016: chap. 4; Young 2012). Second, the outbreak of a new civil war in December 2013 amounted to nothing less than a failure of peacebuilding. When the war broke out, the SPLM/A, which allegedly had been reformed and consolidated, automatically broke into pieces, and the state systems of administration and judiciary became paralysed. A fragile state collapsed, and it is apparent that all efforts at peacebuilding, strongly supported by the UN and the international community, were in vain. I would argue that the failure was a result of too much emphasis on state building at the expense of nation building. The peace-from-above approach was preoccupied with building up containers, leaving aside the issue of contents. Indeed, very little was done to mend the torn social fabric and achieve peaceful co-existence at the local level, as a starting point to nurture the sense of a nation.

5. Peace from Below and Peace from Above

The salient characteristic of peace from below is that it is endogenous, based on the people's wish for reconciliation and peaceful co-existence. It depends on the genuine wishes of the people. Ultimately, it is focused on the necessities of daily life. From the African Potentials perspective, peace from below demonstrates people's potential capability to resolve conflicts and restore peaceful co-existence. Hostilities among neighbouring communities and insecurity in the area make sustaining a livelihood very difficult. In a place like South Sudan, where the majority of the people are basically engaged in a 'multiple subsistence economy' in which not only agriculture but also pastoralism, fishing, gathering and hunting are practised, each community occupies a large territory, and natural resources in the border zone with neighbours are commonly shared. Thus, neighbours share the lands and waters required for grazing, fishing, gathering and hunting. These border territories are utilised commonly, but without free movement and security, such utilisation becomes impossible, rendering livelihoods very difficult. Free movement across territories of other communities is also necessary for trade and to visit administrative and commercial centres.

Another notable characteristic of peace from below is its flexibility and creativity. To realise reconciliation and peace and make them durable, people may mobilise whatever means are available, both 'traditional' and 'modern'. Traditional conflict resolution mechanisms (TCRMs) are such means, and products of modern technology such as satellite phones, smartphones and computers are actively used.

The people-to-people peace initiatives discussed in this chapter are a typical example of peace from below. They are participatory and consensual. All sections and sectors of the communities need to be represented, and the conclusions reached consensual. The preparation and coordination take time. Often, the final conference also takes weeks, as representatives of warring parties sit down together to report all sufferings and grievances and listen to those of others. The sort of justice embraced in this way is restorative, not retributive, as payment of compensation is the method employed to achieve justice.

Nonetheless, people-to-people peace' initiatives have not always been successful. It is easier to point to failed conferences than to identify successful ones. What is important, then, is to continue these engagements. Conferences need to be repeated, again and again, with good coordination until a final solution is reached.

On the other hand, peace from above is exogenous. It is conceived and planned somewhere else and transplanted to the conflict zones or post-conflict countries and areas. The prototype is the peacebuilding programmes brought by the UN and the international community, which are readymade packages, allegedly universally applicable. Also included in this category are initiatives and programmes by regional and sub-regional bodies such as the African Union (AU) and Inter-Governmental Authority for Development (IGAD), national and local governments and international NGOs.

The typical and influential peace-from-above approach seen in the UN-led peacebuilding programmes originates from *An Agenda for Peace* (1992) by UN Secretary General Boutros-Ghali. Other basic

UN documents are Secretary General Kofi Annan's report *The Causes of Conflict and the Promotion of Durable Peace and Sustainable Development in Africa* (1998) and the *Report of the Panel on United Nations Peace Operations* (2000), usually called the 'Brahimi Report' after the chairperson of the commission, Lakhdar Brahimi. In Annan's report, which is focused on Africa, the causal relations between poverty and conflict and the linkage between conflict resolution and sustainable economic development were made clear. In Brahimi's report, the notion of peacebuilding was expanded as an integral part of peace keeping in general. Thus, during the 1990s, a new framework of UN-led peacebuilding emerged, and it emphasised building institutions in a post-conflict country based on a market economy and democracy; this approach has been termed 'liberal peacebuilding' (Duffield 2001; Newman, Paris and Richmond (eds) 2009: 10–1).

Hideaki Shinoda, a leading Japanese scholar on peacebuilding, summarises the idea as follows: 'Peacebuilding operations are the conceptual framework to make a comprehensive and integrative strategy for endurable peace in society' whose nature is to 'focus on the root causes, not on superficial phenomena' (2003: 21). The principle is right, but in practice, there have been both successful and failed cases. In my opinion, those failures should be attributed to the fact that the programmes were not comprehensive and integrative enough and did not address root causes, as they were focused only on superficial issues.

We already have excellent critical studies on the success and failure of UN peacebuilding operations, which overlap with studies on international humanitarianism (Duffield 2001; Kennedy 2005; Paris 2004; Newman and Richmond (eds) 2006; Doyle and Sambanis 2006; Oberschall 2007; Newman, Paris and Richmond (eds) 2009). The criticism basically concerns two points; one is that of technical shortcomings in implementation, and the other involves questions about the legitimacy of liberal peacebuilding, especially when it is imposed on a country where a market economy and democracy are insufficiently developed. In a sense, it is about the existing gap between the 'internationals' and the 'locals'. Representing this line of argument, Newman, Paris and Richmond put it as follows:

International peacebuilding currently revolves around a distinction between the 'international' and 'locals.' ... It may well be that this points to the need for a non-liberal type of peacebuilding, or at least for a greater consideration and respect for alternative modes of politics or polities, if this can be done without creating even greater problems for the population of the host countries. We might even wish to explore more hybridised forms of peacebuilding that involve a mixture of conventionally liberal and local practice and models (Newman et al. 2009: 14).

Although this was written from the 'Above' perspective, I agree with their point. To translate their comments into my own words, there is a dire need to bridge and harmonise the peace-from-below with the peace-from-above approaches. Conceptually, I consider the two approaches opposites, but in reality, they merge. First, 'below' and 'above' are relative notions. At the one end of spectrum, we find the 'grassroots' stakeholders, villagers who are parties to the conflict, who can be both assailants and victims. At the other end are UN agencies and the international community. In between, we find local NGOs, local government, national government and international NGOs. They intermingle and interact in different ways.

From the peace from below perspective, a peace-from-above component is necessary for two reasons. First, the former needs support from outside for mediation and logistics. Negotiations for peace and reconciliation require neutral mediators, and someone from outside is more suitable for the job than is an insider. Thus, churches and national and international organisations can provide mediators. Needless to say, in South Sudan, transportation and lodging are chronic problems. Local people do not have the means to transport themselves or accommodate guests. Means of transport and necessary food and water must be provided, and makeshift sleeping and meeting spaces must be constructed. Often those who are living in diaspora and are respected by and influential to the people and those who live in East Africa, Europe and North America need to be invited. This also requires financial support. Outside support includes technical support as well. Any meeting or conference should be recorded and documented. If an agreement is reached, it should be signed by stakeholders. So, they need computers, printers and electricity. The other requirement is that for the implementation of agreements, administrative support is necessary. So, unless governments of all sorts support it, whether they be internationally recognised or de facto governments created by the liberation movement, the agreement reached in a conference cannot be fully implemented.

Therefore, the distinction between peace from below and peace from above does not pose a question with two choices. What is needed is a way to bridge the gap and find harmony between the two.[40]

Considering South Sudan again, it is very unfortunate that peace from below and peace from above were not simply bridged and harmonised. Instead, the former has been neglected by successive governments of South Sudan since the CPA. The momentum for people-to-people peace that emerged during Sudan's civil war was discontinued. To understand this requires a full analysis of the post-CPA era. Here, it suffices to note a common saying among ordinary people who lived in liberated areas during the war: 'During the war, the SPLM/A was close to us. Now it is very far.' After the CPA era, new national elites concentrated in Juba were occupied with the task of state building. Very little attention was paid to nation building in general or local peace and reconciliation programmes in particular. These elites were also busy 'getting positions to eat', i.e., seeking positions in the government for their own benefit. This 'eating', of course, involved embezzling from the government budget and arranging kickbacks from government contracts. In some extreme cases, the money disappeared entirely and the contracted projects were never implemented (Johnson, H. 2016: 23–42; De Waal 2014). As a result, many SPLM/A leaders became extremely wealthy.

6. Conclusions

South Sudan has been a huge experimental field for peace making and peacebuilding. As the new civil war that broke out in December 2013 ended in February 2020, these efforts should have begun again. What was done between 2005 and 2013, with massive intervention by the UN and international community, proved to be a total failure.

We are obliged to reconsider seriously why peacebuilding programmes in South Sudan failed. There is a dire need for us to learn from past mistakes so that they will not be repeated again. In doing so, the distinction between peace from below and peace from above is useful, and peace from below initiatives during Sudan's civil war (1983–2005) hold a key. They embody local people's will and capability for peace and reconciliation and are considered to constitute African Potentials.

It is meaningful to recall what Salva Kiir said on the first day of the Wunlit Conference as part of his concluding speech: 'This Conference is not based on dreams but on reality. It has sprung from the grass roots. It was not concocted in some foreign capital and brought to you in a package. It is you who made this Conference. It is you who are making peace. It is you who are making this effort on the ground. This is the basis of my confidence in the success of the Conference.' He was right in saying that peace from above is 'a package concocted in some foreign capital' and in stressing the importance of the people's will for peace and reconciliation. After 2005, however, during his presidency, he failed to nurture the people's will.

People's capacity for peace needs to be activated again, first, to secure and improve their livelihood and, ultimately, to fashion a strong nation. To achieve this, it will be necessary to bridge and harmonise this peace from below with peace from above.

Given the degree of dire damage done during the new civil war, in which the very fabric of society is almost completely destroyed, and the South Sudanese became so hostile and divided among themselves, it may be too naïve to reply on the people's will for peace and reconciliation. Certainly the government and people of South Sudan are in a much worse condition in 2020, than they were in 2005. It is a sort of desperate condition that one is tempted to ask, "What hope is left?" (Martell 2018: 273). Nevertheless, I believe that there can be no any other alternative than counting on people's will for peace and reconciliation by reviving and reconstituting it under the current context. It is a way of realising African Potentials.

Endnotes

[1] The Republic of South Sudan became independent on 9 July 2011. Before that, it was called Southern Sudan, i.e., the southern part of Sudan. For the sake of simplicity, I call it South Sudan throughout this chapter unless otherwise noted.

[2] The Dinka as a people (ethnic group), as well as the Nuer, are divided into various territorial sections or 'tribes', and members of each 'tribe' recognise a common ancestry. For instance, the Twic is a Dinka section and the Dok is a Nuer section (Evans-Pritchard 1940).

[3] Under the Anglo–Egyptian Condominium rule (1899–1956), Southern Sudan consisted of three provinces, Equatoria, Upper Nile and Bahr al-Ghazal. This administrative division continued in post-independence Sudan after 1956. During the transitional period (2005–11) after the signing of the Comprehensive Peace Agreement (CPA) ended the second civil war (1983–2005), ten 'states' were created within the administrative boundaries of old provinces. Equatoria and Upper Nile were divided into three and Bhar al-Ghazal into four. Each state had a governor, a government and a legislative assembly.

[4] The power of the political wing, the SPLM, was nominal, and it was considered a weakness in the liberation movement. During the war, people referred to it simply as the SPLA, not the SPLM/SPLA.

[5] In Sudanese English, ethnic groups are called 'tribes'. Notably, tribal militias were recruited from the pastoral Arabs of Southern Kordofan and Southern Blue Nile (which are in Northern Sudan), Murle in the Upper Nile, Fartit in Bahr al-Ghazal and Mundari and Toposa in Equatoria.

[6] The two factions were initially named according to their bases; Garang's faction was called the SPLM/A-Torit and that of Riek the SPLM/A-Nasir. The former was also called the SPLM/A-Mainstream.

[7] For a discussion of the physical and moral significance of automatic rifles among the Nuer, see Hutchinson (1996: chap. 3).

[8] In anthropology, they are well-known peoples through the classic works of Oxford anthropologists E. E. Evans-Pritchard and G. Lienhardt. In today's South Sudan, population-wise, the Dinka are the largest ethnic group, followed by the Nuer. Many top politicians in the government and generals in the army hail from these two peoples.

[9] Oil was a major factor in Sudan's civil war (Kurimoto 1996: 62–4).

Sudan became an oil-exporting country in 1999.

¹⁰ Now, the official documents are available on the internet. 'Dinka-Nuer West Bank Peace and Reconciliation Conference' (https://www.southsudanpeaceportal.com/wp-content/uploads/1999/03/Wunlit-Dinka-Nuer-West-Bank-Peace-and-Reconciliation-Conference.pdf) (https://www.peaceagreements.org/viewmasterdocument/1813) (accessed: 17 October 2020).

¹¹ I am grateful to Mr N. M. Shackleton, associate professor at Osaka Gakuin University, who kindly introduced me to Rev. William Lowrey.

¹² It should also be pointed out, however, that the congregations of all denominations are ethnicised to one degree or another.

¹³ For the master of the fishing spear, see Lienhardt (1961). The earth priest is also called the leopard skin chief/priest in the literature (Evans-Pritchard 1940; Hutchinson 1996).

¹⁴ 'Dinka–Nuer West Bank Peace and Reconciliation Conference', pp. 9–11, 146–8 (https://www.southsudanpeaceportal.com/wp-content/uploads/1999/03/Wunlit-Dinka-Nuer-West-Bank-Peace-and-Reconciliation-Conference.pdf) (accessed: 17 October 2020).

¹⁵ See 'Chronological and geographical table of peace meetings' and also 'List of peace meetings by region and date' (Bradbury et al. 2006: 147–79). The counting is mine. The report also covers the cases in Northern Sudan.

¹⁶ At the time, it was called the SPLM/A-United. In 1994 the name changed again to the Sudan Independence Movement/Sudan Independence Army (SIM/SIA). For the sake of simplicity, I maintain the name, SPLM/A-Nasir.

¹⁷ The power of Nuer prophets in making both war and peace should not be underestimated. A prophet was instrumental in maintaining agreements at the Wunlit Conference. In fact, the large village where he resided was a sort of sanctuary, or free zone, where anyone, irrespective of friend/enemy dividing lines, could visit and stay (Hutchinson and Pendle 2015).

¹⁸ I appreciate the invitation by my long-term friend and co-researcher, Dr Simon Simonse, who is a Dutch anthropologist and senior advisor for Pax Christi Netherlands.

¹⁹ I understand that not all cattle were returned to the owners. Some were eaten by SPLA soldiers, and some were taken to the Agoro cattle

market in Uganda and sold.

[20] In fact, in an effort to restructure the movement and to regain national support from the people, the SPLM/A-Mainstream organised the first-ever National Convention in Chukudum in 1994. As a result, a civil administration structure was established in liberated areas (Rolandsen 2005; Johnson, D. 2016: 106).

[21] The Sudan Peace Fund was set up with USAID money in 2002. Its funds have supported many grassroots peace programmes.

[22] Cdr Longole was the most senior Buya officer in the SPLA and had held the position of SPLM Deputy Governor of the Equatoria region.

[23] This 'government' means the SPLM/A.

[24] According to skin colour categories of the South Sudanese, East Asians are recognised as 'white'. Other categories are 'black' and 'red'. 'Arabs' in northern Sudan and Ethiopian highlanders are considered 'red'.

[25] Alluvial gold is found in this area. Gold panning is an important source of cash income for the locals and, allegedly, for the SPLM/A senior personnel.

[26] See also 'Didinga community: killing of 54 civilians by Toposa is political', 2 July 2007 (https://sudantribune.com/spip.php?article22658) (accessed: 18 October 2020).

[27] I have maintained close relations with the people of Pachidi (Pugeri) since 1978.

[28] '20 killed in communal violence in Torit', 28 March 2019 (https://radiotamazuj.org/en/v1/news/article/20-killed-in-communal-violence-in-torit) (accessed: 16 October 2020). 'Lafon County official urges government to end communal violence', 3 April 2019 (https://radiotamazuj.org/en/v1/news/article/lafon-county-official-urges-government-to-end-communal-violence) (accessed: 16 October 2020).

[29] I understand that at the background of the Lokiri incident lies in the issue of land and borders, namely the utilisation of natural resources for cultivation, grazing, fishing and hunting in the inter-ethnic border zone.

[30] For the mandate of the UNMIS, see UN Security Council Resolution 1590 (2005) (https://www.un.org/ga/search/view_doc.asp?symbol=S/RES/1590(2005)) (accessed: 19 October 2020).

[31] 'The Government budget in 2005 was $14.5 million; in 2006 it

budgeted $1.34 billion and spent $1.56 billion' (Johnson, H. 2016: 28).

[32] There are ten states. Each state has a government headed by a governor and a state legislature. Administratively, a state is divided into counties and then into *payam*s and *boma*s.

[33] After the independence of South Sudan in 2011, a new currency, the South Sudanese Pound, was introduced. Initially, 1 dollar was equal to 2.7 SSP. As of 15 October 2020, the value was 510 SSP on the black market (personal communication). Therefore, salaries for government employees are absolutely far from adequate.

[34] On several occasions during the CPA period, I visited villages of the Pari people in Lafon County of Eastern Equatoria State, where I had conducted long-term fieldwork until 1985. Apart from an administrative office and a health centre in the County centre, the government had provided absolutely nothing to the people.

[35] For a detailed and in-depth analysis by an insider of the failure of the SPLM during the CPA period, see Nyaba (2011).

[36] For the mandate of the UNMISS, see UN Security Council Resolution 1996 (2011) (http://unscr.com/en/resolutions/doc/1996) (accessed: 19 October 2020).

[37] For the African Forum in Juba, see the link below (https://www.africapotential.africa.kyoto-u.ac.jp/en/research_activites-en/internationalsymposium-en/5359.html) (accessed: 15 October 2020).

[38] Initial reports spoke of 1,000 deaths. For instance, see a Human Rights Watch report (https://www.hrw.org/news/2014/01/16/south-sudan-ethnic-targeting-widespread-killings) (accessed: 16 October 2020). Note that it is commonly assumed that more than 20,000 were massacred, although the truth has yet to be determined.

[39] For the White Army, see Young (2007, 2012: 318, 320–3) and Hashimoto (2018: 292–337).

[40] See the conference that Dr Simon Simonse and I organised in Torit in 2009 as a trial for bridging the gap (Simonse and Kurimoto (eds) 2011).

Acknowledgement

This work was supported by JSPS KAKENHI Grants Numbers JP16H06318, 13571017, 17401005, 22242029, 15K03041, and 19K12527.

References

Bradbury, M., Ryle, J., Medley, M. and Sansculotte-Greenidge, K. (2006) *Local Peace Processes in Sudan: A Baseline Study*, Commissioned by the UK Government Department for International Development, London and Nairobi: The Rift Valley Institute (https://www.sudanarchive.net/) (accessed: 11 November 2020).

De Waal, A. (2014) 'When Kleptocracy becomes insolvent: Brute causes of the civil war in south Sudan', *African Affairs*, Vol. 113, No. 452, pp. 347–69.

Doyle, M. W. and Sambanis, N. (2006) *Making War and Building Peace: United Nations Peace Operations*, Princeton: Princeton University Press.

Duffield, M. (2001) *Global Governance and New Wars: The Merging of Development and Security*, London: Zed Books.

Evans-Pritchard, E. E. (1940) *The Nuer: A Description of Modes of Livelihood and Political Institutions of a Nilotic People*, Oxford: Clarendon Press.

Hashimoto, E. (2018) *E Kuoth: An Ethnography of Prophecy and Suffering among the Nuer of South Sudan*, Fukuoka: Kyushu University Press (in Japanese).

Hutchinson, S. E. (1996) *Nuer Dilemmas: Coping with Money, War, and the State*, Berkeley: University of California Press.

Hutchinson, S. E. and Pendle, N. R. (2015) 'Violence, legitimacy and prophecy: Nuer struggles with uncertainty in South Sudan', *American Ethnologist*, Vol. 42, No. 3, pp. 415-30.

ICG (International Crisis Group) (2009) *Jonglei's Tribal Conflicts: Countering Insecurity in South Sudan*, Africa Report No. 154, Brussels: International Crisis Group.

_____ (2014) *South Sudan: Jonglei – 'We Have Always Been at War'*, Africa Report No. 221, Brussels: International Crisis Group.

Johnson, D. H. (2016) *Root Causes of Sudan's Civil Wars: Old Wars and New Wars*, revised edition, Woodbridge: James Currey.

Johnson, H. F. (2016) *South Sudan: The Untold Story, from Independence to Civil War*, London: I. B. Tauris.

Kennedy, D. (2005) *The Dark Sides of Virtue: Reassessing International Humanitarianism*, Princeton: Princeton University Press.

Kurimoto, E. (1996) *People Living through Ethnic Conflicts: State and Minorities in Modern Africa*, Kyoto: Sekaishisōsha (in Japanese).

———— (2000) '"Peace from Above" and "Peace from Below": On the Sudan's civil war,' *NIRA Seisakukenkyū* (*NIRA Policy Studies*), Vol. 13, No. 6, pp. 46–9 (in Japanese).

———— (2004) 'A report of the evaluation survey on Peacebuilding Programmes in the East Bank, Equatoria Region, South Sudan, sponsored by Pax Christi Netherlands' (https://www.sudanarchive.net/) (accessed: 11 November 2020).

———— (2011) 'Creating peace from the community: A perspective from the southern Sudan', in K. Fujiwara, R. Oshiba and T. Yamada (eds) *Introduction to Peacebuilding*, pp. 126–50, Tokyo: Yūhikaku (in Japanese).

———— (2014) 'Limits and possibilities of grassroots peacebuilding in the southern Sudan', in H. Oda and Y. Seki (eds) *Anthropology of Peace*, pp. 27–8, Tokyo: Hōritsubunkasha (in Japanese).

LeRiche, M. and Arnold, M. (2012) *South Sudan: From Revolution to Independence*, London: Hurst & Co.

Lienhardt, G. (1961) *Divinity and Experience: The Religion of the Dinka*, Oxford: Clarendon Press.

Lowrey, W. (1997) '"Passing the Peace": The role of religion in peacemaking among the Nuer in Sudan', in A. Wheeler (ed.) *Land of Promise: Church Growth in a Sudan at War*, Nairobi: Paulines Publications Africa, pp. 129–50.

Martell, P. (2018) *First Raise a Flag: How South Sudan Won the Longest War but Lost Peace*, London: Hurst & Co.

Newman, E. and Richmond, O. P. (eds) (2006) *Challenges to Peacebuilding: Managing Spoilers during Conflict Resolution*, Tokyo: United Nations University Press.

Newman, E., Paris, R. and Richmond, O. P. (2009) 'Introduction', in E. Newman, R. Paris and O.P. Richmond (eds), *New Perspectives on Liberal Peacebuilding*, Tokyo: United Nations University Press, pp. 2-25.

New Sudan Council of Churches (2004) *Building Hope for Peace Inside Sudan: People-to-People Peacemaking Process, Methodologies and Concepts among Communities of Southern Sudan*, Nairobi: New Sudan Council of Churches.

Nyaba, P. A. (2000) *The Politics of Liberation in South Sudan: An Insider's View*, second edition, Kampala: Fountain Publishers.

_____ (2011) *South Sudan: The State We Aspire to*, CASAS Book Series No. 85, Cape Town: CASAS.

_____ (2014) *South Sudan: The Crisis of Infancy*, CASAS Book Series No. 108, Cape Town: CASAS.

Oberschall, A. (2007) *Conflict and Peacebuilding in Divided Societies*, New York: Routledge.

Paris, R. (2004) *At War's End: building Peace after Civil Conflict*, New York: Cambridge University Press.

Rolandsen, Ø. (2005) *Guerrilla Government: Political Changes in the Southern Sudan during the 1990s*, Uppsala: Nordic Africa Institute.

Schlee, G. (1989) *Identities on the Move: Clanship and Pastoralism in Northern Kenya*, Manchester: Manchester University Press.

_____ (1997) 'Cross-cutting ties and interethnic conflict: The example of Gabra Oromo and Rendille', in K. Fukui, E. Kurimoto and M. Shigeta (eds.) *Ethiopia in Broader Perspective, Vol. II*, pp.577–96, Kyoto: Shokado.

Schomerus, M. (2008) *Violent Legacies: Insecurity in Sudan's Central and Eastern Equatoria*, HSBA Working Paper 13, Geneva: Small Arms Survey.

Shinoda, H. (2003) *Peacebuilding and the Rule of Law: Theoretical and Functional Analyses of International Peace Operations*, Tokyo: Sōbunsha (in Japanese).

Simonse, S. and Kurimoto, E. (eds) (2011) *Engaging Monyomiji: Bridging the Governance Gap in East Bank Equatoria, Proceeding of the Conference, 26-28 November 2009, Torit*, Nairobi: Pax Christi Horn of Africa.

Thomas, E. (2015) *South Sudan: A Slow Liberation*, London: Zed Books.

Young, J. (2007) *The White Army: An Introduction and Overview, Sudan Working Papers 5*, Geneva: Small Arms Survey.

_____ (2012) *The Fate of Sudan: The Origins and Consequences of a Flawed Peace Process*, London: Zed Books.

_____ (2019) *South Sudan's Civil War: Violence, Insurgency and Failed Peacemaking*, London: Zed Books.

Chapter 7

Institutional Bricolage in Responses to Public Health Crises in South Africa: Between Path Dependency and Flexibility

Kumiko Makino

1. Introduction

The novel coronavirus has changed the world as we know it. The outbreak started in Wuhan City, China, in late 2019, but Europe and the United States soon became the new epicentres. The spread of the virus to Africa began relatively late, but the number of positive cases in Africa increased continuously in the first half of 2020. Many countries, including at least 42 African countries as of May 2020, have imposed local or national 'lockdown' measures to slow the spread of the virus (UNECA 2020). Governments across the world have tightened entry restrictions, forbidding or severely restricting entry except for their own citizens' return. Under the lockdown measures, people are asked to stay home as much as possible, and their outings and economic and social activities are restricted. Restrictions on economic activities have caused many people to lose their jobs and incomes and have had significant impacts on their livelihoods. Although lockdowns have been effective in slowing the spread of the virus, they cannot be continued indefinitely, as they have serious negative impacts on lives and livelihoods. In Africa and elsewhere, 'hard lockdowns' last only for a few weeks at best, after which restrictions are gradually relaxed and economic activity starts resuming. However, there are still restrictions on the movement of people across borders. It seems that the new coronavirus has put globalisation into reverse, at least temporarily. Even when the regulations are lifted altogether, we do not yet know whether the world will completely return to the 'old normal'.

Considering the magnitude of the impact of the new coronavirus on the lives of people at various levels, African Potentials, the main concept of the international research project on which this book is based, is arguably being put to the test in the response to the new coronavirus. The concept of African Potentials was introduced by Gebre, Ohta and Matsuda (2017: 3) to refer to 'philosophies, knowledge, institutions, values and practices that African societies have developed, modified and utilised in handling conflicts and achieving peaceful coexistence'. According to those authors, 'African potentials are characterised by dynamism, which is expressed in flexibility, adaptability, receptivity, proactivity and consensus', and '[t]he ability to adapt positively to changing environments and stay relevant helps individuals and groups to achieve what they want and avoid risks of getting into trouble' (Gebre, Ohta and Matsuda 2017: 23).

World leaders spearheading the response to COVID-19 often say they are waging a 'war' against the virus. For instance, Chinese President Xi Jinping called the government's efforts against the virus the 'people's war' (Chris and Myers 2020), and the former United States' President, Donald Trump, declared that America continued to 'wage all-out war to defeat the virus' (White House 2020). On the other hand, some argue that the metaphor of war is problematic, as it demands subordination from people for the sake of winning the 'war' and forces sacrifices upon the weak (Takahashi 2020). In any case, the new coronavirus will not go away any time soon. At least for a while, until an effective vaccine or treatment is widely available, we have no choice but to coexist with the virus.

If that is the case, it would be worthwhile to start looking at responses to the new coronavirus from the perspective of African Potentials, i.e., responses characterised by flexibility, adaptability, receptivity, proactivity and consensus. This chapter takes South Africa as a case study and examines its policy responses in the first few months of the COVID-19 pandemic. Specifically, I will focus on how the South African government has drawn lessons from past experiences with another deadly epidemic, namely human immunodeficiency virus/acquired immunodeficiency syndrome (HIV/AIDS), and adopted measures built upon existing policies, institutions and networks. Of course, it is still too soon to discuss fully the impact of the new coronavirus on South Africa and other African countries, yet I would argue that we can sense a kind of African Potentials in South Africa's agile responses.

Such arguments may not be well accepted by Africanist scholarship, which is accustomed to viewing governments and political leaders as incompetent and irrelevant or, even worse, evil and predatory. In contrast, the agency of people, demonstrated in their daily lives, has been highlighted in the African Potentials literature.[1] However, it is also true that, in 21st century Africa, the role of governments with regard to protecting and promoting people's health and livelihood has increased against the backdrop of both democratisation and international development goals such as the Millennium Development Goals (MDGs) and Sustainable Development Goals (SDGs), which emphasise the importance of investment in health and social protection. Despite these changes, we still often see media reports based on negative preconceptions that African governments are doomed to fail.[2] This chapter constitutes a call for a fair assessment and a challenge to these persistent negative stereotypes of Africa.

2. COVID-19 in Africa

While the spread of the virus to Africa began relatively late, the number of COVID-19 cases on the African continent continued to rise in the first half 2020. According to the World Health Organization (WHO) news release in May 2020, it was estimated that up to 190,000 people could die of COVID-19 in Africa in the first year of the pandemic if it was not properly controlled (WHO Africa 2020). However, early records of the infection's spread in the African continent belied this initial pessimism. Although a variety of factors might have contributed to reductions in the initial spread of infection,[3] one plausible explanation is that African countries were able to respond quickly to the coronavirus partly because, compared to other regions in the world, they have had richer experiences of handling serious epidemics of various communicable diseases in the recent past (Endo 2020).

HIV/AIDS, tuberculosis (TB) and malaria have been the three

major global health threats in the 21st century, and the African continent has been the epicentre of them all. More recently, Western African countries including Guinea, Liberia and Sierra Leone saw the ebola outbreak in 2014. The Africa Centres for Disease Control and Prevention (Africa CDC) was established in 2017 following the ebola outbreak, which highlighted the critical need for a continental entity to address disease control and prevention (Ordu 2020). The Africa CDC has played a key role in developing the African joint response to the COVID-19 outbreak. One example of the joint response in the continent is the Africa Medical Supplies Platform, a digital platform for procurement of COVID-19-related critical medical equipment across the African continent. It was jointly launched by the African Union (AU), the Africa CDC, the African Export–Import Bank (Afreximbank) and the United Nations Economic Commission for Africa (ECA) in June 2020.[4] In other words, this coronavirus is new, but the institutions that have been shaping responses to this virus are not entirely new. Rather than building from scratch, African responses to COVID-19 have been informed by existing institutions and networks, and enacted through flexible and agile adaptation of whatever tools were available to the new situations.

The observation that existing institutions can be utilised in responding to novel sets of problems is not new or unique to Africa. In fact, it is rather common and normal, as it has been long discussed as 'path dependency' in the historical institutionalist literature that existing institutions constrain the responses to new situations. The main assumption of this school of thought is that 'policymaking systems tend to be conservative and find ways of defending existing patterns of policy, as well as the organisations that make and deliver them' (Peters, Pierre and King 2005: 1276). Although the emphasis is put on institutional stability, historical institutionalism has evolved by incorporating theories of institutional change (Mahoney and Thelen (eds) 2010). One of the key concepts of institutional change is the 'critical juncture', a period of significant change in which distinct legacies are produced in a time of crisis (Collier and Collier 1991). With regard to COVID-19, some have argued that, similar to the Black Death in European history, COVID-19 may become a critical juncture that disrupts the status quo and opens the door to previously unthinkable reforms (Green 2020). What kind of changes, then, are taking place in Africa in this critical period? Although it remains to be seen what the outcome might be, of greatest interest to me is the observation that, in the context of the African crisis of COVID-19, we are observing less an abrupt change than a flexible adaptation of existing institutions. This could be understood as an expression of 'institutional bricolage', i.e., gradual institutional change in a time of crisis in which existing institutions provide the tool kit or repertoire for actors to use in modifying institutions (Carstensen 2017).

With the above conceptual considerations and contexts in mind, the rest of the chapter examines the background and context of South African responses to COVID-19.

3. HIV/AIDS: Experiences from Another Epidemic[5]

As a disease requiring a global response, HIV/AIDS is an important precedent for COVID-19. COVID-19 and HIV/AIDS have several things in common. First, both are potentially fatal infectious diseases that affect every corner of the world, taking many lives in both richer and poorer countries. Second, both COVID-19 and HIV/AIDS are more than just health problems; they are entangled with other issues such as the global economy, trade and security. Third, therefore, responses to these diseases require global governance that involves diverse actors. In addition to sovereign state governments and agencies, various non-state actors engage in policy development and implementation, including international organisations, multinational corporations, private foundations, medical and other experts, NGOs and social movements, as well as individuals, families and communities who are affected by the diseases.

The disease that was later called AIDS was initially thought in Western developed countries to be an illness that only affected men who had sex with men (MSM). However, it soon became clear that HIV, the virus that causes AIDS, was also transmitted through heterosexual contact or from mother to child or by blood transfusion. HIV was also found to be much more widespread in sub-Saharan

Africa than in any other region of the world. Sub-Saharan Africa has been the constant epicentre of the HIV/AIDS epidemic, with South Africa having the highest number of HIV-positive people in the world.

Initially, HIV infection amounted to a certain death sentence. However, as life-saving antiretroviral therapy (ART) was introduced in the late 1990s and then became widely available in less affluent regions, including sub-Saharan Africa, in the past two decades, HIV/AIDS has come to be regarded as a chronic but manageable disease. ART literally saved the lives of millions of people living with HIV who otherwise could not have survived. ART is also known to be effective in preventing new infections because the medication suppresses the amount of virus in the blood. According to WHO, access to ART has increased from just 2.0 million people in 2005 to 23.3 million by the end of 2018, with the estimated ART global coverage increasing from 7 per cent in 2005 to 62 per cent in 2018. The greatest increase occurred in Africa: in the WHO Africa Region, fewer than 1 million people were on ART in 2005, and the number increased to 16.3 million in 2018 (WHO n.d.). The world is now working towards the ambitious 90-90-90 target, i.e., that 90 per cent of the people living with HIV know their status, 90 per cent of the people who know they are living with HIV are on ART and 90 per cent of people on treatment are virally suppressed (UNAIDS 2017).

The rapid increase in ART's global coverage in the last two decades would not have been possible without a drastic reduction in the price of antiretroviral drugs. Although the cost of the original products of a first-line antiretroviral regimen was greater than 10,000 United States dollars per person per year in 2000, nowadays, the generic price for the first-line regimens can be as low as 100 United States dollars (MSF 2016). The fact that HIV/AIDS became one of the top global issues around the turn of the century certainly accelerated the change. The United Nations General Assembly Special Session (UNGASS) on HIV/AIDS in 2001 and establishment of the Global Fund in 2002, among others, were some highlights of this progress. That said, it should be also noted that NGOs and social movements played significant roles in putting this issue on the global agenda. They were key driving forces behind the drastic changes in global HIV/AIDS policy.

The issue of 'access to medicines' was highlighted in the late 1990s by international NGOs such as Médecins Sans Frontières (MSF), Oxfam International and Health Action International (HAI). These NGOs campaigned against the World Trade Organization (WTO) agreement on Trade-Related Aspects of Intellectual Property Rights (TRIPS), which came into force in 1995, for having detrimental effects on access to medicines in poorer countries (Hein 2007). In addition, people living with HIV/AIDS also became increasingly aware of the importance of issues surrounding intellectual property as the critical barrier to patients' access to life-saving antiretroviral drugs. These groups started to organise in various parts of the world and sought partnership with each other as well as with international NGOs to overcome this barrier. Against this backdrop, South Africa became one of the main battlefields for NGOs and social movements in their struggle for global access to ART, with the Treatment Action Campaign (TAC) taking a leading role in mobilising activism among people living with HIV/AIDS. Numerous books and articles on TAC's activism have been published by researchers who were often activist-scholars themselves (Mbali 2003, 2013; Robins 2004; Grebe 2011; Heywood 2017; Friedman and Mottiar 2005). I will not repeat all of the findings of previous research here, limiting myself to a few sketches about their activism.

Launched in 1998 by a group of people living with HIV/AIDS and their friends, the TAC focused on demanding greater access to antiretroviral treatment, which was at that time only available at private clinics. To gain universal access to ART, the TAC campaigned on two fronts. First, it demanded that the pharmaceutical industry lower the prices of antiretroviral drugs, which were kept high due to patent monopolies. Second, its campaign was directed at the South African government to roll out antiretroviral treatment in the public sector (Mbali 2003: 322–3). The health-care system of South Africa has been characterised by large disparities between the private sector, which mainly serves relatively high-income (historically, primarily white) people and the public sector used by low-income (historically, primarily black) people; these disparities are, of course, a legacy of apartheid. ART became available in the private sector at roughly the same time as in Western countries, whereas its availability in the public sector, which depends on government health spending, was delayed. People in rich countries could get treatment and continue to live, while people in poor countries could not get the same treatment and therefore died; within a country, those who were better off and had access to private sector health care could get treatment, whereas poor people depending on public health care could not. Ultimately, the aim of the TAC's activism was overthrowing this 'medical apartheid'. Many TAC founders had previous experience in the anti-apartheid struggle. They drew on their experiences and networks from that struggle to build the new movement. Thus, they appropriated the repertoire of anti-apartheid struggles including freedom songs, calls and responses (such as 'Amandla' and 'Awethu') and *toyi toyi* (Grebe 2011; Robins 2004).

The TAC and the South African government stood on the same side in the court case between the South African government and the Pharmaceutical Manufacturers' Association (PMA) regarding the Medicines and Related Substances Control Amendment Act (No. 90 of 1997). The aim of the Act was to lower the cost of medicines by allowing parallel importation and promotion of generic substitutes for medicines. However, the PMA claimed that the Act violated its intellectual property rights and sued the South African government. In the process of campaigns protesting against pharmaceutical companies in relation to the court case, the TAC built links with international NGOs and AIDS activist groups such as the MSF and the AIDS Coalition to Unleash Power (ACT UP), and it successfully organised internationally coordinated demonstrations such as a Global March for HIV/AIDS Treatment at the XIII International AIDS Conference in July 2000 in Durban and a Global Day of Action against Drug Company Profiteering in March 2001. In addition to demonstrations and protests outside the court, the TAC was admitted as an *amicus curia* (friend of the court). Eventually, the PMA decided to drop the case against the South African government in April 2001 (Heywood 2017: 114–8; Grebe 2011: 860–5; Makino 2009: 116–7).

The trajectory of TAC's campaigns would have been much simpler were it not for the so-called AIDS denialism of then

President Thabo Mbeki. After the court case, there were high expectations for increased access to antiretrovirals in South Africa. However, such expectations were betrayed as the government procrastinated over introducing ART in the public sector. It is widely acknowledged that the South African government's sluggishness had to do with the AIDS denialism of Mbeki and Manto Tshabalala-Msimang, who served as Health Minister in Mbeki's cabinet.[6] Mbeki embraced the position of AIDS dissidents who questioned the causal link between HIV and AIDS, using this to justify his decision not to supply antiretrovirals to people living with HIV/AIDS on the grounds that the drugs were 'toxic'. Fourie and Meyer argued that although official denial has been seen in various governments since the apartheid era, further opportunities for official denial were created under the Mbeki government, which pursued the 'African renaissance' vision that aimed at restoring African dignity and intellectual enlightenment (Fourie and Meyer 2010).

The TAC protested against the government and campaigned for a change in AIDS policy. In August 2001, the TAC took the South African government to court, challenging its policy of restricting the provision of Prevention of Mother-to-Child Transmission (PMTCT) programmes to a limited number of pilot sites. Judgements from both the Pretoria High Court and the Constitutional Court supported the TAC's argument and ordered the government to expand public PMTCT programmes in 2002. After the court victory for PMTCT programmes, the focus of the TAC campaign moved on to access to ART for the HIV-positive population in general. After many protests and demonstrations and the loss of many lives that could have been saved had ART been introduced earlier, South Africa's public ART programme was finally introduced in 2004 (Makino 2009).

The current high uptake of ART in South Africa is a result of protests, legal battles, and advocacy by a network of people living with HIV/AIDS, their families and friends along with various supporters in South Africa and beyond its borders. In this process, the South African National AIDS Council (SANAC) was progressively restructured, increasing the space for civil society representatives and health professionals to make inputs to policy making on HIV/AIDS. This important institutional change was brought about by a combination of two factors: a new wave of international donor funding that made civil society's participation in decision making a condition for aid, and domestic criticism of the Mbeki government's policies based on an unorthodox view of HIV/AIDS (Powers 2013, 2015). As a result, ART, which used to be accessible only through private clinics and NGO projects, is now widely available through the public health system. Since 2016, with the 'test and treat' strategy in place, everyone with a positive diagnosis is eligible for treatment regardless of how advanced the HIV might be. This change more than doubled the number of people eligible for treatment in recent years, from 3.39 million in 2015 to 7.7 million people in 2018. As a result, South Africa's ART programme is now the largest in the world. It is estimated that 62 per cent of the 7.7 million people living with HIV are receiving HIV treatment. Testing has been also encouraged through interventions such as a national HIV testing and counselling (HTC) campaign in 2010 and an HTC revitalisation strategy in 2013. South Africa has now met the first of the 90-90-90 targets, with 90 per cent of people living with HIV being aware of their status in 2018 (Avert n.d.).

4. South African Responses to COVID-19

At the time of writing, South Africa has the highest number of coronavirus cases in the African continent, with 615,701 confirmed COVID-19 cases and 13,502 deaths as of 26 August 2020.[7] The short timeline of the South African responses to COVID-19 during its first two months (March and April 2020) is as follows. On 5 March, South Africa confirmed its first case of COVID-19; on 15 March, a National State of Disaster was declared; and on 23 March, to delay the peak of infection and to buy time for strengthening the health-care system to prepare for the peak, it was announced that a national lockdown would be implemented from 27 March. Since the beginning of the lockdown, the government has deployed more than 28,000 community health workers (CHWs) to undertake mass screening and testing in the communities at highest risk (Karim 2020). Mass community screening has been conducted in vulnerable areas such as former black townships around cities, and more than one million people were tested by mid-June.[8] During the strict lockdown, now known as 'level five', which lasted for five weeks from 27 March to 30 April, people were not allowed to go to work or participate in any economic activity unless they were providing essential goods or essential services. On 21 April, to mitigate the negative economic impact of the lockdown measures, the government announced a R500 billion 'stimulus package' including an allocation of R50 billion toward social grants for the most vulnerable people (Ramaphosa 2020).

Despite the fact that South Africa has one of the largest economies in Africa, it is characterised by structural inequality in every aspect of life, including access to quality health care. With the expectation that the already overstretched public health-care system, which mainly serves the black African majority, would be overwhelmed by the rapid increase of COVID-19 cases, the South African government had to make swift moves in responding to the virus after the first positive cases were confirmed among people who returned from Europe in March 2020.

Bricolage is a useful strategy in such a context, when quick decisions must be made even as available resources are limited. Specifically, existing institutions and networks in this country that had been in place to respond to HIV/AIDS have been repurposed in the context of the COVID-19 crisis. The nation's unique pre-corona experiences in dealing with the challenges of the HIV/AIDS epidemic make South Africa a notable case study for exploring African Potentials in the context of responding to the current COVID-19 crisis by employing 'institutional bricolage'. As noted in the previous section, South Africa has the highest disease burden of HIV/AIDS in the world. In addition, co-infection of HIV and TB is common. While this situation apparently makes South Africa vulnerable to COVID-19, the availability of HIV and TB testing, treatment and surveillance systems has been an advantage in rapidly responding to the new pandemic.

The activities of CHWs are notable as an example of how systems that were shaped and used in the context of HIV/AIDS and TB have been adapted for the COVID-19 response. The fact that tens of thousands of CHWs were in the country at the start of outbreak of the COVID-19 pandemic has much to do with the development of South Africa's AIDS response with grassroots mobilisation. In the process of mobilisation of people at the grassroots through AIDS activism, many people from poor communities (typically young, black African, unemployed women, many of them HIV positive) were trained as volunteers and engaged in AIDS awareness and treatment literacy campaigns (Robins 2004: 663–5). Lay health workers and counsellors have undertaken various HIV/TB-related tasks including home-based care, lay counselling, ART adherence counselling, advocacy/activism and DOTS[9] support in South Africa (Schneider and Lehmann 2010).

Internationally, CHWs became part of the health systems of many developing countries in the period following the 1978 Alma Ata Declaration on Primary Health Care. Recently, CHW programmes have re-emerged globally, particularly in the context of the HIV/AIDS epidemic (Schneider, Hlope and Van Rensburg 2008). In South Africa, CHW programmes were used in apartheid times mainly by NGOs, and after the 1990s they were slowly integrated into the post-apartheid government programme (Lund and Budlender 2009). Lay CHWs have been acknowledged in major government policy documents including the National Development Plan 2030 as playing an important complementary role to support health professionals (doctors and nurses) in carrying out public health-care policies. However, their work initially started as a non-governmental, grassroots effort, which was only later given public recognition. During the period of governmental AIDS denialism in South Africa, care for HIV-positive people in communities was primarily performed by volunteers, as these patients could not receive adequate care from the public health-care system. After 2003, volunteer community workers were brought under the banner of an Expanded Public Works Programme (EPWP) (Schneider, Hlope and Van Rensburg 2008). The EPWP is a government programme with a dual purpose: to provide opportunities for unemployed and poor people to work and earn an income, and to provide social services and public goods to the general population. The institutionalisation of CHWs was facilitated under this system. It was because tens of thousands of CHWs, whose origins lay in these grassroots volunteer efforts, were working on a daily basis that mass screening by CHWs became possible soon after the new coronavirus arrived in the country.

The situation in Japan is very different from this. In Japan, where most members of the 'African Potentials' research project are based, infectious diseases are often regarded as a problem of the past, and the government has made light of infectious disease control measures and reduced the budgets and personnel of the National Institute of Infectious Diseases (NIID) and local health centres over the years (Tokyo Shimbun 2020). A shortage of NIID testing capacity has been identified as one of the reasons for the relatively low volume of PCR testing for the new coronavirus, especially in the early stages of the epidemic (Kubota 2020). In contrast, South Africa has performed more than 3.6 million tests by the end of August 2020, of which 34 per cent were conducted by the public sector through community screening and testing (NICD 2020). The health-care system, developed to respond to the high disease burdens of HIV/AIDS and TB, has been adapted to respond to COVID-19.

The second important aspect in which the experience of the HIV/AIDS response appears to be utilised is the close communication between the government and the scientific community in policy making on the fight against coronavirus. As discussed in the previous section, in the process of leaving the era of denialism behind, the SANAC was reformed to increase the representation of civil society and the scientific community. The South African scientific community had a bitter experience with the Mbeki government's HIV/AIDS policy, but its visibility in the current COVID-19 response is high.

Specifically, it is worth noting the personal background of Salim S. Abdool Karim, who is spearheading South Africa's COVID-19 response as the chair of South Africa's Ministerial Advisory Committee on COVID-19. He is an infectious disease expert and, along with his wife Quarraisha Abdool Karim, one of South Africa's top specialist scientists on HIV/AIDS. Karim was the scientific programme chair at the International AIDS Conference in Durban in 2000 at which the TAC, together with international NGOs, organised the Global March for Treatment. Karim drew the ire of the Mbeki government for his opposition to dissident theories and for criticising the government's AIDS policy from a scientific perspective (*Sunday Times* 2020; Karim, Coovadia and Makgoba 2009). In contrast, Karim is currently helping the South African government to make policy decisions on COVID-19 measures as chair of the 45-person Ministerial Advisory Committee.

Karim was actually a medical school classmate of the current Health Minister, Zweli Mkhize, and also of Aaron Motsaledi, the former Health Minister and predecessor of Mkhize, at the University of Natal. The school was one of the few educational institutions that opened its doors to black students who wished to pursue professional careers during the apartheid era, and was also a stronghold of anti-apartheid student activism. Karim, who grew up in an Indian township in Durban, had experienced forced removal as a child. As his mother was active in the anti-apartheid movement, he was already involved in human rights and anti-apartheid activism by the time he went to medical school (Maxmen 2009). Karim's personal network from his student days is likely to have been a factor that has facilitated his working smoothly with political leaders, rebuilding the trust between the political leadership and the scientific community that had been destroyed during the Mbeki era.

As a result of Mbeki's AIDS denialism, it is estimated that more than 330,000 people died prematurely from HIV/AIDS between 2000 and 2005 (Chigwedere et al. 2008). Even this painful experience seems to have been used as a lesson for the current collaboration between political leaders and scientific and medical experts in response to COVID-19.

5. Conclusion

This chapter has argued that, when faced with the challenge of the sudden crisis of COVID-19, South African responses have been guided by flexibly adapting institutions and networks that had emerged to combat HIV/AIDS.

We do not yet know when and how the COVID-19 epidemic in South Africa may end. When President Cyril Ramaphosa announced the lockdown measures on 23 March 2020, no death due to the new coronavirus had yet been reported in the country. During the hard lockdown, the number of cases increased at a moderate pace. However, since the lockdown level was gradually softened from 1 May, the pace of increase in new cases in South Africa has accelerated as economic activity has resumed and the movement of people increased. At the time of writing (August 2020), South Africa ranks fifth in the world in the number of COVID-19 cases, after the United States, Brazil, India and Russia.

It has been reported that some public hospitals in the Eastern Cape Province are overwhelmed and doctors and nurses are exhausted and overcome with fear and fatigue (Harding 2020). The number of COVID-19 cases in the Eastern Cape is low compared to the Western Cape and Gauteng Provinces. Nonetheless, these problems have occurred because of the fewer medical resources the Province had to begin with. In fact, the few weeks of lockdown were too short for South Africa, which has large disparities between private and public hospitals and where public health care was already overstretched and underperforming even in the pre-corona period, to prepare fully for the COVID-19 peak. Despite the ability to utilise past infectious disease control institutions flexibly, as well as the country's responses to COVID-19 being facilitated by existing networks, the effectiveness of these measures is diminished by the unchanging structural inequality. In addition, it is also becoming clear that existing networks also have a negative impact on the COVID-19 response, as the corruption scandals surrounding procurement of personal protection equipment (PPE) have shown.[10]

In retrospect, South African responses might seem to have been far from the best choices. However, imperfections and inadequacies notwithstanding, I would argue that we can see elements of African Potentials in South Africa's responses to the COVID-19 crisis. South Africans have learned at great cost over the past two decades that it is possible to resist Western intellectual hegemony and yet to be locked into a subservient position. The South African case also shows that Africa is not a unilateral importer and receiver of public policy established in the North. Innovations and breakthroughs can take place in Africa as well.

Endonotes

[1] See Ohta (2016) for a summary of the findings of the first phase of the 'African Potentials' research project.

[2] For instance, an article written by the Africa correspondent of the Japanese public broadcaster, NHK, emphasised the vulnerability of African countries to the coronavirus and concluded with a call for 'strong' countries to give aid to vulnerable countries, a typical example of representation of Africa as incapable and powerless (Beppu 2020).

[3] As of May 2020, Africa was the least affected region globally, with 1–5 per cent of the world's reported COVID-19 cases and 0–1 per cent of the world's deaths. The suggested hypotheses as to why Africa is less affected by the virus include 'sensitivity of the virus to ambient temperature, Africa's comparatively young population, lower rates of obesity, and familiarity with infectious disease outbreaks' (*The Lancet* 2020).

[4] Africa Medical Supplies Platform website (https://amsp.africa/) (accessed: 24 November 2020).

[5] Some parts of this section are based on my previous publications (Makino 2009, 2018).

[6] See Nattrass (2007) and Geffin (2010) for critical documentations of the AIDS denialism of the Mbeki government and the TAC's fight against it.

[7] 'Latest Confirmed Cases of COVID-19 in South Africa (26 Aug 2020),' National Institute for Communicable Diseases (https://www.nicd.ac.za/latest-confirmed-cases-of-covid-19-in-south-africa-26-aug-2020/) (accessed: 24 November 2020).

[8] 'SA Reaches 1 Million Covid-19 Tests Milestone, Says Mkhize', *Eyewitness News*, 11 June 2020 (https://ewn.co.za/2020/06/11/sa-reaches-1-million-covid-19-tests-milestone-says-mkhize) (accessed: 24 November 2020).

[9] DOTS stands for 'directly observed therapy, short course'.

[10] See for instance BBC (2020).

Acknowledgement

This work was supported by JSPS KAKENHI Grant Number

JP16H06318.

References

Avert (n.d.) 'HIV and AIDS in South Africa', Avert (https://www.avert.org/professionals/hiv-around-world/sub-saharan-africa/south-africa) (accessed: 30 July 2020).

BBC (2020) 'Coronavirus in South Africa: Misuse of Covid-19 funds "frightening"', *BBC*, 2 September 2020 (https://www.bbc.com/news/world-africa-54000930) (accessed: 24 November 2020).

Beppu, S. (2020) 'African vulnerabilities revealed by the Coronavirus', *Gaikō (Diplomacy)*, Vol. 61, pp. 86–9 (in Japanese).

Carstensen, M. B. (2017) 'Institutional bricolage in times of crisis', *European Political Science Review*, Vol. 9, No. 1, pp. 139–60 (https://doi.org/10.1017/S1755773915000338) (accessed: 24 November 2020).

Chigwedere, P., Seage III, G. R., Gruskin, S., Lee, T. and Essex, M. (2008) 'Estimating the lost benefits of antiretroviral drug use in South Africa', *Journal of Acquired Immune Deficiency Syndromes*, Vol. 49, No. 4, pp. 410–5.

Chris, B. and Myers, S. L. (2020) 'Where's Xi? China's leader commands Coronavirus fight from safe heights', *New York Times*, 8 February 2020 (https://www.nytimes.com/2020/02/08/world/asia/xi-coronavirus-china.html) (accessed: 24 November 2020).

Collier, R. B. and Collier, D. (1991) 'Critical junctures and historical legacies', in R. B. Collier and D. Collier (eds) *Shaping the Political Arena: Critical Junctures, the Labor Movement, and Regime Dynamics in Latin America*, Princeton: Princeton University Press, pp. 27–39 (https://ssrn.com/abstract=1750509) (accessed: 24 November 2020).

Endo, M. (2020) 'African responses to the new Coronavirus are surprisingly swift due to accumulation of experiences of responding to Ebola outbreaks', *Toyo Keizai Online*, 3 April 2020 (https://toyokeizai.net/articles/-/341038) (accessed: 24

November 2020) (in Japanese).

Fourie, P. and Meyer, M. (2010) *The Politics of AIDS Denialism: South Africa's Failure to Respond*, Farnham: Ashgate.

Friedman, S. and Mottiar, S. (2005) 'A rewarding engagement? The Treatment Action Campaign and the politics of HIV/AIDS', *Politics & Society*, Vol. 33, Issue 4, pp. 511–65.

Gebre, Y., Ohta, I. and Matsuda, M. (2017) 'Introduction: Achieving peace and coexistence through African potentials', in Y. Gebre, I. Ohta and M. Matsuda (eds) *African Virtues in the Pursuit of Conviviality: Exploring Local Solutions in Light of Global Prescriptions*, Bamenda: Langaa RPCIG, pp. 3–37.

Geffin, N. (2010) *Debunking Delusions: The Inside Story of the Treatment Action Campaign*, Johannesburg: Jacana.

Grebe, E. (2011) 'The Treatment Action Campaign's struggle for AIDS treatment in South Africa: Coalition-building through networks', *Journal of Southern African Studies*, Vol. 37, Issue 4, pp. 849–68.

Green, D. (2020) 'Covid-19 as a critical juncture and the implications for advocacy', *Global Policy*, 23 April 2020 (https://www.globalpolicyjournal.com/sites/default/files/pdf/Green%20-%20Covid-19%20as%20a%20Critical%20Juncture%20and%20the%20Implications%20for%20Advocacy_0.pdf) (accessed: 24 November 2020).

Harding, A. (2020) 'Coronavirus in South Africa: Inside Port Elizabeth's "hospitals of horrors"', *BBC News*, 15 July 2020 (https://www.bbc.com/news/world-africa-53396057) (accessed: 24 November 2020).

Hein, W. (2007) 'Global health governance and WTO/TRIPS: Conflicts between "global market-creation" and "global social rights"', in W. Hein, S. Bartsch and L. Kohlmorgen (eds) *Global Health Governance and the Fight against HIV/AIDS*, Basingstoke and New York: Palgrave Macmillan, pp. 38–66.

Heywood, M. (2017) *Get Up! Stand Up!: Personal Journeys Towards Social Justice*, Cape Town: Tafelberg.

Karim, S. S. A. (2020) 'The South African response to the pandemic', *The New England Journal of Medicine*, Vol. 382, e95 (https://doi.org/10.1056/NEJMc2014960) (accessed: 24 November 2020).

Karim, S. S. A., Coovadia, H. M. and Makgoba, M. W. (2009) 'Scientists stand by decision to join Mbeki's AIDS panel', *Nature*, Vol. 457, No. 7228, pp. 379 (https://doi.org/10.1038/457379a) (accessed: 24 November 2020).

Kubota, A. (2020) 'Reasons that the expansion of the testing system for the new Coronavirus was delayed', *Nikkei Biotechnology and Business*, 28 February 2020 (https://bio.nikkeibp.co.jp/atcl/news/p1/20/02/28/06625/) (accessed: 24 November 2020) (in Japanese).

Lund, F. and Budlender, D. (2009) *Paid Care Providers in South Africa: Nurses, Domestic Workers, and Home-Based Care Workers*, South African Research Report 4 for the Political and Social Economy of Care Project, UNRISD, Geneva: UNRISD (http://www.unrisd.org/unrisd/website/document.nsf/(httpPublications)/57355F8BEBD70F8AC12575B0003C6274) (accessed: 24 November 2020).

Mahoney, J. and Thelen, K. (eds) (2010) *Explaining Institutional Change: Ambiguity, Agency, and Power*, Cambridge: Cambridge University Press.

Makino, K. (2009) 'Institutional conditions for social movements to engage in formal politics: The case of AIDS activism in Post-Apartheid South Africa', in S. Shigetomi and K. Makino (eds) *Protest and Social Movements in the Developing World*, Cheltenham and Northampton: Edward Elgar Publishing, pp. 110-33.

——— (2018) 'Global AIDS governance and Africa', in H. Watanabe, K. Fukuda and M. Shuto (eds) *Global Governance Research II*, Kyoto: Hōritsubunkasha (in Japanese), pp. 185-202.

Maxmen, A. (2009) 'Salim "Slim" Abdool Karim: Attacking AIDS in South Africa', *Journal of Experimental Medicine*, Vol. 206, Issue 11, pp. 2306–7 (https://doi.org/10.1084/jem.20611pi) (accessed: 24 November 2020).

Mbali, M. (2003) 'HIV/AIDS policy-making in Post-Apartheid South Africa', in J. Daniel, A. Habib and R. Southall (eds) *State of the Nation: South Africa 2003-2004*, Cape Town: HSRC Press, pp. 312–29.

_____ (2013) *South African AIDS Activism and Global Health Politics*, London: Palgrave Macmillan.

MSF (Médecins Sans Frontières) (2016) *Untangling the Web of Antiretroviral Price Reductions, 18th edition July 2016*, MSF Access Campaign (https://msfaccess.org/untangling-web-antiretroviral-price-reductions-18th-edition) (accessed: 24 November 2020).

Nattrass, N. (2007) *Mortal Combat: AIDS Denialism and the Struggle for Antiretrovirals in South Africa*, Durban: University of KwaZulu-Natal Press.

NICD (National Institute for Communicable Diseases) (2020) 'National COVID-19 daily report, 30 August 2020', National Institute for Communicable Diseases, South Africa (https://www.nicd.ac.za/wp-content/uploads/2020/08/COVID-19-Daily-Report-National-Public-30Aug2020.pdf) (accessed: 24 November 2020).

Ohta, I. (2016) 'Outcome and prospects of the "African Potentials" research project', *Afurika Kenkyū (Journal of African Studies)*, Vol. 90, pp. 93–5 (in Japanese).

Ordu, A. U. (2020) 'The coming of age of the Africa centers for disease control', Brookings Institution, 15 April 2020 (https://www.brookings.edu/blog/africa-in-focus/2020/04/15/the-coming-of-age-of-the-africa-centers-for-disease-control/) (accessed: 24 November 2020).

Peters, B. G., Pierre, J. and King, D. S. (2005) 'The politics of path dependency: Political conflict in historical institutionalism', *The Journal of Politics*, Vol. 67, No. 4, pp. 1275–300 (https://doi.org/10.1111/j.1468-2508.2005.00360.x) (accessed: 24 November 2020).

Powers, T. (2013) 'Institutions, power and para-state alliances: A critical reassessment of HIV/AIDS politics in South Africa, 1999-2008', *The Journal of Modern African Studies*, Vol. 51, Issue 4, pp. 605–26.

_____ (2015) 'Negotiating state and market: The South African HIV/AIDS movement and social change', in K. Hart (ed.) *Economy for and against Democracy*, New York and Oxford: Berghahn Books.

Ramaphosa, C. (2020) 'Statement by President Cyril Ramaphosa on further economic and social measures in response to the COVID-19 epidemic', 21 April 2020, The Presidency, Republic of South Africa (http://www.thepresidency.gov.za/speeches/statement-president-cyril-ramaphosa-further-economic-and-social-measures-response-covid-19) (accessed: 24 November 2020).

Robins, S. (2004) '"Long live Zackie, long live": AIDS activism, science and citizenship after Apartheid', *Journal of Southern African Studies*, Vol. 30, No. 3, pp. 651–72.

Schneider, H., Hlope, H. and Van Rensburg, D. (2008) 'Community health workers and the response to HIV/AIDS in South Africa: Tensions and prospects', *Health Policy and Planning*, Vol. 23, Issue 3, pp. 179–87 (https://doi.org/10.1093/heapol/czn006) (accessed: 24 November 2020).

Schneider, H. and Lehmann, U. (2010) 'Lay health workers and HIV programmes: Implications for health systems', *AIDS Care*, Vol. 22, Supplement 1, pp. 60–7.

Sunday Times (2020) 'Salim Abdool Karim: The man outsmarting Covid-19', *Sunday Times*, 19 April 2020.

Takahashi, F. (2020) 'Stop using the phrase "war against the virus": We can not accept the expression that allows sacrifices of the weak: Calls from experts on new Coronavirus', *Huffpost*, 23 April 2020 (https://www.huffingtonpost.jp/entry/story_jp_5ea13673c5b699978a3365a0) (accessed: 24 November 2020) (in Japanese).

The Lancet (2020) 'Editorial: COVID-19 in Africa: No room for complacency', *The Lancet*, Vol. 395, Issue 10238, pp. 1669 (https://doi.org/10.1016/S0140-6736(20)31237-X) (accessed: 24 November 2020).

Tokyo Shimbun (2020) 'New Coronavirus: The National Institute of Infectious Diseases has suffered from budget cuts by successive administrations', *Tokyo Shimbun*, 7 March 2020 (https://www.tokyo-np.co.jp/article/14466) (accessed: 24 November 2020) (in Japanese).

UNAIDS (Joint United Nations Programme on HIV/AIDS) (2017) *Ending AIDS: Progress towards the 90-90-90 Targets, Global AIDS Update 2017*, Geneva: UNAIDS (https://www.unaids.org/sites/default/files/media_asset/Globa

l_AIDS_update_2017_en.pdf) (accessed: 24 November 2020).

UNECA (United Nations Economic Commission for Africa) (2020) *COVID-19 Lockdown Exit Strategies for Africa*, Addis Ababa: Economic Commission for Africa (https://www.uneca.org/sites/default/files/uploaded-documents/COVID-19/ecarprt_covidexitstrategis_eng_9may.pdf) (accessed: 24 November 2020).

White House (2020) 'Remarks by President Trump, Vice President Pence, and members of the Coronavirus task force in press briefing', White House, 1 April 2020 (https://www.whitehouse.gov/briefings-statements/remarks-president-trump-vice-president-pence-members-coronavirus-task-force-press-briefing-16/?utm_source=link) (accessed: 24 November 2020).

WHO (World Health Organisation) (n.d.) 'Antiretroviral therapy (ART) coverage among all age groups', Global Health Observatory (GHO) data (https://www.who.int/gho/hiv/epidemic_response/ART_text/en/) (accessed: 16 September 2020).

WHO Africa (World Health Organisation Regional Office for Africa) (2020) 'New WHO estimates: Up to 190 000 people could die of COVID-19 in Africa if not controlled', WHO Africa, 7 May 2020 (https://www.afro.who.int/news/new-who-estimates-190-000-people-could-die-covid-19-africa-if-not-controlled) (accessed: 24 November 2020).

Chapter 8

Kusina Amai Hakuendwe: Diasporan Zimbabweans, COVID-19 and Nomadic Global Citizenship

Artwell Nhemachena

1. Introduction

Although nomadic subjectivity is being celebrated by some scholars as overcoming the binaries between the local and the global, the particular and the universal and the past and the present (Rowan 2016; Braidotti 2010; 2014), I will argue that COVID-19 has revealed tensions in the praxis of nomadic global citizenship. While some imperial states have refused and/or are shuffling their feet when it comes to repatriating the skulls and skeletons of African ancestors that were assassinated during the early colonial era, COVID-19 has witnessed speedy repatriations of living African human beings back to their states. Put otherwise, the fact that imperial states prefer to retain the artefacts, skeletons and skulls of African ancestors while ironically repatriating, with alacrity, living Africans in the context of COVID-19 is indicative of what I call 'necrozenship' – a situation where the empire prefers to retain remains of the dead Africans while happily repatriating living Africans who happen to stray to the imperial centres. Thus, what I call necrozenship is a situation where the skulls and skeletons of the dead are preferred over living citizens; where the dead are preferred over the living – the dead are offered residence even where the living are denied the same. In other words, COVID-19 has revealed that states across the world are more prepared to cooperate in repatriating living African human beings than cooperate in repatriating the skulls and skeletons of African anticolonial heroes that have been lodged in Western museums for centuries now.

Using the Shona (a people of Zimbabwe) saying that *kusina amai hakuendwe* (do not wander off too far away from your mother), this chapter examines the repatriations of Zimbabweans during COVID-19, in the context of discourses on nomadic global citizenship and nomadic subjectivity. While the concept of nomadic subjectivity underscores fluidity of identities, identity flux, flows, de-territoriality rather than territoriality, a shift from nation states to universalism, bridging of binaries between citizens and noncitizens (Braidotti 2010; Rowan 2016; Deleuze and Guattari 1987), the global practices of managing COVID-19 have exposed the resilience of the binaries and the absence of fluidity, flows and fluxes in regard to nomadic subjectivities and nomadic identities. Zimbabweans who had migrated to various countries such as USA, Britain, South Africa, Namibia, Botswana and so on have been repatriated back to Zimbabwe in spite of the well-publicised poverty, joblessness, suffering, political repression, oppression and general penury (Maromo 2020; Ncube 2020; Chibamu 2020; Vinga 2020; Mutsaka and Magome 2020; Bothoko 2020; Staff Reporter 2020; Chipunza 2020; Mavhunga 2020; BBC News 2020; Mushava 2020; Case Number 0 2020; Nyathi 2020; Scoones 2020; Dube 2020). In this regard, I argue in this chapter that while some scholars and thinkers argue for a New World Order, a One World Government, a Global State with a Global Constitution that would supposedly be more able to guarantee security and peace (Yunker 2012; Mogoatlhe 2020; Inayatullah 1999; Wendt 2003; Elliot 2020; Erman 2019; Baratta 2004; Yang 2011; Shaw 2000; Suzuki 2020; Chimni 2004; Culbertson 1949; Martin 2010), global governance is enamoured in global capitalist logics of outsourcing responsibility to its victims worldwide. Thus, in the context of evidence about the global practices of handling COVID-19, this chapter argues that the Global State and Global One World Government promises to underwrite the interest, security and peace for global capital more than it will do for the rest of humanity. In fact, the rest of humanity is set to be genetically and technologically transformed into post-humans, cyborgs and trans-humans such that they also cease to be human subjects of the Global Government or Global State. In so far as post-humanism and trans-humanism underscore transformations of human identities, this chapter argues that the net effect is to extirpate citizenship and also to transform subjects into post-subjectivity, which implies the death of the human subject as well as the death of the citizen. In a trans-humanist and post-humanist world, human beings become neither subjects nor human citizens in the world. In this regard, a post-humanist and trans-humanist world order is necessarily a post-subjectivity and post-citizenship world order for some sections of humanity who, in terms of the Shona saying *kusina amai hakuendwe*, happen to be so reckless as to wander too far from their mothers.

2. Contextualising Zimbabweans

Zimbabwe is a former British colony that gained notional political independence in 1980, following a protracted liberation war. Following colonisation in the late 1800s, the colonialists dispossessed the precolonial Zimbabweans of their fertile and well-watered land in the Highveld region. The Zimbabweans were resettled in the marginal land with poor sandy/rocky soils and with poor rainfall. Dispossessing Zimbabweans of their land and livestock was a way of forcing them to seek jobs, as cheap labour, in the colonial factories, mines and farms. In these ways, many Zimbabweans became nomadic as they engaged in what is called circulatory labour migration (Stichter 1985) – oscillating between the colonial factories, mines and farms for some months and then moving back to their rural areas and staying there for other months. Having fought the liberation war, Zimbabweans were debarred by the Lancaster House Agreement from repossessing their land immediately after independence in 1980. Thus, in the year 2000, peasants, war veterans and the post-independence government of Zimbabwe embarked on land redistribution by compulsorily acquiring farms under the control of white farmers. The white farmers and some blacks, particularly members of the opposition party, the Movement for Democratic Change (MDC), suffered violence which saw many of them becoming nomadic in the sense of migrating to the diaspora, becoming refugees and asylum seekers or residents of other countries. In other words, their identities as subjects and as citizens of Zimbabwe were unmoored such that they assumed nomadic identities and became nomadic subjects around the world. Put differently, they became post-subjects and post-citizens in the sense

205

of lacking fixed and crystallised identities. In different regions of the world, Zimbabweans have suffered xenophobia and Afrophobia as they were victimised and assaulted or even killed on the basis that they were outsiders and not citizens of the countries to which they migrated (Nyamnjoh 2006; Neocosmos 2008). Receiving states have at various points in time repatriated Zimbabweans back to their country but with the pandemic caused by COVID-19 some Zimbabweans in the diaspora have been forced to 'voluntarily' request repatriations because they experienced hardships caused by COVID-19 lockdowns in the states where they resided. Under the lockdowns, economies tumbled, some people were retrenched, others could not continue with their informal economic activities and some students were ordered to go back to Zimbabwe because their universities had introduced online learning which did not require their physical presence in the countries to which they had migrated (Scoones 2020; Case Number 0 2020).

As the Zimbabweans returned, some from the global epicentres of COVID-19, those that had remained in Zimbabwe feared that the returnees were bringing the virus home; some returnees even escaped from quarantine which they detested as they complained that the conditions in the quarantine centres were deplorable and subhuman in the sense of lacking running water and decent beds and that they were forced to share bathrooms while in the quarantine centres (Case Number 0 2020; Staff Reporter 2020; Chipunza 2020). Some Zimbabweans who had run away from the government, allegedly as a result of political persecution of opposition party members, were forced to return and subject themselves to the government in spite of them having earlier become nomadic global subjects. Upon return, they expected the government to treat and regard them as human subjects or citizens, paradoxically in a world that is already shifting toward post-humanism and trans-humanism which deny preeminent consideration to humans as a species – post-humanism and trans-humanism would place humans and coronavirus on the same plane because the human subject is being decentred and deconstructed in contemporary post-humanist and trans-humanist discourses. In other words, trans-humanism and post-humanism do not privilege human subjectivity or the human condition because there is an assumption that the human beings and the virus are on the same plane or level such that human life does not assume pre-eminence over the life of nonhuman viruses (Nhemachena & Mawere 2020). In fact, it is argued that there is no human essence and therefore, by extension, there is no human subject essence.

Arguing that Zimbabweans ran away from violence and human rights abuses because they considered themselves to have human essence, this chapter draws on the Shona saying *kusina amai hakuendwe* to contend that no mother would treat her son or daughter as lacking human essence. In this sense, the chapter argues that it is when people stray too far from their mothers that they lose human essence or are deemed to lack human essence. Similarly, the chapter argues that human beings, worldwide, are fighting COVID-19 precisely because the human beings are convinced that they have human essence which warrants the human rights to health. For this reason, it is argued that a global citizenship, in an emergent Global State and One World Government, which treats some human beings as lacking human essence is in fact a negation of citizenship. Put differently, global citizenship cannot be premised on assumptions that human beings lack human essence or have no human essence – to contend so would in effect be to deny humans global citizenship because if one does not have human essence then it follows that one cannot be a human citizen of the world. In this sense, citizenship is a function of human essence – and one would add to say citizenship is a function of the essence of ubuntu. Yet, premised as they were on dispossession and exploitation of indigenous people, colonial states could not grant citizenship on the basis of the essence of ubuntu precisely because dispossession and exploitation of other humans is a negation of the essence of ubuntu. Because colonial forms of citizenship were not premised on ubuntu, but on dispossession and exploitation of others, this chapter argues that a global citizenship that does not undo the dispossession and exploitation of other people lacks the essence of ubuntu. For these reasons, nomadic subjectivity and nomadic identities can be understood to be a negation of ubuntu in the sense that they unmoor Africans from their essence of ubuntu. In this vein, nomadising subjectivities and nomadising identities risk intensifying the colonial practices of dispossession and exploitation – in this sense they imply the dispossession not only of materialities but also dispossessing humanity of their human identities, including the identities of their mothers. In ubuntu, human beings have human essence – if human mothers did not have essence how would one guard against wondering too far away from one's mother?

3. *Kusina Amai Hakuendwe* and Its Implications on Nomadic Global Citizenship

Some scholars, thinkers and activists are agitating for and celebrating the constitution of a One World Government, Global State and One World Federation of governments which are supposedly set to usher in global citizenship towards which COVID-19 is pushing the world (Elliot 2020; Mogoatlhe 2020). However, *kusina amai hakuendwe* signals the dangers of reckless mobility, reckless changes and footlooseness that disconnect or separate Africans from their mothers, cultures, human essence, humanity, societies, polities and materialities. In this regard, the phrase *kusina amai hakuendwe* is taken to refer not only to reckless physical mobility but also it refers to cognitive, spiritual, social mobility, cultural mobility or changes that disconnect or separate Africans from their ubuntu essence. For this reason, mobility is interpreted broadly to encompass changes and it is argued that while the Shona people do not encourage humanity to be imprisoned in their immediate physical and social contexts, they nevertheless advise people to avoid reckless mobility that disconnects or separates them from their essence – in this sense *kusina amai hakuendwe* underscores one's mother as constituting one's essence. Also, it is argued in this chapter that *kusina amai hakuendwe* underscores the need for change that recognises one's essence as an African. For the Shona people, reckless mobility and reckless changes result in troubles that would make one wish one was close to and still connected to the mother or to one's human essence. Shrewd mobility retains connections to the human essence and to the mothers as proverbial shoulders upon which to cry in times of trouble.

It does not matter how big, grown up or how old one is, the phrase *kusina amai hakuendwe* advises Africans, young and old/strong and weak, to always retain such connections with their essences and desist from wandering from their human essence or from their mothers. Understood together with the Shona phrase *hakuna mhou inokumira mhuru isiri yayo* (no cow lows for a calf that is not its own), the Shona people advise Africans to be able to distinguish genuine concern from one's mother from appearances of concern by other mothers who may pretend to care while having other ulterior motives. Put differently, for the Shona people, not every lowing must be recklessly heeded because it may in fact be a trap for one to wander off from one's mother. These sayings, by the Shona, need not be taken to mean parochialism or even particularism because in Shona culture, a mother's sisters are also addressed as mothers (they are not addressed as aunts like the English people do). Rather, through these phrases, the Shona people are simply advising humanity to be careful about various noises in the world that may tempt Africans to recklessly wander away from their mothers and human essences. In view of the above sayings, I argue herein that although precolonial Africa is noted by some scholars as having had no borders or boundaries, Africans were advised to desist from reckless mobility that would imperil them by taking them away from their mothers. In other words, for the Shona people, security and peace are never realised after wandering away from one's mother – whether or not the mother is small, skinny, strong or weak, deprived or seemingly poor. As much as the Shona state that *hakuna nzou inoremerwa nenyanga dzayo* (no elephant feels the weight of its tusks), it can be noted that security, peace and citizenship originate from mothers who always possess the fortitude to provide for their progenies – no matter how seemingly poor or weak or small the mothers are. In short, to be a good citizen, one has to be connected and to be close to one's mother – and not otherwise. A good citizen does not despise the mother's human essence or even her ability to provide for the progeny.

If a mother is seemingly unable to perform, is poor, old, is seemingly weak and so on, ubuntu advises Africans to assist the mother rather than to desert her, abandon her, disparage her or even look down on her. The advice is to assist the mother without questioning her human essence or her identity or ability. By extension, this implies that Africans in diaspora are advised to invest in their countries of origin, to help their governments and states back home wherever possible such that when they return or when they are repatriated back home, they find the states in order and they do not experience and complain of poor conditions, subhuman conditions and inhuman conditions such as in quarantine centres for COVID-19. In precolonial Africa, able-bodied people would wander away in hunting expeditions and they would ensure that they sent back home whatever they caught so that their mothers would be catered for. They would not even keep the meat to themselves and their immediate families but they would share with the whole community. Even colonialists and slave drivers who dispossessed, captured and exploited Africans sent back the proceeds to their metropolitan centres. Hundreds of universities, museums, companies and institutions in America and Britain (Reuters Staff 2019; Francois 2019), for example, were built on the basis of proceeds repatriated by slave drivers and colonialists who remembered to take care of their mothers even though they used proceeds from dispossessing and exploiting enslaved and colonised Africans.

One might argue that Africans in the diaspora have been treated inhumanely by their states and governments but then even the colonialists that came to Africa were escaping impoverishment and dispossession as a result of ongoing enclosure systems back in Europe. Yet that did not stop them from repatriating proceeds and investing back in their metropolitan countries. Even Cecil John Rhodes, the British arch-imperialist, invested back in Britain sponsoring and funding a number of universities including the famous Oxford University which has recently refused to pull down Rhodes's statue in spite of student demonstrations to the contrary (Rawlinson 2016). In this case, it can be argued that even Cecil John Rhodes took care not to stray too far away from his own mother – he guarded against wandering too far away from Britain. In order not to stray too far away from Britain, Rhodes repatriated proceeds of colonising Africans and invested them back in Britain yet when Africans wander into the diaspora, they often do not repatriate and invest back home to assist not only their immediate family members but also their states and governments. However, when they are repatriated and returned due to COVID-19, and quarantined in dilapidated colleges and universities in the country, they complain of the supposedly subhuman conditions. The point is why not invest in one's families and in one's state and governments in the same way slave drivers and colonialists helped to fund universities and colleges back in their metropolitan centres? The point here is that citizenship implies as much rights as obligations and so Africans need not only demand rights from states when they do not also perform their obligations to them.

The argument here is that if one does not build a house for one's mother or grandmother, then one must not complain when, after circumstances have forced one to go to the village, one is forced to stay in a hovel. Similarly, when one neglects one's state and government, one must not complain when, after being forced by circumstances to go back to one's state, one is quarantined in a hovel. Citizenship is not only about rights vis-à-vis one's state; citizenship is also about obligations to one's state. The point here is that if one assumes nomadic citizenship and chameleon identities, one may not know which state one has obligation to or even one may end up asserting citizenship rights to the wrong state. One has to know one's mother and in as much as the mother's identity should not be chameleon/nomadic but has to have human essence, the progeny's identity also has to have human essence and be without chameleon/nomadic subjectivity. Chameleon or nomadic identities create confusion in that one may end up claiming motherly rights from someone other than one's mother or a mother may end up claiming rights from someone other than her progeny. Colonialism was similarly about mistaking other people's heritage for one's own – this is because colonialism was about nomadic/chameleon subjectivity/identities.

With the enslavement era, Africans were physically forcibly moved away from their mothers; with colonialism, Africans were also physically and forcibly moved from their mothers whose sons and daughters were forced to provide cheap labour in distant colonial industries away from home (Stichter 1985; van Onselen 1980). Even in the postcolonial era, Africans are lured by so-called greener pastures to drift away from their mothers and from their countries

211

that are ravaged by dispossession, exploitation and impoverishment. As if African mothers, cultures, customs, mores and values that are often left behind are not green enough, Africans have been cultured away from heeding the lowing of their mothers. African cultures, customs, social norms and values that constitute the essence of Africans are consistently demonised in Eurocentric scholarship that seeks to uproot Africans in their efforts to create global citizenship by pulling Africans away from their mothers. In fact, since the colonial era, African mothers have been demonised as illiterate, as barbaric, as backward, as savage, as beastly and so on. Colonial subjectivity and citizenship were, in essence, predatory in the sense of thriving on the basis of cannibalising Africans' connections and relations with their mothers and human essence. Colonial anthropologists might have learnt, taught and published treatises on genealogies but the colonial context hardly valued African genealogies and rootedness. While colonial anthropologists researched African genealogies, the colonial administrations were busy uprooting Africans from their genealogies and rootedness, thereby turning them into colonial subjects that would despise their own roots and their own mothers. In fact, colonial religious leaders usurped the roles of African fathers and mothers such as when Catholic officials described themselves as fathers (*mafata*) to Africans. In this way, African mothers and fathers were retrenched from their roles as parents of Africans who were being turned into colonial subjects and citizens. In this regard, colonial 'subjectivity' and 'citizenship' lacked rootedness for Africans.

As hinted above, while colonialists migrated from their own countries when they colonised Africans, the colonialists still retained their rootedness by keeping their connections with their metropoles. Even Cecil John Rhodes, the arch-imperialist retained his connections with Britain into which he invested much of his wealth that was realised by dispossessing and exploiting Africans. He even had statues erected in his honour back in Britain even as he dispossessed and exploited Africans on the continent. Colonialists retained their connections and relations with their own mothers back in the metropoles even as they destroyed connections and relations among Africans and their mothers. Thus, even as they fought the

Ndebele King Lobengula, the British colonialists sang 'God Bless the Queen' (Kaplan 1965). Similarly, even as they dispossessed and exploited Africans in ways that made them unable to care for and provide for their mothers, colonialists invested the proceeds of colonisation back into their metropoles and they used the proceeds from dispossessing and exploiting Africans to provide for and take care of their own mothers back in the imperial centres. Even as they retrenched African fathers and mothers from parenthood over their sons and daughters that were forced into forced labour, colonialists entrenched their own connections and relations with their fathers and mothers back in the metropoles.

Similarly, even as they retrenched African ancestors whom they condemned as demons, colonialists venerated their own ancestors whom they addressed and revered as saints. Also, even as they destroyed African religions, colonialists engaged in their own religions including Christianity and freemasonry of which rituals they conducted often using material resources stolen from Africans whose land and livestock were lost to colonialists. The point here is that colonial dispossession left Africans without ownership and control over land and shrines which they could have used to perform their rituals for their mothers and grandmothers (Nhemachena 2017). Colonial dispossession left Africans without ownership of livestock which they could have also used to perform their own rituals in honour of their ancestry – for their mothers and grandmothers. In this regard, this chapter contends that what is often called colonial citizenship was in fact 'conizenship' and 'conizenisation' in the sense that colonialists conned Africans by pretending that they were civilising them. Global citizenship should not be premised on such logics of colonial conizenship, otherwise we would need to think in terms of global conizenship instead of global citizenship.

Conizenship is a concept that I use here to render weight to the historiography of the formation of 'citizenship' since the colonial era. It is a term that I use to render traction to the colonial history of citizenship. The term allows one to picture the world not simplistically in term of subjectivity, subjection, domination, oppression and citizenship but *a fortiori* in terms of the process by which colonialists became 'citizens' on the basis of colonial

213

conizenship. Africans were not merely subjected, dominated or oppressed by colonialists but there is a historiography of dispossession and exploitation which have quite different valences from mere subjection, domination and oppression. It is such dispossession and exploitation that are referred to by conizenship or conizenisation. When someone is dispossessed, it would be quite imprecise to describe them simply as having been dominated, subjected or oppressed. Therefore, what colonialists set up in Africa was not mere subjectivity and citizenship but rather they set up conizenship and conizenisation of Africa. When Africans fought against colonialism, they should be understood as having fought against conizenship and conizenisation. When Africans fought against colonialism, they should not be understood as having sought to reject outsiders but what they sought to reject was conizenship and conizenisation that characterised colonisation outsider-ness. The Shona people have an idiom called *kuwanda huuya* (which celebrates becoming many owing to immigration or owing to outsiders coming in) – however, colonialists were not merely outsiders coming in and so what the Shona people detested was the dispossession and exploitation – the conizenship – that characterised colonial outsider-ness. In this regard, to be colonised refers to being conizenised and to be infiltrated by conizens (called *vapambe pfumi* in Shona). To describe the world in terms of citizenship – as those who have entitlements against the state – and subjects – or as comprising those that are dominated and oppressed, would be to ignore the historiography of colonisation and the attendant conizenisation of Africa.

In the contemporary era, when states vet applicants for citizenship, they should be understood as sifting for conizens. The idea in vetting applicants for citizenship is to prevent societal infiltration by conizens. But colonialists evaded vetting for citizenship, in precolonial Africa, by describing their colonial victims as open, as barbaric, savage, backward, beastly, as without laws, without borders, as without states, as devoid of sovereignty and autonomy and so on. Colonialists knew that once they admitted that precolonial African states had sovereignty and borders, were civilised, had laws and so on, then they would be bound to submit to the requisite vetting for

214

citizenship, and this would have prevented the colonial conizenship that Africans have suffered. For this reason, this chapter argues that discourses of openness and borderlessness risk conizenship and conizenisation and that therefore there must be mechanisms to prevent conizenship in the emergent global citizenship. The experience that Africans have had with enslavement and colonisation shows that assumptions of openness and borderlessness do not guarantee security and peace – instead, they risk replication of colonisation.

4. COVID-19 and the Emergent Global Citizenship

Although it is often argued that global peace and security can be achieved by becoming open, borderless; by letting go of sovereignty, national politics and autonomy (Engelbrecht 2014; Morales-Moreno 2004; Gumplova 2015; Taskale 2016; Husain, Roep and Franklin 2020; Harsin 2015), this chapter argues that there is a risk of creating not necessarily global citizens but global conizens if the world becomes open and borderless. In other words, given the history of colonial conizenship that was premised on colonial assumptions that the territories that were being colonised were open, borderless, savage, barbaric, beastly, backward and so on, contemporary celebrations of borderlessness and openness should consider the risks of infiltration and penetration by conizens of the world. The risk in becoming open and borderless does not merely lie in terrorism as colonially and imperially defined but the risk of becoming open and borderless should also be connected to the kind of conizenship that characterised colonisation. The question is about how to create a safe world that is free not only from terrorists, as traditionally and imperially defined, but how to create a world that is safe from conizens and from conizenisation such as happened during the colonial era. Put differently, the risk lies in premising global citizenship on colonial conizenship that further supplants and conveys Africans away from their mothers and ancestry. In other words, historically, conizenship has been mistaken for citizenship.

In a contemporary world that celebrates genetic modification, editing and deleting memories and genomic modifications

(Nhemachena, Hlabangane and Kaundjua 2020; Reardon and TallBear 2012; Collier-Robinson et al. 2019; Hamilton 2020), there is no guarantee that African rootedness and ancestry will be valued. In a world that celebrates nomadic subjectivity and nomadic identities, there is no guarantee that African identities are going to be valued in the same way African mothers celebrate the identities of their children. In a world that celebrates cyborgs and hybrid identities, there is no guarantee that African identities will be valued. Further, in a world where everything African is dismissed as backward, savage, uncivilised, barbaric and so on, there is no guarantee that Africans will be accorded real citizenship in the world. Besides, in a world that celebrates cloning, there is no guarantee that African mothers will enjoy their role of mothering. It is a continuation of the colonial retrenchment of African mothers from their roles and perquisites of mothering. In a contemporary world that celebrates humanoid sex robots, there is no guarantee that African husbands and wives will be valued for their roles and perquisites. This is another retrenchment of African husbands and wives from their roles and perquisites as sexual partners. Arguably, this is an intensification of the retrenchment of the neoliberal era foisted by the Bretton Wood institutions; it is a form of retrenchment that decentres African husbands and wives not only from their jobs but from their sexual roles and obligations towards one another. The effect is to transform sexual citizenship at a global level. If humans become cyborgs in the emergent global citizenship, the question then is how do they retain their human subjectivity and do they become global human citizens or they become global cyborg citizens? If Africans lose their human subjectivity, their African identities and African citizenship in the global citizenship that is emerging, the question is whether all these do not amount to conizenship and conizenisation that historically characterised colonisation? Might these not be ways by which to negate African ancestry, genealogies, identities, heritages and therefore to push Africans further from where their mothers are?

While historically, social theory has been preoccupied with dichotomies between the local and the global, this chapter posits the notion of conizenship, which notion already transcends the binaries between the global and the local. The point is that while social theory

216

has historically been preoccupied with binaries between subject and citizen, this chapter posits the notion of conizenship which also bridges the binary between subject and citizen. In fact, the notions of conizenship and conizenisation build on post-modernism, post-humanism, trans-humanism and post-structuralism in the sense of conjoining conmanship and citizenship that characterise the world. It is a term that speaks to hybrid identities that characterised colonialists and post-colonies. Noting that colonialists adopted hybrid identities as colonisers, as civilisers, as exploiters, as dispossessors and as murderers in the colonial territories, this chapter argues that hybrid identities are not necessarily a feature of the post-colonial theorisation or moment in Africa – hybrid identities have a long colonial history in Africa. In this regard, hybridity of global citizenship may not speak to contemporary decolonial postulations as evident in contemporary decolonial scholarship. To become a hybrid may as well be to become a conizen and to be conizenised. Similarly, if colonisation was about destroying African institutional structures, how might the contemporary global citizenship be different when it is premised on the destruction of African sovereignty, autonomy, cultures, identities, social norms and values, polities, economies and humanity? The question is whether it might not be fruitful for Africans to trace the genealogy of post-structuralism and post-modernism to the early colonial era which destroyed African forms of modernism and civilisation? The point is that colonisation and the attendant conizenship and conizenisation were not necessarily about establishing modernisation but about the destruction of African modernity and civilisation (see Chirikure 2010; Taiwo 2010). The question then is whether the contemporary global destruction of sovereignties and autonomy of humanity should be construed as modernisation, civilisation, development or industrialisation or growth?

In the context of COVID-19, humanity is becoming global citizens in circumstances marked by deindustrialisation and degrowth. In this sense, while COVID-19 destroys human lives, polities, economies, cultural and social ways of behaving and so on, humanity is noted as simultaneously becoming global citizens. Scholars and thinkers are advocating for degrowth and postgrowth in the sense of ceasing to prioritise economic growth and industrialisation (Drew and Antal 2016; Kallis, Kerschner and Martinez-Alier 2016). In this regard, the question is whether humanity will be better off in the emergent global state that is marked by deindustrialisation, post-growth, degrowth, post-development and post-industrialisation. Might the global state and global citizenship be set to become a state of penury and tribulations for some sections of humanity that lose jobs due to ongoing deindustrialisation, degrowth, post-growth, post-industrialisation, post-development and the robotisation of work? Similarly, in a context of degrowth and post-growth in a demographic sense, might some sections of humanity not be reduced to the misery of cohabiting with humanoid sex robots and technologies of masturbation that are set to replace reproductive sex? In so far as the COVID-19 social distancing regulations have resulted in an increase in purchases of humanoid sex robots (Nhemachena and Mawere 2020), this chapter argues that in a post-COVID-19 world order, humanoid sex robots will increasingly become popular and traditional African marriages will become moribund. If historically marriages have united different people, of different genealogies and heritages, the disappearance of the marriage institutions would entail the disappearance of society and the disappearance of socialisation into marriages and families in the historical cultural sense. In short, the world is getting into an era where citizenship will not be defined on the basis of the right to employment or job because the oncoming post-COVID-19, post-industrial, degrowth and post-growth society promises to be workless or jobless for what Yuval Noah Harari (2018) calls a 'useless class of humans'. The oncoming global state also promises a world wherein citizenship is not defined on the basis of tenets of marriage and birth because humanoid sex robots will increasingly take over the roles of sexual and marriage partners. Equally the post-COVID-19 world order promises global citizenship that is not premised on birth because the world is increasingly being populated with robotic and electronic persons (Bulman 2017; Stancati and Gallo 2020) which, as some scholars argue, will eventuate in 'robocalypse' for humans.

In the light of the foregoing, one wonders whether we are not witnessing a world that thrives as much on conizenry as on what I call necrozenry, wherein death is celebrated even as life is being destroyed. In a world that prefers to retain the skulls and skeletons of the dead even as the states deport and repatriate live human beings, I would describe this in terms of necrozenship. With necrozenship, the world prefers to be populated by remains of the dead than to be populated by living human beings. Also, necrozenry is a world in which inanimate matter is celebrated as much as spirits of the dead that are portrayed as animate and immanent in matter. Necrozenry marks a world in which inanimate technological substrates are celebrated as animate even as live humans are being killed; it is a world in which human consciousness is transferred into technological substrates for what is being celebrated as second virtual lives when minds are uploaded to pieces of technology (Kurzweil 2005) – immortal lives wherein the consciousness of dead humans is uploaded onto technological substrates. Necrozenry characterises a world in which zombies, or the so-called living dead are celebrated in lieu of living human beings. In such a world where the dead and zombies are celebrated, global citizenship becomes not only conizenship but also necrozenship: binaries between the living and the dead are elided and so the dead become 'citizens' or necrozens as do the living in the emergent world. In a world that is premised on conizenship and necrozenship, indigenous people, cultures and spirituality are conveniently attuned and celebrated as helping to overcome binaries between the dead and the living.

5. Conclusion

Using the Shona saying that *kusina amai hakuendwe*, this chapter critically interrogates the emergent Global State and citizenship. While taking cognisance of the Shona saying that *chitsva chirimurutsoka*, the chapter contends that the Shona people were not and are not static in their cultural outlook but the saying *kusina amai hakuendwe* advises Africans to be circumspect about becoming recklessly mobile or becoming recklessly amenable to change. Situating these Shona sayings in the context of the emergent Global State and global citizenship that is being ushered in as a result of COVID-19, the chapter contends for a delicate balance between change and stasis.

Postulating the theories of conizenship and necrozenship, the chapter anticipates a world in which the dead and death are celebrated even as life is being destroyed. Arguing that such an emergent world is one that dwells on the philosophy of brinkmanship between death and life, the chapter wonders about the fate of human citizens in a world that dispenses with the binaries between the dead and the living. In this regard, the chapter argues that the emergent post-binary world promises to be penumbral in the sense of being suspended between life and death, between the dead and the living – and global 'citizens' live both lives supposedly without the necessity of drawing binaries. This becomes a world of necrozenship – celebrating the dead and the half dead.

Acknowledgement

This work was supported by JSPS KAKENHI Grant Number JP16H06318.

References

Baratta, J. P. (2004) *The Politics of World Federation: United Nations, UN Reform, Atomic Control*, Westport: Praeger Publishers.

BBC News (2020) 'Coronavirus: Zimbabwe arrests 100,000 for violations of measures', *BBC News*, 19 July 2020 (https://www.bbc.com/news/world-africa-53462259) (accessed: 23 November 2020).

Bothoko, P. (2020) 'Zimbabwean voluntary repatriation ongoing', *Mmegi Online*, 7 May 2020 (https://www.mmegi.bw/index.php?aid=85395&dir=2020/may/07) (accessed: 23 November 2020).

Braidotti, R. (2010) 'Nomadism: Against methodological nationalism', *Policy futures in Education*, Vol. 8, No. 3–4, pp. 408–18.

——— (2014) 'Writing as a nomadic subject', *Comparative Critical Studies*, Vol. 11, No. 2–3, pp. 163–84.

Bulman, M. (2017) 'EU to vote on declaring robots to be "electronic persons"', *Independent*, 14 January 2017 (https://www.independent.co.uk/life-stle/gadgets-and-tech/robots-eu-vote) (accessed: 23 November 2020).

Case Number 0 (2020) "The government is lying to you': UK returnees on conditions at Belvedere', *ZimLive*, 21 April 2020 (https://www.zimlive.com/2020/04/21/the-government-is-lying-to-you) (accessed: 23 November 2020)

Chibamu, A. (2020) 'Govt fails to buy air tickets for stranded Zimbos in UAE', *New Zimbabwe*, 9 June 2020 (https://www.newzimbabwe.com/govt-fails-to-buy-air-tickets-for-stranded) (accessed: 23 November 2020).

Chimni, B. S. (2004) 'International institutions today: An imperial global state in the making', *EJIL*, Vol. 15, No. 1, pp. 1–37.

Chipunza, P. (2020) '65 returnees from UK demand hotel quarantine', *The Herald*, 21 April 2020 (https://www.herald.co.zw/65-returnees-from-uk-demand-hotel-quarantine) (accessed: 23 November 2020)

Chirikure, S. (2010) *Indigenous Mining and Metallurgy in Africa*, Cambridge: Cambridge University Press.

Collier-Robinson, L., Rayne, A., Rupene, M., Thoms, C. and Steeves, T. (2019) 'Embedding indigenous principles in genomic research of cultural significant species: A conservation genomics case study', *New Zealand Journal of Ecology*, Vol. 43, No. 3, pp. 1–9.

Culbertson, E. (1949) 'The preliminary draft of a world constitution, by the committee to frame a world constitution', *Indiana Law Journal*, Vol. 24, No. 3, pp. 474–82.

Deleuze, G. and Guattari, F. (1987) *A Thousand Plateaus: Capitalism and Schizophrenia*, Minneapolis and London: University of Minnesota Press.

Drew, S. and Antal, M. (2016) 'Degrowth: A "missile word" that backfires?' *Ecological Economics*, Vol. 126, pp. 182–87.

Dube, M. (2020) 'On the edge of starvation, hundreds of Zimbabweans in Botswana want to go home', *VOA*, 15 April 2020 (https://www.voanews.com/covid-19-pandemic/edge-starvation-hundreds-zimbabweans-botswana-want-go-home) (accessed: 23 November 2020).

Elliot, L. (2020) 'Gordon Brown calls for global government to tackle coronavirus', *The Guardian*, 26 March 2020 (https://www.theguardian.com/politics/2020/mar/26/gordon-brown-calls-for-global-government-to-tackle-coronavirus) (accessed: 23 November 2020).

Engelbrecht, S. F. (2014) 'Can autonomy be limited- An ethical and legal perspective in a South African context?', *Journal of Forensic Odonto-Stomatology*, Vol. 32, No. 1, pp. 34–9.

Erman, E. (2019) 'Does global democracy require a world state?', *Philosophy Papers*, Vol. 48, No. 1, pp. 123–53.

Francois, M. (2019) 'It's not just Cambridge University – All of Britain benefited from slavery', *The Guardian*, 7 May 2019 (https://www.theguardian.com/commentisfree/2019/may/07/cambridge-university-britain-slavery) (accessed: 23 November 2020).

Gumplova, P. (2015) 'On sovereignty and post-sovereignty', *Philosophica Critica*, Vol. 1, No. 2, pp. 3–18.

Hamilton, J. A. (2020) 'Genetic ancestry tests: Materializing race and indigeneity across law, medicine and society', in M.-A. Jacob. and A. Kirkland (eds) *Research Handbook on Socio-Legal Studies of Medicine and Health*, Northampton: Edward Elgar Publishing.

Harari, Y. N. (2018) *21 Lessons for the 21st Century*, London: Jonathan Cape.

Harsin, J. (2015) 'Regimes of posttruth, postpolitics, and attention economies', *Communication, Culture and Critique*, Vol. 8, Issue 2, pp. 327–33.

Husain, S. O., Roep, D. and Franklin, A. (2020) 'Prefigurative post-politics as strategy: The case of government-led blockchain projects', *The JBBA*, Vol. 3, No. 1, pp. 1–11.

Inayatullah, S. (1999) *World Government, Globalization and UN Reform*, Global Policy Forum (https://www.globalpolicy.org/component/content/article/228/32402.html) (accessed: 23 November 2020).

Kallis, G., Kerschner, C. and Martinez-Alier, J. (2016) 'The economics of degrowth', *Ecological Economics*, Vol. 84, pp. 172–80.

Kaplan, M. (1965) 'Their Rhodesia', *Transition*, Vol. 23, pp. 32-44.

Kurzweil, R. (2005) *The Singularity Is Near: When Humans Transcend*

Biology, New York: Penguin Books.

Maromo, J. (2020) 'Hundreds of Zimbabweans leave South Africa in assisted repatriation', *African News Agency*, 16 May 2020 (https://www.iol.co.za/news/africa/hundreds-of-zimbabweans-leave-south-africa-in-assisted-repatriation-47997944) (accessed: 23 November 2020).

Martin, G. T. (2010) *A Constitution for the Federation of Earth*, 2nd edition, Virginia: Institute for Economic Democracy Press.

Mavhunga, C. (2020) 'Zimbabwe disregards WHO COVID-19 quarantine guidelines', *VOA*, 22 April 2020 (https://www.voanews.com/covid-19-pandemic/zimbabwe-disregards-who-covid-19-quarantine-guidelines) (accessed: 23 November 2020).

Mogoatlhe, L. (2020) 'These world leaders shared vital messages for "One World: Together at Home"', *Global Citizen*, 21 April 2020 (https://www.globalcitizen.org/en/content/world-leaders-message-one-world-together-at-home/) (accessed: 23 November 2020).

Morales-Moreno, I. (2004) 'Postsovereign governance in a globalizing and fragmenting world: The case of Mexico', *Review of Policy Research*, Vol. 21, No. 1 pp. 107–27.

Mushava, E. (2020) 'Returning Zimbos expose govt', *Newsday*, 22 April 2020 (https://www.newsday.co.zw/2020/04/returning-zimbos-expose-govt) (accessed: 23 November 2020).

Mutsaka, F. and Magome, M (2020) 'Zimbabwe nurses protest; South Africa reopens some classes', *AP News*, 6 July 2020 (https://apnews.com/article/5e35cd3e8c0d61a04d1b9215b2bf7eab) (accessed: 23 November 2020).

Ncube, T. (2020) 'Thousands return home as COVID-19 bites', *ZBC News*, 12 July 2020 (https://www.zbcnews.co.zw/thousands-return-home-as-covid-19-bites/) (accessed: 23 November 2020).

Neocosmos, M. (2008) *From Foreign Natives' to 'Native Foreigners' Explaining Xenophobia in Post-Apartheid South Africa*, Dakar: CODESRIA.

Nhemachena, A., Hlabangane, N. and Kaundjua, M. (2020) 'Relationality or hospitality in twenty-first century research? Big data, internet of things and the resilience of coloniality on Africa',

Modern Africa: Politics, History and Society, Vol. 8, No. 1, pp. 105–39.

Nhemachena, A and Mawere, M. (2020) *Securitising Monstrous Bottoms in the Age of Posthuman Carnivalesque: Decolonising the Environment, Human Beings and African Heritages*, Bamenda: Langaa RPCIG.

Nhemachena, A. (2017) *Relationality and Resilience in a Not So Relational World? Knowledge, Chivanhu and (De-)Coloniaity in 21st Century Conflict-Torn Zimbabwe*, Bamenda: Langaa RPCIG.

Nyamnjoh, F. B. (2006) *Insiders and Outsiders: Citizenship and Xenophobia in Contemporary South Africa*, London: Zed Books.

Nyathi, K. (2020) 'Zimbabwe fears returnees will rev up coronavirus spread', *The EastAfrican*, 5 April 2020 (https://www.theeastafrican.co.ke/news/africa/Zimbabwe-fears-returnees-will-rev-up-corona-virus-spread/4552902-5514058-npyjmpz/index.html) (accessed: 23 November 2020).

Rawlinson, K. (2016) 'Cecil Rhodes' statue to remain at Oxford after 'overwhelming support'', *The Guardian*, 29 January 2016 (https://www.theguardian.com/education/2016/jan/28/cecil-rhodes) (accessed 25 December 2020)

Reardon, J. and TallBear, K. (2012) '"Your DNA is our history" Genomics, anthropology, and the construction of whiteness as property', *Current Anthropology*, Vol. 53, No. 5, pp. 233–45.

Reuters Staff (2019) 'How have British Universities Grappled with Links to the Slave Trade', *Reuters*, 30 April 2019 (https://www.reuters.com/article/us-britain-slavery-universities-factbox-idUSKCN1S61TX) (accessed: 23 November 2020).

Rowan, L. (2016) 'Nomadic subject', in N. A. Naples (ed.) *The Wiley Blackwell Encyclopaedia of Gender and Sexuality Studies*, 1st edition, Hoboken: Wiley & Sons Ltd.

Scoones, I. (2020) '"Know your epidemic": Reflections from Zimbabwe', *Chronicle*, 30 September 2020 (https://www.chronicle.co.zw/know-your-epidemic-reflections-from-zimbabwe/) (accessed: 23 November 2020).

Shaw, M. (2000) *Theory of the Global State: Globality as an Unfinished Revolution*, Cambridge: Cambridge University Press.

Staff Reporter (2020) 'Outrage as 65 Returning UK Zimbos refuse college quarantine, demand hotel', *New Zimbabwe*, 20 April 2020 (www.newzimbabwe.com/outrage-65-returning-uk-zimbos-refuse-college) (accessed: 23 November 2020).

Stancati, C. and Gallo, G. (2020) 'Could an electronic person exist? Robots and personal responsibility', in R. Giovagnoli and R. Lowe (eds) *The Logics of Social Practice (Studies in Applied Philosophy, Epistemology and Rational Ethics Vol. 52)*, Berlin: Springer.

Stichter, S. (1985) *Migrant Laborers*, Cambridge: Cambridge University Press.

Suzuki, K. (2020) 'After COVID, time to consider a UN parliament and a world federation', Democracy Without Borders, 29 June 2020 (https://www.democracywithout borders.org/13857/after-covid-time-to-con) (accessed: 23 November 2020).

Taiwo, O. (2010) *How Colonialism Preempted Modernity in Africa*, Bloomington and Indianapolis: Indiana University Press.

Taskale, A. R. (2016) *Post-Politics in Context*, London: Routledge.

Van Onselen, C. (1980) *Chibaro: African Mine Labour in Southern Rhodesia, 1900-1933*, Johannesburg: Ravan Press.

Vinga, A. (2020) 'Zimbabwe: No plans to assist repatriate COVID-19 victims based abroad-Mangwana', *New Zimbabwe*, 27 March 2020 (https://www.newzimbabwe.com/no-plans-to-assist-repatriate-zim-covid-19-victims-based-abroad-mangwana/) (accessed: 23 November 2020).

Wendt, A. (2003) 'Why a world state is inevitable', *European Journal of International Relations*, Vol. 9, No. 4, pp. 491–542.

Yang, U. (2011) *A Global State through Democratic Federal World Government: How the World Works Better Hidden Benefits of a New World Political Economy*, London: AuthorHouse.

Yunker, P. (2012) 'Evolutionary world government', *Peace Research*, Vol. 44, No. 1, pp. 95–126.

Chapter 9

Epidemics, Negotiability and Futurity in Africa and Beyond

Ato Kwamena Onoma

1. Introduction

The mobilisation of epidemics by actors in social interactions is the subject of a significant body of work. In relations between communities some have seized on these outbreaks to cleanse their homelands of long-undesired others (Onoma 2017; Markel and Stern 2002; Eichelberger 2007) while others have used the cover of epidemic control and prevention measures to further long-held ambitions of segregating cities along racial lines (Curtin 1985; Goerg 1998; Echenberg 2002). In earlier work, I showed that interactions within the same community are not immune to the exploitation of epidemics, demonstrating how migrants invoke the hardships caused by these public health crises to relieve themselves of some of the pressures they face from their relatives back in their places of origin (Onoma 2018).

In this chapter I invoke such manipulation of these hardships caused by epidemics in intra-communal interactions to highlight the pervasiveness of negotiability in African social interactions. This constant negotiability points to the limited weight that the past exerts on future social dynamics on a continent that has all too often been portrayed as a place of tradition, where the past exerts overwhelming influence on the future. Scholars and policy actors alike have blamed this limited ability of the past, when considered in the form of established institutions and structures, to shape future events for the economic challenges of Africa and other societies in the Global South (Acemoglu and Robinson 2012; De Soto 2000). But as recent advances in the new institutionalism indicate (Hacker, Pierson and Thelen 2015; Mahoney and Thelen 2010; Onoma 2010), the limited capacity of institutions to structure the future in definitive ways, thus limiting the room for negotiations by agents is not another peculiarity of the African continent. Negotiability may not only be more pervasive than is often portrayed, I conclude that it may have positive potentials that are not always acknowledged in the rush to decry the African continent's weak institutions.

While this chapter is significantly rooted in my ongoing research on the interactions between epidemics and xenophobia, I also draw on earlier and other current work conducted on a broad range of issues, including land rights, refugee–host relations and interment practices. In almost all of this work, I have privileged ethnographic methods along with archival research and have covered areas of West, Central, East and Southern Africa. Immediately below, I highlight the mobilisation of the possibilities presented by migrants and by epidemics, as well as their relatives back home in continual negotiations of ties and status. The section following this invokes the pervasiveness of negotiability in African life before highlighting its implications for the weight of the past on the future. I then connect these reflections to work on institutional ambiguity before concluding.

2. Mobilising 'the Boon' of Public Health Crises

In June 2020 many Senegalese families like those elsewhere in many countries in the Global South who rely on remittances from emigrants in European countries and the United States (US) were suffering the economic ill-effects of the COVID-19 pandemic. The outbreak, which was later determined to be caused by the severe acute respiratory syndrome coronavirus 2 (*SARS-CoV-2*) was first signalled in the city of Wuhan in Hubei Province, China in December 2019 (WHO 2020). By March 2020 the outbreak had spread to other East Asian countries as well as the US and Europe (Rothan and Byrareddy 2020; WHO 2020). South America and Africa were the areas last hit by the outbreak, which the World Health Organization (WHO) declared a pandemic on 11 March 2020 (WHO 2020). By August 2020, there was still no WHO-approved cure or vaccine against the disease. Most countries have placed emphasis on limiting physical contact between people and rendering those interactions that happen safe through the maintenance of physical distance, use of face masks and encouragement of the regular washing of hands. Measures to limit physical interactions have included the suspension of gatherings beyond thresholds that have varied across territories, the closure of schools, places of worship and non-essential businesses, lockdowns of regions and whole national territories and closure of international borders (Wilder-Smith, Chiew and Lee 2020).

European countries, like Spain, Italy and France were badly hit by the pandemic leading authorities there to impose stringent lockdown measures from March 2020 that were eased later in the year only for some to be re-imposed as infection numbers rose again in the summer and autumn of 2020 (Ruktanonchai et al. 2020). Similar measures were adopted in areas like New York City in the United States of America that also suffered high infection rates early on in the pandemic (CBS/AFP 2020). Lockdown measures in these European countries and areas of the US significantly slowed economic activities, particularly affecting hospitality and tourism sectors that offer both formal and informal employment opportunities for many migrants (Kalantaryan and McMahon 2020). Non-contractual workers and those who depend on activities like hawking, categories among whom migrants lacking legal working permits are over-represented, suffered particularly from these disruptions (Causa and Cavalleri 2020). The pandemic badly affected the ability of migrants to make a living and led to significant drops in their remittances to families in their places of origin (Kalantaryan and McMahon 2020) who depend on their remittances to help cover daily expenses, the payment of utility bills, school fees and hospital bills as well as the cover of important family events including funerals and baptisms. As is the case in other contexts in the Global South (Manuh 2001), migrants contribute significantly to the livelihood of many families in Senegal (Daffe 2008), and as the spread of the pandemic to the country jeopardised the economic activities of many in the country, their inability to count on the usual help from emigrants was particularly damaging.

During an interview that I had with a young professional that I will give the apocryphal name Oumy Fall for reasons of anonymity, in Dakar on 1 April 2020, she detailed the high number of members of her extended family that were emigrants, especially in France, Italy and Spain. She described the contributions of these migrant kin to various sections of her family and pointed at the challenges that segments of her family were enduring on account of the decline or complete cut-off of remittances from these migrants. While commiserating with her migrant kin who were facing difficult times abroad far from their families, she voiced the suspicion that:

> Some of the more irresponsible migrants are using the cover of Corona (COVID-19) to avoid assuming their responsibilities here. They say 'Because of Corona I can't send money. There is no work here. We are all confined. We can't even go outside'. But some of them actually can afford to send money if they want to. After all there are still people working in Italy and Spain. Some of them are just always looking for ways to avoid their responsibilities.

Oumy's suspicions about migrants' mobilisation of the possibilities presented by public health crises in their constant negotiations of ties and status with home communities sounded familiar to me. During my investigation of social dynamics in Senegal in the shadow of the 2013–2016 West African ebola virus disease (EVD) epidemic which centred on Guinea, Sierra Leone and Liberia, I had interviewed Peul migrants from Guinea based in Senegal who detailed the mobilisation of the EVD epidemic by members of their migrant community in negotiations with relatives in Guinea. The Peul of Guinea are part of Fulfulde-speaking people that can be found in many countries in West and Central Africa (Diallo 2009; Onoma 2020a). Many Peul from Guinea migrated to Senegal during the political economic crises that bedevilled the reign of Guinea's first president, Sekou Touré. Since the death of Sekou Touré in 1984, the search for economic opportunities has motivated the continued migration of Peul Guineans to Senegal, where they form a large and highly visible migrant community that dominates the retailing of fruits and running of neighbourhood corner shops in the capital city of Dakar, in addition to being involved in many other sectors of the economy (Bah, Keita and Lootvoet 1989; Diallo 2009; Onoma

2020b; Lefebvre 2003: 11; Groelsema 1998).

During interviews on how the 2013–2016 EVD epidemic had influenced their relations with their Senegalese hosts and their relatives back in Guinea, many of these migrants detailed how the travel curbs during the epidemic had affected their activities. They also reflected on how anti-Peul xenophobia in Senegal had negatively affected their lives and livelihoods. While these migrants insisted that the disruptions of the epidemic had made life difficult for them and made it harder for them to 'assume their responsibilities', in Guinea, some pointed out that the EVD epidemic had become a cover for some that had been seeking for a while to shirk certain responsibilities. Some, seeking to free themselves of obligations to remit to certain people in Guinea complained that the downturn in economic activities deprived them of funds, making it hard for them to send money to the country. Others, trying to avoid certain trips to Guinea, claimed that the closure of the land border between Senegal and Guinea made it impossible for them to return even though the porosity of the border allowed people to travel between the two countries even after Senegal closed its borders with Guinea. Some seeking to avoid hosting certain guests visiting from Guinea cited the same border closure and general hostility toward Peul migrants in Senegal during the pandemic to dissuade people from making the trip.

Migrants are not the only ones guilty of mobilising the possibilities presented by epidemics in these intra-group negotiations. Their relatives back home similarly exploit the possibilities presented by epidemics in their relations with their migrant kin. In a telephone interview I had with a primary school teacher in Sierra Leone on 12 October 2015, she noted how the 2013–2016 EVD epidemic had become a formidable talking point for people there seeking to squeeze ever greater remittances out of their relatives abroad and to convince these relatives to help them migrate. They fashioned narratives stressing the disruption of economic activities in the country by the epidemic and the general hardship the outbreak had engendered to argue for more help from relatives abroad and to demonstrate why it was best for them to leave the country. They pointed out that food had become scarce and more expensive due to disruptions in agriculture and curbs on international and internal mobility just as lockdowns and the fear of contracting the disease had undermined activities in certain sectors of the economy. The devastating economic consequences of the epidemic on the worst affected countries is the subject of significant work (Economic Commission for Africa 2015a, 2015b), and this interviewee readily acknowledged these. But she pointed out that the epidemic did not negatively affect everyone and that it was a boon for some who were able to build fortunes due to the outbreak, a point underlined by scholars working on the subject (Shepler 2017). She claimed that even those whose livelihoods may not have been negatively affected by the epidemic had eagerly latched on to it in their negotiations with relatives abroad.

The allure of epidemics for those involved in these negotiations of identity, belonging, place and status within communities partly lies in the multi-dimensional character of their disruptive influences. The fear of contagion motivates measures to avoid contamination by private individuals and public officials alike that often involve the reduction of physical interactions and curbs on mobility, undermining economic activities. Scapegoating that tends to portray certain categories of people, especially migrants, as disease vectors often fuel curbs on the mobility of members of targeted groups and the boycotting of their businesses. All of this can undermine the economic activities of migrants and infringe on their ability to travel home or host relatives from their places of origin.

The visible character of these health crises increases their utility as key elements of the structured narratives mixing elements of fact and the apocryphal that people deploy in these intra-communal negotiations (Onoma 2018). Tales of personal misfortune woven by migrants that mix elements of fact and the apocryphal to 'escape responsibilities' often raise suspicions and sometimes fail to obviate retaliation from relatives in home communities. Unlike personal misfortunes, epidemics and their negative consequences are public knowledge. The clever exploitation of the interstices between these public calamities and their generally disruptive effects on the one hand and myriad individual fortunes, which are not always linearly correlated with these public health crises is something that each party in these negotiations of ties eagerly partakes in while suspecting and condemning others of exploiting.

These ties that bind migrants to their home communities are regulated by institutions and intersubjective norms on what constitutes a good emigrant, what a good emigrant is supposed to do and what constitutes proper punishment for 'bad emigrants' and just rewards for 'good emigrants'. These norms also lay out the obligations of home communities and the courses of action that an emigrant can take against family members that do not fulfil their promises at home. A large segment of the initial literature tended to emphasise harmonious and convivial relations between migrants and their home communities within the scope of these norms with each playing their 'expected roles'. Migrants were said to remit money in cash and kind home in support of their families, support local development efforts there and pursue investment opportunities in these spaces. They are said to always seek to visit these spaces, often laden with gifts. Further, they are said to desire that their bodies be returned to these places for burial on their death (Ferguson 1999; Geschiere and Gugler 1998; Arhinful 2001; Grillo 1973; Curtis 1995; Hickey 2011; Fall 2008; Mazzucato, Kabki and Smith 2006; Page 2007; Eyoh 1999). Home communities are in turn said to contribute to help fund the cost of migration for their members and provide them with moral and spiritual support while they are away. They are also said to welcome and treat them as returning heroes when they visit and accord their remains befitting burials when they are returned in death (Nyamnjoh and Rowlands 1998; Ndegwa 1997; Smith 2001; Geschiere and Gugler 1998; Dietz et al. 2011; Mazzucato, Kabki and Smith 2006). This literature in many ways coincides with dominant understandings of social interactions in Africa that emphasise intra-group conviviality and harmony while stressing inter-communal tensions and contestations (Ekeh 1975; Osaghae 1995; Berman 1998; Lewis 1992; De Sardan 1999).

Another strand of literature seeks to problematise conviviality between migrants and their home communities (Onoma 2018; Tazanu 2012; Geschiere 2014; Hay 2014; Lindley 2007; Englund 2004; Tabappsi 1999). In place of the understanding of conviviality as a tranquil and placid state produced by norms and institutions that are efficacious in their ability to shape behaviour, it infuses

233

conviviality with significant turbulence and perturbation. In place of the view of conviviality as a state, it casts it as a process, an open-ended one, that is subject to constant negotiation and whose results are never certain and open to reverses. It casts the norms, regulations and institutions within which these relations are played out as themselves being the object of constant negotiations and contestations (Nyamnjoh 2005, 2016; Onoma 2018). The tensions that fuel these perturbations in relations between migrants and home communities include what many migrants see as the endless material demands on them that are often in disproportion with their earnings (Geschiere 2014; Hay 2014; Lindley 2007; Englund 2004; Tabappsi 1999). Coupled with these excessive demands are what they characterise as a lack of empathy from these relatives for the hard lives they live far away from their loved ones (Nyamnjoh 2005). Migrants also complain about what many (Diop 2008; Lindley 2009; Nyamnjoh 2011, 2016; Daffe 2008: 124; Azam and Gubert 2002; Barro 2008; Onoma 2018) recognise as the misuse of funds they send home to build houses and invest in businesses. This exploitation is only worsened by the fact that migrants that protest too much about such misappropriation or misuse of funds are likely to draw the ire and condemnation of their relatives at home (Fouquet 2008).

Migrants are not the only ones that harbour frustrations in these relations. Those at home tend to decry the tendency of migrants to shirk their responsibilities, including remitting home for various causes, visiting home, aiding others to migrate and hosting others from their home areas abroad (Nyamnjoh 2005; Fouquet 2008). Home communities also complain about migrants' insistence on accountability for funds that may have been misused or misappropriated by their relatives. They see this insistence as tantamount to ruining the image of their families and fracturing familial unity.

Given genuine feelings of warmth on both sides and the costs of extreme measures, interactions take the form of constant negotiations over the nature of ties and their meanings and implications. Name-calling is a weapon of choice for bringing migrants to order with relatives in home communities accusing recalcitrant migrants of having forgotten their roots, 'becoming

234

European' and so on (Tazanu 2012; Lindley 2009; Onoma 2018; Nyamnjoh 2005, 2011). Migrants that fail to yield in the face of name-calling can expect ostracism by their families. They will no longer hear from their families and will be excluded from family discussions and activities. When they visit home, they can expect to be ignored and denied of the welcome reserved for 'good migrants'. They may even be threatened with witchcraft attacks (Nyamnjoh 2005; De Sardan 1999: 41; Lindley 2007; Geschiere and Nyamnjoh 2000; Onoma 2018). Migrants on the other hand can denounce exploitative relatives and threaten to and actually cut off support to these relatives. Many migrants craft tales of woe that involve accounts of personal misfortune and social perturbations to justify their inability to fulfil their responsibilities. Others just lie low and try to evade detection by changing phone numbers and closing social media accounts (Tazanu 2012; Lindley 2009; Onoma 2018; Nyamnjoh 2005, 2011).

3. Negotiability

The mobilisation of the possibilities presented by public health crises in these negotiations between migrants and their home communities attests to the centrality of negotiability in African social relations, which has been noted by scholars like Mbembe (2000) and Berry (1993). It points to the limited influence of structures, rules and regulatory systems in everyday interactions. It does not signal an absence or paucity of these structures, rules and laid down procedures. Instead, it shows the ways in which people not only play within these structures but also play with the structures, recasting them as they interact. The structures and norms, while governing and regulating interactions between migrants and their home communities, are themselves also simultaneously the subject of constant negotiations and contestations by these groups. Who can be qualified as a 'good emigrant'? What are the responsibilities of the home community to their sons and daughters abroad? What rights and privileges can a 'good emigrant' expect at home? Under what circumstances can emigrants justifiably not fulfil their responsibilities to home, or relatives at home not fulfil their responsibilities to migrants? What sorts of punishment can be justifiably imposed on shirking emigrants? These are all questions that are constantly posed and debated.

There are many domains in which the centrality of negotiability in African life is apparent. In Ghana, the Akan saying *'abusua do funu'* (the family loves a dead body) does not point to an unhinged fascination with morbidity. Instead, it points to the eager exploitation of the space for (re)negotiating social relations that deaths, especially those of elderly and important people permits. The period between death and the conclusion of funerals is an occasion for renegotiating ties among the living partly through the highly contested elaboration of ties between the dead and the living (Arhin 1994; Jindra and Noret 2011a). The corpse becomes the arena for contesting, renegotiating and renewing ties among the living (De Witte 2001; Van der Geest 2000). Evolutions in technology and religious orientations have prolonged periods of mourning, radically magnifying the space for negotiations during these social events (Jindra and Noret 2011b).

Works on land rights and the institutions that govern them have also displayed the centrality of negotiations in the process of claiming, conserving and contesting rights. Rights tend to be the subject of endless negotiations and contestations that are hardly ever foreclosed by rules, various forms of documentation and judicial pronouncement. Narratives of origins, belonging and relatedness form the core of discourses that continually bring rights that were ostensibly settled in earlier rounds of negotiations and contestations back into play (Berry 2000). Various archives have become important sites in these negotiations and the documents they hold are critical resources in the building up of narratives (Onoma 2009). The courts are also key parts of these processes with cases lasting generations as rights over parcels are contested multiple times with earlier judicial decisions acting more to unleash new contestations than to close debates on rights to ownership and use (Berry 2000; Onoma 2009).

The privileging of negotiations is evident in work on the incorporation of strangers in African communities as well. Murphy and Bledsoe (1987) and Colson (1970) have all noted the tendency of communities to privileging the negotiation of ties between hosts and newcomers instead of the invocation of jural ties and the obligations they ostensibly carry. During my research on relations between refugees and host communities in the Mano River Basin, I noticed a similar tendency of hosts to privilege relations borne out of open-ended negotiations with those they have no obligations to over those with relatives that are delineated by established rules and norms (Onoma 2013a).

This negotiability is also apparent in the nomadism of political life in many spaces on the continent. The constant movement of politicians between parties, the fabrication, abandonment, fusion and scission of parties that is common in many countries are parts of constant negotiations between political actors whose results are almost never predictable. Sworn opponents and their supporters during one round of contestation can become inseparable allies during the next only to fall out again after that (Bindra 2007). These incessant moves point to the malleability of political parties as well as their limited constricting influence on actors involved in the important game of politics.

4. Futurity

The paramountcy of negotiability in African social interactions points to the immense weight of futurity in African life. The past settles little. The ability of the past to structure the future is limited. Things are constantly put into play as old 'settlements' become the object of negotiation as time evolves. Settlements and resolutions take on a decidedly temporary hue, making them not the end to processes of negotiations but as junctures that facilitate, influence and enable new rounds without definitively foreclosing many possibilities.

Life and the social interactions that constitute it take the form of an 'ambiguous adventure', to borrow the famous term of Cheikh Hamidou Kane (1972). Social relations are adventurous not in the sense of being overly risky but on account of their having contours that are uncertain and unsteady, bounded in only a limited sense by the past. The adventures that they constitute are ambiguous in being very open-ended and having 'end results' that are constantly put into play again, ensuring that what exists is an endless process defined above all by negotiations. Souleymane Bachir Diagne's view of 'Africanity as an open question' (2001) is worth invoking here partly because, in its contemplation of Africanity, it shifts from a focus on certainties to questions and installs the endless process of searching for answers, the work of negotiating ties, as the defining feature of Africanity. It insists on process and the constant work of exploration as the defining character of Africanity. Nyamnjoh, in similar fashion, emphasises incompleteness in his reflections on Africanity and interactions on the continent (2015a, 2015b).

This view of Africanity fundamentally undermines the trope of Africa as a place of tradition that Nyamnjoh (2015a) questions; a locale where the past reigns and is constantly invoked or 're-enchanted' as Mbembe puts it (2001a: 22). It subverts the idea of the continent as a place where the weight of the past on the present and future is overwhelming, acting as a repository of answers that people can and should readily consult in interactions. The recognition of the place of negotiability in African life instead views tradition as part of the broad ensemble of resources that are mobilised to pursue the constant process of negotiations. In this reading, the types of traditions invoked among the multiplicity that exist, the form and content of traditions preferred among the multitude that could be invoked as well as the timing of their invocation are all influenced by current processes of bargaining and negotiations that they are 're-enchanted' to support.

Traditions do not constitute clear slates from which answers can be read and solutions derived in a straightforward manner. They are not mechanisms that severely constrict the present and completely determine forms of sociability. Instead, the present and future shape traditions, reminding one of the thesis of the invention of tradition to which Mudimbe (1988) and Ranger (1983) have contributed. The question of what traditions exist, the forms they take and their meanings are the subject of negotiations today and will continue to be tomorrow. The past in a sense is continuously recreated as time evolves through negotiations and contestations.

5. Institutional Ambiguity

What some note as the weak institutional landscape in Africa facilitates the constant negotiability of social relations. Scholars argue that the weakness of institutions is one of the characteristics that defines less developed countries compared to more developed areas of the planet (De Soto 2000; Clague 1997; North 1990; Acemoglu and Robinson 2012). The institutions touched on include political parties, the courts, legislative bodies, local governments, property rights regimes and so on. The African state as a whole is often characterised as weak and even failed (Bayart 1993; Chabal and Daloz 1999; Mkandawire 2001; Callaghy 1987). Legal regimes, regulatory bodies and various state structures are said to be plagued by ambiguity, allowing actors to cleverly interpret and exploit them in ways that accord with their interests (Mbembe 2001b). Instead of shaping social dynamics in uniform ways, these institutions permit and may even facilitate contrasting sets of actions and outcomes (Onoma 2010).

Going beyond the ontological fact of weak institutions and their exploitation some scholars have noted the tendency by some in African societies to view the ambiguity, incompleteness and pluralism that facilitate negotiability in a positive light. The literature provides evidence of some efforts to cultivate and preserve forms of ambiguity. This is evident in work on property rights that highlights the deliberate cultivation of ambiguity in boundaries and claims. The subversion of mapping, surveying and titling efforts and the deliberate promotion of multiple and contradictory maps and titles all serve to create ambiguity over land rights (Berry 2000; Onoma 2009). The choice of this strategy in the pursuit of rights and their benefits instead of efforts to clarify and then claim exclusive rights constitute a good example of this cultivation of ambiguity. Far from being traps that people just cannot escape despite their interest in and efforts to do so, what is portrayed as the weak institutions that facilitate negotiability may be structures that do not entirely lack support in these societies.

The costs of weak institutions have been a major pre-occupation of the New Institutional Economics, a major school, that has won multiple Nobel Prizes in Economics in recent times. The Peruvian economist, Hernando de Soto, in his work *The Mystery of Capital* (2000) and the World Bank's 2002 World Development Report titled 'Building Institutions for Markets' (2002), have put the reflections of this school on the costs of weak institutions and the benefits of their opposite for economic activities and growth (De Soto 2000; Clague 1997; North 1990; Acemoglu and Robinson 2012) in more accessible form. Poor contract enforcement, weak property rights and the absence of the rule of law reduce the predictability of social dynamics (Clague 1997). They severely raise transaction costs and so undermine economic activities and growth. The New Institutional Economics' thesis implies that strong institutions that allow us to predict the future by severely constricting it are both possible and desirable. This perspective sees the banishment of negotiability as possible and critical for economic prosperity.

Scholars have explained economic development in the Global North and economic backwardness in the Global South in terms of the wealth of institutions in the former and its lack in the latter. This view explains the World Bank's transition in the early 2000s from simply getting the prices right through structural adjustment programmes to the broader goal of building institutions (World Bank 2002). Beyond the purely economic sphere, scholars and policy actors alike have identified the lack of strong institutions as the reason for the lack of democratic consolidation in African countries (Cheeseman 2018; Adebanwi and Obadare 2011; Randall and Svåsand 2002; Obi 2011). Democratic consolidation, then, has been framed as a process of reinforcing institutions that include political parties and party systems, electoral commissions, constitutional courts and so on to limit the room for manoeuvre of political actors (Branch and Cheeseman 2009; Lynch and Crawford 2011).

Recent work in historical and sociological institutionalism may suggest that the problem of weak institutions is not a peculiarity of the Global South. Pluralism, ambiguity and problems of enforcement have been shown to characterise the institutional terrain in advanced industrial countries (Mahoney and Thelen 2010). The ability of actors to cherry pick among multiple regulatory structures, their proclivity to interpret ambiguous institutions and cleverly

240

exploit enforcement regimes in these countries is the subject of a growing literature (Mahoney and Thelen 2010; Hacker, Pierson and Thelen 2015; Jackson 2005). It is not only in Africa that institutions do not entirely foreclose future possibilities. It is not only on the continent that negotiability is pervasive. This literature also shows how institutions themselves are the subject of gradual change as actors exploit the interstices permitted by ambiguity, pluralism and enforcement to continually reshape and recast these structures (Mahoney and Thelen 2010).

These insights undergird a shift from punctuated equilibrium models of institution change where long periods of institutional continuity and path dependence are punctuated by critical junctures when exogenous shocks shatter existing equilibriums and permit agency to initiate new paths (Pierson 2000). Scholars instead insist on the gradual and incremental evolution of institutions over time and recognise the ability of actors to continually rework institutions instead of just working within these structures (Mahoney and Thelen 2010; Onoma 2010). There has also been a subtle shift in how scholars understand institutional persistence. First, there is a greater focus on the ways in which what appears as institutional persistence masks small but incremental gradual changes that result in massive transformations over the *longue durée* (Mahoney and Thelen 2010). The view here is that the literature may have exaggerated institutional persistence while underestimating institutional change. Second, even where institutional persistence is recognised, there has been a shift from always seeing it as the result of positive feedback mechanisms to a focus on the contributions of continual negotiations to this persistence (Onoma 2013b). Persistence, in this view, is no longer automatically attributed to the constriction or banishment of negotiations.

6. Conclusion

Advances in historical and sociological institutionalism pose the fundamental question of whether institutions, regardless of their strength and form can structure social realities and constrain future interactions in the ways indicated by the new institutional economics and earlier versions of institutionalism that emphasised path-dependence. Because of their heavy focus on the political economies of advanced industrialised countries this literature has the potential of provoking a broader discussion about institutions and social life that goes beyond the condemnation of weak institutions in Africa and other areas of the Global South that are almost always defined by lack, failure and pervasion.

Escaping this focus on 'weak institutions' as failure also allows a contemplation of some of the potentially positive consequences of the inability of the past, including institutions to severely constrict room for negotiability in the future. First, the fact that structures have limited weight on the future and all things are constantly negotiated provides greater room for recalibrating social relations and structures and correcting social inequalities. Inequalities borne out of one moment of negotiation can always be over turned in the future. Second, and related to the first point, is the impact of constant negotiability on the nature of conflicts. The possibility of future negotiations transforms conflicts from one-off do-or-die events to open-ended processes in which there are potentially no permanent losers or winners. Today's losers can always harbour hopes of winning the next round just as the winners of one round are mindful that they may be the losers of the next round. Losing ceases to be a moment of permanent loss that has to be avoided at all costs and winning ceases to be a moment of triumph that should be exploited to the worst disadvantage of the losers.

Acknowledgement

This work was supported by JSPS KAKENHI Grant Number JP16H06318.

References

Acemoglu, D. and Robinson, J. (2012) *Why Nations Fail: The Origins of Power, Prosperity, and Poverty*, New York: Crown Business.

Adebanwi, W. and Obadare, E. (2011) 'The abrogation of the electorate: An emergent African phenomenon', *Democratization*, Vol. 18, No. 2, pp. 311–35.

Arhin, K. (1994) 'The economic implications of transformations in Akan funeral rites', *Africa*, Vol. 63, Issue 3, pp. 307–22.

Arhinful, D. K. (2001) '"We think of them": How Ghanaian migrants in Amsterdam assist relatives at home', *Research Report 62*, Leiden: African Studies Centre.

Azam, P. and Gubert, F. (2002) 'Ceux de kayes: L'effet des transferts des emigres maliens sur leur famille d'origine', in F. Héran, M. Aoudaï and J. L. Richard (eds) *Commissariat General au Plan, Immigration, Marché du Travail, Intégration*, Paris: La documentation française, pp. 203–30.

Bah, A., Keita, B. and Lootvoet, B. (1989) 'Les Guinéens de l'extérieur: Rentrer au pays?', *Politique Africaine*, No. 36, pp. 22–37.

Barro, I. (2008) 'Emigration, transferts financiers et creation de PME dans l'habitat', in M.-C. Diop (ed.) *Le Sénégal des Migrations: Mobilités, Identités et Sociétés*, Paris: Karthala, pp. 133–52.

Bayart, J-F. (1993) *The State in Africa: The Politics of the Belly*, New York: Longman.

Berman, B. (1998) 'Ethnicity, patronage and the African state: The politics of uncivil nationalism', *African Affairs*, Vol. 97, Issue 388, pp. 305–341.

Berry, S. (1993) *No Condition is Permanent: The Social Dynamics of Agrarian Change in Sub-Saharan Africa*, Madison: The University of Wisconsin Press.

———— (2000) *Chiefs Know their Boundaries: Essays on Property, Power, and the Past in Asante, 1896-1996*, Portsmouth: Heinemann.

Bindra, S. (2007) 'This political Matatu race retards our progress', *Sunwords*, 16 September 2007 (https://sunwords.com/2007/09/16/this-political-matatu-race-retards-our-progress/) (accessed: 11 September 2020).

Branch, D. and Cheeseman, N. (2009) 'Democratization, sequencing, and state failure in Africa: Lessons from Kenya', *African Affairs, Vol.* 108, Issue 430, pp. 1–26.

Callaghy, T. (1987) 'The state as lame leviathan: The patrimonial administrative state in Africa', in Z. Ergas (ed.) *The African State in Transition*, London: Palgrave Macmillan, pp. 87-116.

Causa, O. and Cavalleri, M. C. (2020) 'How non-standard workers are affected and protected during the Covid-19 crisis: Stylised facts and policy considerations', *VOX EU/CEPR*, 30 June 2020 (https://voxeu.org/article/how-non-standard-workers-are-affected-and-protected-during-covid-19-crisis) (accessed: 30 September 2020).

CBS/AFP (2020) 'Lockdown extended for most of Coronavirus-battered New York', *CBS News*, 15 May 2020 (https://www.cbsnews.com/news/new-york-stay-at-home-extended-coronavirus-lockdown/) (accessed: 10 September 2020).

Chabal, P. and Daloz, J.-P. (1999) *Africa Works: Disorder as Political Instrument*, Bloomington: Indiana University Press.

Cheeseman, N. (2018) 'Political institutions and democracy in Africa', in N. Cheeseman (ed.) *Institutions and Democracy in Africa: How the Rules of the Game Shape Political Developments*, New York: Cambridge University Press, pp. 351–75.

Clague, C. (1997) 'The new institutional economics and economic development', in C. Clague (ed.) *Institutions and Economic Development: Growth and Governance in Less-Developed and Post-Socialist Countries*, Baltimore: The Johns Hopkins University Press, pp. 13–36.

Colson, E. (1970) 'The assimilation of aliens among Zambian Tonga', in R. Cohen and J. Middleton (eds) *From Tribe to Nation in Africa: Studies in Incorporation Processes*, San Francisco: Chandler Publishing Company, pp. 35–54.

Curtin, P. (1985) 'Medical knowledge and urban planning in tropical Africa', *The American Historical Review*, Vol. 90, Issue 3, pp. 594–613.

Curtis, J. (1995) *Opportunity and Obligation in Nairobi: Social Networks and Differentiation in the Political Economy of Kenya*, Münster: Lit Verlag.

Daffe, G. (2008) 'Les transferts d'argent des migrants Sénégalais entre espoir et risques de dépendance', in M-C. Diop (ed.) *Le Sénégal des Migrations: Mobilités, Identités et Sociétés*, Paris: Karthala, pp. 105–32.

De Sardan, O. (1999) 'A moral economy of corruption in Africa?', *The Journal of Modern African Studies*, Vol. 37, Issue 1, pp. 25–52.

De Soto, H. (2000) *The Mystery of Capital: Why Capitalism Triumphs in the West and Fails Everywhere Else*, New York: Basic Books.

De Witte, M. (2001) *Long Live the Dead! Changing Funeral Celebrations in Asante, Ghana*, Amsterdam: Aksant Academic Publishers.

Diagne, S. B. (2001) 'Africanity as an open question', in S. B. Diagne, A. Mama, H. Melber and F. B. Nyamnjoh (eds) *Identity and Beyond: Rethinking Africanity*, Nordic Africa Institute Discussion Paper 12, pp. 19–24.

Diallo, P. (2009) *Les Guinéens de Dakar: Migration et Intégration en Afrique de l'Ouest*, Paris: L'Harmattan.

Dietz, T., Kabki, M., Mazzucato, V. and Smith, L. (2011) 'Ghanaians in Amsterdam, their "good work back home" and the importance of reciprocity', *Journal of Global initiatives*, Vol. 6, No. 11, pp. 132–43.

Diop, M-C. (2008) 'Présentation. Mobilités, État et société', in M-C. Diop (ed.) *Le Sénégal des Migrations: Mobilités, Identités et Sociétés*, Paris: Karthala, pp. 13–36.

Echenberg, M. (2002) *Black Death, White Medicine: Bubonic Plague and the Politics of Public Health in Colonial Senegal, 1914-1945*, Oxford: James Currey.

Economic Commission for Africa (2015a) *Socio-economic impacts of Ebola on Africa*, Addis Ababa: Economic Commission for Africa.

—— (2015b) *A case for external debt cancellation for Ebola-affected countries*, Addis Ababa: Economic Commission for Africa.

Eichelberger, L. (2007) 'SARS and New York's Chinatown: The politics of risk and blame during an epidemic of fear', *Social Science and Medicine*, Vol. 65, No. 6, pp. 1284–95.

Ekeh, P. (1975) 'Colonialism and the two publics in Africa', *Comparative Studies in Society and History*, Vol. 17, Issue 1, pp. 91–112.

Englund, H. (2004) 'Cosmopolitanism and the devil in Malawi', *Ethnos*, Vol. 69, Issue 3, pp. 293–316.

Eyoh, D. (1999) 'Community, citizenship and the politics of ethnicity in postcolonial Africa', in P. T. Zeleza and E. Kalipeni (eds) *Sacred Places and Public Quarrels: African Cultural and Economic Landscapes*,

Trenton: Africa World Press.

Fall, A. S. (2008) *Bricoler pour Survivre: Perceptions de la Pauvreté dans l'Agglomération Urbaine de Dakar*, Paris: Karthala.

Ferguson, J. (1999) *Expectations of Modernity: Myths and Meanings of Urban Life on the Zambian Copper Belt*, Berkeley: University of California Press.

Fouquet, T. (2008) 'Migrations et "glocalisation" Dakaroises', in M-C. Diop (ed.) *Le Sénégal des Migrations: Mobilités, Identités et Sociétés*, Paris: Karthala, pp. 241–76.

Geschiere, P. (2014) '"The funeral in the village: Urbanites" shifting imaginations of belonging, mobility, and community', in M. Diouf and R. Fredericks (eds) *The Arts of Citizenship in African Cities: Infrastructures and Spaces of Belonging*, New York: Palgrave Macmillan, pp. 49–66.

Geschiere, P. and Gugler, J. (1998) 'The Urban–rural connection: Changing issues of belonging and identification', *Africa*, Vol. 68, Issue 3, pp. 309–19.

Geschiere, P. and Nyamnjoh, F. (2000) 'Capitalism and autochthony: The seesaw of mobility and belonging', *Public Culture*, Vol. 12, No. 2, pp. 423–52.

Goerg, O. (1998) 'From hill station (Freetown) to downtown Conakry (first ward): Comparing French and British approaches to segregation in colonial cities at the beginning of the twentieth century', *Canadian Journal of African Studies*, Vol. 32, Issue 1, pp. 1–31.

Grillo, R. (1973) *African Railwaymen: Solidarity and Opposition in an East African Labour Force*, Cambridge: Cambridge University Press.

Groelsema, R. (1998) 'The dialectics of citizenship and ethnicity in Guinea', *Africa Today*, Vol. 45, No. 3–4, pp. 411–21.

Hacker, J., Pierson, P. and Thelen, K. (2015) 'Drift and conversion: Hidden faces of institutional change', in J. Mahoney and K. Thelen (eds) *Advances in Comparative Historical Analysis*, Cambridge: Cambridge University Press, pp. 180–208.

Hay, P. (2014) *Negotiating Conviviality: The Use of Information and Communication Technologies by Migrant Members of the Bay Community Church in Cape Town*, Bamenda: Langaa RPCIG.

Hickey, S. (2011) 'Toward a progressive politics of belonging?

Insights from a pastoralist "hometown" association', *Africa Today,* Vol. 57, No. 4, pp. 28–47.

Jackson, G. (2005) 'Contested boundaries: Ambiguity and creativity in the evolution of German codetermination', in W. Streeck and K. Thelen (eds) *Beyond Continuity: Institutional Change in Advanced Political Economies,* New York: Oxford University Press, pp. 229–54.

Jindra, M. and Noret, J. (2011a) 'Funerals in Africa: An introduction', in M. Jindra and J. Noret (eds) *Funerals in Africa: Explorations of a Social Phenomenon,* New York: Berghahn Books, pp. 1–15.

—— (2011b) 'African funerals and sociocultural change: A review of momentous transformations across a continent', in M. Jindra and J. Noret (eds) *Funerals in Africa: Explorations of a Social Phenomenon,* New York: Berghahn Books, pp. 16–40.

Kalantaryan, S. and McMahon, S. (2020) *Covid-19 and Remittances in Africa,* Luxembourg: Publications Office of the European Union.

Kane, C. H. (1972) *Ambiguous Adventure,* Oxford: Heinemann.

Lefebvre, G. (2003) 'La ville Africaine et ses immigrants: Les Guinéens au Sénégal et à Dakar', in M. Lesourd (ed.) *L'Afrique: Vulnérabilité et défis,* Nantes: Éditions du Temps.

Lewis, P. (1992) 'Political transition and the dilemma of civil society in Africa', *Journal of International Affairs,* Vol. 46, No. 1, pp. 31–54.

Lindley, A. (2007) 'Remittances in fragile settings: A Somali case study', HiCN Working Papers 27, Households in Conflict Network.

—— (2009) 'The early-morning phonecall: Remittances from a refugee diaspora perspective', *Journal of Ethnic and Migration Studies,* Vol. 35, No. 8, pp. 1315–34.

Lynch, G. and Crawford, G. (2011) 'Democratization in Africa 1990–2010: An assessment', *Democratization,* Vol. 18, No. 2, pp. 275–310.

Mahoney, J. and Thelen, K. (2010) 'A theory of gradual institutional change', in J. Mahoney and K. Thelen (eds) *Explaining Institutional Change: Ambiguity, Agency, and Power,* New York: Cambridge University Press, pp. 1–37.

Manuh, T. (2001) 'Ghanaian migrants in Toronto, Canada: Care of kin and gender relations', *Research in Review,* Vol. 17, pp. 17-26.

247

Markel, H. and Stern, A. (2002) 'The foreignness of germs: The persistent association of immigrants and disease in American society', *Milbank Quarterly*, Vol. 80, Issue 4, pp. 757–88.

Mazzucato, V., Kabki, M. and Smith, L. (2006) 'Transnational migration and the economy of funerals: Changing practices in Ghana', *Development and Change*, Vol. 37, Issue 5, pp. 1047–72.

Mbembe, A. (2000) 'Everything can be negotiated: Ambiguities and challenges in a time of uncertainty', in B. Berner and P. Trulsson (eds) *Manoeuvring in an Environment of Uncertainty: Structural Change and Social Action in Sub-Saharan Africa*, Aldershot: Ashgate, pp. 265–76.

—— (2001a) 'African Modes of Self-Writing', *Identity, Culture and Politics*, Vol. 2, No. 1, pp. 1–39.

—— (2001b) *On the Postcolony*, Berkeley: University of California Press.

Mkandawire, T. (2001) 'Thinking about developmental states in Africa', *Cambridge Journal of Economics*, Vol. 25, Issue 3, pp. 289–313.

Mudimbe, V. Y. (1988) *The Invention of Africa: Gnosis, Philosophy, and the Order of Knowledge*, Bloomington: Indiana University Press.

Murphy, W. and Bledsoe, C. (1987) 'Kinship and territory in the history of a Kpelle Chiefdom (Liberia)', in I. Kopytoff (ed.) *The African Frontier: The Reproduction of Traditional African Societies*, Bloomington, IN: Indiana University Press, pp. 121-147.

Ndegwa, S. (1997) 'Citizenship and ethnicity: An examination of two transition moments in Kenyan politics', *American Political Science Review*, Vol. 91, Issue 3, pp. 599–616.

North, D. (1990) *Institutions, Institutional Change and Economic Performance*, New York: Cambridge University Press.

Nyamnjoh, F. (2005) 'Images of Nyongo amongst Bamenda Grassfielders in Whiteman Kontri', *Citizenship Studies*, Vol. 9, Issue 3, pp. 241–69.

—— (2011) 'Cameroonian bushfalling: Negotiation of identity and belonging in fiction and ethnography', *American Ethnologist*, Vol. 38, Issue 4, pp. 701–13.

—— (2015a) 'Incompleteness: Frontier Africa and the currency of conviviality', *Journal of Asian and African Studies*, Vol. 52, Issue 3, pp. 253–70.

—— (2015b) 'Amos Tutuola and the elusiveness of completeness', *Stichproben Wiener Zeitschrift für kritische Afrikastudien*, Vol. 15, No. 29, pp. 1–47.

—— (2016) 'Mobility and the challenge of obligation and reciprocity: The case of Cote d'Ivoire', in F. Nyamnjoh and I. Brudvig (eds) *Mobilities, ICTs and Marginality in Africa: Comparative Perspectives*, Cape Town: HSRC Press, pp. 98–120.

Nyamnjoh, F. and Rowlands, M. (1998) 'Elite association and the politics of belonging in Cameroon', *Journal of International African Institute*, Vol. 68, No. 3, pp. 320–37.

Obi, C. (2011) 'Taking back our democracy? The trials and travails of Nigerian elections since 1999', *Democratization*, Vol. 18, No. 2, pp. 366–87.

Onoma, A. K. (2009) *The Politics of Property Rights Institutions in Africa*, New York: Cambridge University Press.

—— (2010) 'The contradictory potential of institutions: The rise and decline of land documentation in Kenya', in J. Mahoney and K. Thelen (eds) *Explaining Institutional Change: Ambiguity, Agency, and Power*, New York: Cambridge University Press, pp. 63–93.

—— (2013a) *Anti-refugee Violence and African Politics*, New York: Cambridge University Press.

—— (2013b) 'Animating institutional skeletons: The contributions of subaltern resistance to the reinforcement of land boards in Botswana', in G. Berk, D. Galvan and V. Hattam (eds) *Political Creativity: Reconfiguring Institutional Order and Change*, Philadelphia: University of Pennsylvania Press, pp. 123–45.

—— (2017) 'The making of dangerous communities: The "Peul-Fouta" in Ebola-Weary Senegal', *Africa Spectrum, Vol. 52*, Issue 2, pp. 29–51.

—— (2018) 'Epidemics and intra-communal contestations: Ekeh, 'Les Guinéens' and Ebola in West Africa', *The Journal of Modern African Studies*, Vol. 56, Issue 4, pp. 595–617.

—— (2020a) 'Xenophobia's contours during an Ebola epidemic: Proximity and the targeting of Peul migrants in Senegal', *African Studies Review*, Vol. 63, Issue 2, pp. 353–74.

—— (2020b) 'Epidemics, xenophobia and narratives of

propitiousness', *Medical Anthropology*, Vol. 39, Issue 5, pp. 382–97.

Osaghae, E. (1995) 'Amoral politics and democratic instability in Africa: A theoretical exploration', *Nordic Journal of African Studies*, Vol. 4, No. 1, pp. 62–78.

Page, B. (2007) 'Slow going: The mortuary, modernity and the hometown association in Bali-Nyonga, Cameroon', *Africa*, Vol. 77, Issue 3, pp. 419-41.

Pierson, P. (2000) 'Increasing returns, path dependence, and the study of politics', *The American Political Science Review*, Vol. 94, No. 2, pp. 251–67.

Randall, V. and Svåsand, L. (2002) 'Political parties and democratic consolidation in Africa', *Democratization*, Vol. 9, No. 3, pp. 30–52.

Ranger, T. (1983) 'The invention of tradition in colonial Africa', in E. Hobsbawn and T. Ranger (eds) *The Invention of Tradition*, New York: Cambridge University Press, pp. 211–62.

Rothan, H. A. and Byrareddy, S. N. (2020) 'The epidemiology and pathogenesis of Coronavirus disease (COVID-19) outbreak', *Journal of Autoimmunity*, Vol. 109 (https://doi.org/10.1016/j.jaut.2020.102433) (accessed: 23 November 2020).

Ruktanonchai, N. W., Floyd, J. R., Lai, S., Ruktanonchai, C. W., Sadilek, A., Rente-Lourenco, P., Ben, X., Carioli, A., Gwinn, J., Steele, J. E., Prosper, O., Schneider, A., Oplinger, A., Eastham, P. and Tatem, A. J. (2020) 'Assessing the impact of coordinated COVID-19 exit strategies across Europe', *Science*, Vol. 369, Issue 6510, pp. 1465–70.

Shepler, S. (2017) '"We know who is eating the Ebola money!": Corruption, the state, and the Ebola response', *Anthropological Quarterly*, Vol. 90, No. 2, pp. 451–73.

Smith, D. (2001) 'Kinship and corruption in contemporary Nigeria', *Ethnos*, Vol. 66, Issue 3, pp. 344–64.

Tabappsi, T. (1999) *Le Modèle Migratoire Bamiléké (Cameroun) et sa Crise Actuelle: Perspectives Economique et Culturelle*, Leiden: CNWS.

Tazanu, P. (2012) *Being Available and Reachable: New Media and Cameroonian Transnational Sociality*, Bamenda: Langaa RPCIG.

Van der Geest, S. (2000) 'Funerals for the living: Conversations with elderly people in Kwahu, Ghana', *African Studies Review*, Vol. 43,

Issue 3, pp. 103–29.

WHO (World Health Organization) (2020) 'Timeline of WHO's response to Covid-19: Last updated July 30, 2020', WHO (https://www.who.int/news-room/detail/29-06-2020-covidtimeline) (accessed: 10 September 2020).

Wilder-Smith, A., Chiew, C. J. and Lee, V. J. (2020) 'Can we contain the COVID-19 outbreak with the same measures as for SARS?', *The Lancet Infectious Diseases*, Vol. 20, Issue 5, e102-e107.

World Bank (2002) *World Development Report 2002: Building Institutions for Markets*, New York: Oxford University Press.

Chapter 10

African Potentials and the Thought of Universal Humanity: The Latent Universalism in African Popular Cultures[1]

Michael Neocosmos

1. Introduction

Humanity currently finds itself at the edge of an abyss. If there is no change in the manner politics are being thought worldwide, the world could easily tip over into nuclear annihilation. I am not being dramatic here; this is fast becoming a distinct possibility. In this context it is absolutely imperative to re-introduce the idea of universal humanity at the centre of intellectual thought. Western liberalism has failed lamentably to establish a real universal thought of the human. While the effects of violence are now slowly entering middle-class consciousness, it is also becoming apparent that the obscene inequalities and colonial domination – both occasioned by capitalism – that currently prevail, are directly connected to a spurious liberal idea of universality from which the overwhelming majority of humanity is excluded. In fact, it is gradually being understood that the liberal conception of 'Man' has no universal validity whatsoever; it is simply a perverted conception of universalism. It has led to a greater and greater emphasis on particularities, interests, identities and, hence, wars and more wars. We are desperately in need of a shift to thinking ideas of unadulterated universal humanity.

The idea of 'African Potentials' began as an intuitive slogan developed by Professor Itaru Ohta and continued by Professor Motoji Matsuda at the University of Kyoto. Japanese scholars have not had a history of colonial relations with Africa. This has enabled the expansion of this brilliant project that puts the innovative aspects of African cultures at the forefront. African Potentials are seen as of central importance for understanding and, maybe, even solving the world's problems. What is more important than an idea of humanity as a whole?

Moreover, Japanese people have had a direct experience of what it is to suffer the effects of atomic weapons. It is not possible to visit Hiroshima and not to be particularly affected by a concept of the fragility of the idea of universal humanity. The real, most important problem today is how to bring the idea of universal humanity back into public and, indeed, private discourse.

African Potentials has proven to be an important conceptual innovation that provides intellectual access to alternative conceptions of thinking the universal, which are of central importance for the world today. What I want to do is to contribute to a shift in academic discourse from a focus on identity (which has been the case over the past 20 years say) to a focus on humanity, from focusing on difference to focusing on the common.

I want to distance myself from the dominant thinking of cultures (African or European or Asian) as coherent entities and even more from the idea of an African culture in general. The reason is simple. There is evidence of a concept of universal humanity in many African cultures but at the same time African cultures (for the most part) are founded on power differentials underpinned by a central authority or state power that reproduces inequalities and hierarchies. Such dominant power systematically contradicts the idea of universality. The latter, although it recognises differences, is founded on what is common to humanity, i.e., on some idea of equality. In fact, the idea of a true human universality can never emanate from power. I take this to be a universal truth for the simple reason that state power is necessarily inimical to the common, to the human. This idea is apparent as far back as ancient Egypt in the *Tale of the Eloquent Peasant*, for example, in which we see an ordinary rural cultivator (Khun-Anup) berate state power for its arbitrariness and thus for undermining justice (*Ma'at*), that is the equal treatment of all irrespective of their position in the hierarchy (Shemsw Bak 2016). The idea of universal humanity, especially when it exists in practice, is usually an exception, even in African cultures.

In Southern Africa, local cultures have been so heavily impacted by colonial and apartheid domination that they have been systematically transformed in the interests of the powerful: Western, local and male. The idea of the 'invention of tradition' put forward by historians such as Ranger and others has shown quite clearly how power – colonial power in particular – systematically transformed traditional cultures in its interest, making them more oppressive, more distant from popular practices. Of course, this process went hand in hand with the formation of a domain of the traditional – of 'traditional society' in opposition to the domain of the modern reserved for Europeans. This colonially modified 'tradition' can then be pointed to by power today as somehow authentic.

Simultaneously, dominant classes in Africa appeared, which were dependent either on the modern or on a tradition transformed in their interests. This was a process that Amílcar Cabral for one understood extremely well. The rising petty-bourgeoisie and bourgeoisie were assimilated into Western culture, or in ex-British colonies (because of indirect rule) systematically benefited from the transformation of custom which the British colonial authorities engaged in. The increased powers of the chieftaincy over peasants and the increased extraction of tribute labour for the purposes of supplying labour power, goods and commodities to growing markets, the transformation of matriarchal societies into patriarchal ones, the systematic entrenchment or even creation of ethnicities ('tribes') when they did not exist, the regulation of gender relations in particular in order to control male labour are all well-known features of colonial domination. In particular, the family was seen by colonial authorities as the foundation of African societies. I cannot survey the literature here but the impact of colonial interventions on traditional cultures has been studied at length. It is abundantly clear that *dominant* traditional culture was transformed in the interests of the powerful: the colonial state, the chieftaincy, dominant nationalities, the missionaries, men, etc. The chieftaincy in particular had not simply been a political institution, but was also a cultural one given that there was no division between the two in Africa. Given all these processes of 'hierarchisation' and division, how then is it possible for some African cultures to recognise conceptions of the universally human?

Whereas the conceptions of African societies viewed from above have been studied at length, it has been assumed that popular beliefs and practices have changed in conformity with them. Yet people have drawn upon memories, beliefs and practices during their resistance to colonial domination which have not always conformed to the dominant view of culture. Many of these refer precisely to what has been unsullied by colonial impact. People hold onto what is theirs and protect it from the interests of the dominant in order to retain their dignity. They still refer to their cherished beliefs in the face of domination and rely on these during times of resistance in order to hold their collectivity together. Thus, it is mistaken to think in terms of the *epistemicide* of African conceptions during the colonial period as Boaventura de Sousa Santos (2014) does, for example. This despairing attitude is largely characteristic of those in the academy assimilated into Western culture and wishing to 'delink' from Western epistemologies prevalent in currently fashionable 'decolonial theory'.[2] Popular resistance and, in particular, popular rebellions have been able to draw on cultural traditions precisely in order to create a collective agency that itself is founded on mutual recognition, i.e., some conception of universal equality. Equality and mutual respect and dignity emanate from collective meetings organised by people themselves. In other words, a political subject is created collectively, not by reference to African culture in general, but by reference to those features of tradition which stress equality, mutual cooperation and support, and popular democratic principles which are activated in popular discussions and struggles.

It follows that it is largely false to think of such practices as given fully fledged features of culture. Rather given the continuous struggle over the content of cultural tradition, these features must be understood as latent aspects, as potentials – and not as givens. They need to be activated in collective popular struggles, which they often are incidentally. This is why I think it important to think in terms of 'the latent universalism in African popular cultures'. Examples of such popular conceptions of universality have included: the palaver (in its various forms of popular assemblies) as a manner of resolving contradictions in community, the *Ngoma* and secret societies of community healing, the idea of the universality of human existence (*a person is a person*), the communal access to land, the idea of social interdependence as in *uBuntu* and many many others.

All of these features appear and are drawn upon by people during periods of struggle and resistance. The potential of these practices is therefore activated during periods of struggle only. Otherwise, it simply exists in a latent form – in the form of sayings or proverbs for example – because it is rooted among popular beliefs and forms part of a panoply of resources that can be drawn upon during periods of crisis (Sekyi-Otu 2018). One can see this latency, for example, in popular sayings such as, for example, 'a chief is a chief by his people', common in all Southern African cultures, but in order to be activated, such sayings need to form part of collective political practices. I want in what follows to expand on these points under three headings:

1.   Colonial domination and the transformation of cultures, dehumanisation and 'thingification' (Césaire 1972) being the destruction of the common and the introduction of state regulated hierarchies.

2.   Resistance against colonialism and its institutions as a way of re-introducing the idea of collective humanity. It is uncanny how universalism is drawn upon during periods of political resistance driven by the necessity of collective self-organisation.

3.   I shall examine the idea of *uBuntu* and shall conclude by suggesting that the contradiction between the inequalities within cultures and the latent potential universalism inherent in popular traditions constitutes a dialectic that is at the core of all human struggles for emancipation from oppression.

What is arguably common to Africa then is the latency or potentiality of the human universal in popular conceptions. The idea of universal humanity cannot be actualised through the exercise of power but only through popular self-organisation.

2. Colonial Domination and the Manipulation of Culture in Favour of 'Traditional Power'

Probably one of the most important features of the colonial

transformation of African cultural practices was the systematic distortion of tribute labour in the interests of chiefly power. Rural Africans (the overwhelming majority) in British colonies in particular were ruled by means of a tradition modified or re-created for the purpose, and able and willing to accommodate extra-economic coercion in the form of forced labour, forced commodities, forced removals, forced monetary levies and so on. The chiefly powers, which under precolonial tradition had always involved an element of popular control, restraint and reciprocal benefits, were administratively distorted (tradition was set in stone and its flexible nature undermined) so that tribute labour was now forcibly extracted for colonial purposes and only legitimised by the invented traditional discourse of power (Vail 1989).

Mahmood Mamdani's account of such 'extra-economic coercion' in his *Citizen and Subject* is extremely important and detailed. I have also insisted on the stark political character of labour extraction and cash exactions in my work on Swaziland – where I referred to this process as 'institutionalised plunder' – and on the history of ethnicity in Southern Africa (Mamdani 1996; Neocosmos 1987). The provision of tribute labour is intimately connected with the chieftaincy's control over land. Throughout Southern Africa (with appropriate variations) the importance of the chieftaincy's control over land is manifold. In the first place, it not only enables them to extract bribes from the peasantry in return for allocating them a plot on which to produce (justified by reference to 'traditional' culture, of course), but in many conditions the threat of banishment from the land constantly hangs over the peasantry, especially in conditions of land scarcity, thus enabling the development of patronage relations which systematically fleece the people of their resources.

As John Dube, the famous spokesman for the Zulu bourgeoisie put it in his evidence to the *Native Economic Commission* of 1930–32 in South Africa: 'the chief's power was largely dependent on his control of the land. A man offending him could be cut off from the land and from subsistence' (Lacey 1981: 109). Moreover, this power provides the basis for the mobilisation of unpaid labour or cash for the construction of public works (roads, contours, dipping tanks, schools, clinics, water points and so on) (Neocosmos 1987). Chiefs can also require payment for any official function and, given the autonomy of their powers, can regularly utilise free labour and extorted funds for personal accumulation. Chiefs of course also have, in most cases, judicial functions of legislating bye-laws and the power to try cases under customary 'traditional' law. The chieftaincy therefore generally combines in one person administrative, judicial, executive and police functions. In Mamdani's apt phrase, these fused powers amount to a 'clenched fist' over the peasantry (Mamdani 1996). Such powers are made plain in the following typical statement by a chief to a plaintiff at a 'traditional' court in Matatiele district in the Transkei in the mid-1980s:

> We shall never solve your problem here in the *pitso* (court) because you did not pay the money for the clinic, you are not a member of the TNIP (Transkei National Independence Party, the local ruling party at the time – MN) ... you haven't paid ... your name is not on the register. For the gifts for the big TNIP meetings to buy Matanzima a present ... your name is not there. You did not pay any money for the *morena* (chief) ... three times we were asking for money for him to make a feast for him after he became chief. Then there is the R1 for the dipping tank. If the people who are still owing are murdered or attacked ... I'll never solve the problem unless they pay these amounts (Segar 1989: 121).

These powers like the ethnic ideology which supports them, were never simply given by tradition. They were themselves the product of struggles as the chieftaincy was confronted 'from below' by the people and 'from above' by the colonial state. Moreover, there is recent evidence in South Africa for the continued use of unpaid tribute labour and other payments to chiefs, including for road construction and funds towards chiefs' homes, cars or legal fees. Amounts cited in a newspaper article from 2012 included family payments of R500 for road construction, from R200 to R1,000 from the parents of a pregnant girl, from R300 to R1,000 for the unveiling of a tomb, and so on. These amount to extortionate amounts for poor rural families.[3]What is important to stress is that such state coercive practices have continued unaltered during the post-colonial period throughout the continent, reproduced by development interventions that regularly require the provision of unpaid labour by rural worker-peasant families, that is justified not only in terms of tradition but also of 'self-sufficiency' or 'food for work' ideologies. Outside traditional society, in civil or uncivil society, labour for public works is always paid of course.

This process of political control by power and economic exploitation led to rural resistance movements during colonialism and apartheid as rural people protested against the distortion of traditional practices in a way which benefited not only the colonial state but also the chieftaincy itself and its supporters.

3. Resistance and the Idea of the Universal

Most rural-based rebellions in Southern Africa attempted to reassert the tradition that 'a chief is a chief by his people' in other words that tribute exactions were out of control and that the chieftaincy was losing its legitimacy. For some, like *Lekhotla la Bafo* (the Commoners' League) in Lesotho in the 1960s, it was a matter of returning to a past tradition of consultation that chiefs were seen to have betrayed (Edgar 1988). They were now clearly chiefs 'by the colonial state'. For others, such as the Mountain Movement in Mpondoland during the same period, the idea was to return power to people themselves by replacing the individual chief with an elected popular assembly, without altering the popularly founded institution of the chieftaincy as such (Lodge 1983; Neocosmos 1995). These were both struggles for accountability within traditional society and both activated politically the common saying or proverb: 'a chief is a chief by his people'. The former movement in Lesotho was successful in abolishing tribute labour in the country just before independence. The latter, although it failed to democratise the chieftaincy, was arguably resurrected in the Marikana revolt in 2012 on the platinum mines as the memories of the Mountain Movement were clearly reflected in the practices of the miners who were mainly migrants from the Eastern Cape.

In sum, a seemingly innocuous cultural proverb can become a guiding principle for political thought and struggle. This is what I mean by potentiality. The same is true regarding not only the legitimacy of the institution of the chieftaincy but of statements regarding universal humanity.

There have been many examples of resistance against oppression – particularly colonial oppression – by Africans. Not all have clearly evoked a concept of universal humanity; many affirmed ethnic identities and the formation of particular states. Nevertheless, in my book *Thinking Freedom in Africa* I referred to three distinct examples of a politics of universality located within African cultures yet separated by long historical periods. In all three cases it is a politics of universality which is affirmed against the dominant emphases on social location and identity. In all three cases these politics are expressed in a very unique statement that emphasises the universality of humanity. Of course, other similar statements exist. The following statements can be linked directly to a popular political process not simply to a culturally transmitted proverb.

'Every Human Life is a life' – the Oath of the Manden Hunters: fighting a culture of slavery

Popular struggles against slavery by Africans have a long history as have more generally struggles against state power. One of the early statements against slavery on the continent itself dates (as far as can be established) from 1222 and is known as *The Hunters' Oath of the Manden* or *the Donsolu Kalikan* or, sometimes, as the *Mandé Charter.* This affirmation is based on the oral traditions of the Mandinka hunters' guild in the area covering parts of modern Mali, Senegal and Guinea and is said to date back to just prior to the reign of King Sunjata of the Mandinka. Statements from the charter are replete with the recognition of the truth of the universal nature of humanity. At the same time this declaration clearly recognises social differences.

Interestingly this is not a statement emanating from a state and seems to have inaugurated an event for a world in which slavery was an accepted practice. By 1236 (six years after Sunjata became king), another Mandinka document much more clearly of state origin – known as the *Kurukan Fuga* charter – rubbed out the thought of human equality and freedom and replaced them with a statement regarding the hierarchical stratification of society and the rights and duties of each social group. It states inter alia: 'Do not ill-treat your slaves. You should allow them to rest one day per week and to end their working day at a reasonable time. You are the master of the slaves but not of the bag they carry' (article 20). Apart from stressing the obvious fact that Africans had been thinking along the lines of a universal conception of humanity long before it had occurred to the European Enlightenment to do so, it seems important to note that the singularity of the subjective affirmation of the *Donsolu Kalikan* evidently asserted a universal and eternal truth of the universality of the human. The fact that this episode has been occluded in the history books does not lessen this truth.

The *Donsolu Kalikan* or *Oath of the Hunters* is concerned with affirming life over death. It is the universality of life associated with the possession of a soul and the need to fight against death, which here provides the essence of universal humanity. Life had to be affirmed in order to overcome the violence of hunger and the evils of slavery, both of which were closely connected with war and death; its language is that of an affirmation regarding what must be done to avoid hunger, war and death, namely the abolition of slavery itself. The *Donsolu Kalikan* exceeds the norms and laws of culture although arising from within it. It is not written in the language of power but in the language of freedom and equality, of the universality of humanity. It is politically prescriptive, not a sociological statement by power.[4]

'Every Person is a Person' – Freedom and Equality: Haiti c1809

The second statement to be considered refers to the freed ex-slaves in Haiti after 1804, the year the country became independent. A society and nation developed at that time which placed itself in opposition to the post-colonial state. Independence opened a new historical sequence in Haiti, that of the struggle for the formation of a peasantry through what is known in the development literature as an 'agrarian reform'. In this literature this issue is treated as a problem of political economy and the state; here however it must be understood fundamentally as a question of politics. The politics of

262

the supposed necessity of maintaining the plantation system was proposed on the basis of its technical superiority, of its 'obviousness'. This probably constituted the first time in which this kind of argument, which was to become the core of a predominant statist approach to development in post-independence economies of 'Third World' countries and a constantly recurring theme in 20th century politics, was deployed. It regularly took the form of an argument for the primacy of 'economic growth' yet central to this debate in newly independent Haiti was the actualisation of freedom and its consequent extension into equality:

> Permanent freedom had been won through independence. But the masses had not yet won the freedom to till their own soil. And this perhaps more than anything else, sums up what the peasant masses expected out of freedom. A personal claim to the land upon which one laboured and from which to derive and express one's individuality was, for the black labourers, a necessary and an essential element in their vision of freedom. For without this concrete economic and social reality, freedom for the ex-slaves was little more than a legal abstraction. To continue to be forced into labouring for others, bound by property relations that afforded few benefits and no real alternatives for themselves, meant that they were not entirely free (Fick 1990: 249).

According to Barthélemy (1991: 28), it is precisely the exceptional character of a society of freed ex-slaves which explains the 'egalitarian system without a state' which gradually emerged in rural Haiti. The African-born *Bossales* managed to acquire ownership of peasant parcels and the plantation estate system was largely destroyed. The process began in 1809 and was initiated by Pétion who ruled the south of the country while (King) Christophe ruled the north. The forced labour system was abandoned, and large private estates were broken up and leased to peasant sharecroppers. As a result, no *Latifundia* developed in Haiti, unlike in most of post-independence Latin America and the Caribbean. The masses of Haiti (*Bossales*) insisted on establishing a parcel-owning peasantry to anchor their political independence in economic independence, successfully as it turns out, so that the new bourgeoisie was deprived of direct access to surplus labour. A merchant bourgeoisie then developed which extracted surplus from beyond the peasant system and it is on this class that the state was founded, which used taxation for the same purpose (Trouillot 1980). Within peasant society itself, a number of methods of self-regulation – largely of African origin – enabled the restriction of differentiation and the dominance of a system of equality which remained at an objective distance from the state power. These included unpaid collective forms of work, witchcraft and secret societies, a common religious ideology, family socialisation and so on (Barthélemy 1991: 30-44). In fact, Barthélemy (1991: 84) makes the point that from 1804 onwards, it gradually became understood by the masses of the *Bossales* that 'the only alternative to the colonial hierarchical system is that of equality, more so than that of liberty, as while the latter enables freedom from external oppression, it is not able to take on board the ideological content of the system. Only equality is able to put into place an anti-system' (my translation).

A society and nation developed which, therefore, placed itself in opposition to the post-colonial state. Barthélemy (2000: 379 [my translation] refers to this kind of politics as a new form of 'marronage, a counter-culture, a structural and collective reaction of escape' that exceeds the idea of formal equality. We can also understand it as a singular form of politics which attempts to distance its thinking from that of the state and which is simultaneously rooted in local traditions of resistance to oppression. Commonly, this subjectivity was expressed in proverbs or sayings the most important of which was '*Tout moun se moun, men ce pa memn moun*' which loosely translated means 'every person is a person even though they are not the same person'. Barthélemy (2000: 293–4) explains this as a statement governing the world view of the Haitian rural people, for it is more than a simple proverb but reflects a fought for rule of social and political practice. The point is that equality cannot exist without difference and that correspondingly, difference makes no sense without equality: 'In order to be different, not to be *memn moun* each man must begin by identifying what he has in common with others; what is the basic identity from which variations can be felt, interpreted and used' (Barthélemy 2000: 293 [my translation]). In other words what is foundational for this way of thinking is what is common to all humanity.

As a result, while such variations obviously exist, they are restricted from becoming hierarchical through group reactions which limit the entrenchment of these forms of behaviour; these reactions include the attribution to one person of various statuses in different contexts so that all status is relativised. 'A good reputation, [social] behaviour, personal relations all contribute to balancing out the purely quantitative [differences]' so that identification is sought with an ideal of a 'middle peasant' (*moun mouayen*) (Barthélemy 2000: 303 [my translation]). Barthélemy insists that while Haitian rural (*bossale*) society is generally understood as a failure, as wedded to traditions and poverty, it is in fact a highly organised social system that is self-regulating without an institutionalised state structure. In order to achieve this, it had to maintain hierarchical *creole* society and the formal state at a distance, to block all attempts at individual enrichment and power-seeking, and to harmonise the group through a kind of automatic regulation of individual behaviour; 'all this outside any "political" dimension of state control' (Barthélemy 1991: 29, [my translation]). In this way the Haitian nation (if by 'nation' we mean the subjectively constituted unity of the people) constituted itself in a manner that distanced it from the state. Nesbitt (2008: 171) notes that this egalitarian system, 'a legacy of the Haitian revolution, functioned in such a state of dynamic equilibrium from the late 1790s to the 1960s until the destruction of the Haitian (natural and social) environment under the regime of Papa Doc (Duvalier) undermined its viability', inter alia, through the systematic use of terror. It should also be recalled that Jean-Bertrand Aristide and *Fanmi Lavalas*, the mass popular movement with which he was associated, resuscitated the popular prescription '*tout moun se moun*' in their politics during the 1990s in order to insist on popular sovereignty (Aristide 1992; Hallward 2007).

'Each Person is a Person' – fighting xenophobia in South Africa today

The third statement emanates from South Africa. It was uttered by Abahlali baseMjondolo, the movement of shackdwellers in Durban, and was explicitly geared against xenophobic attacks. In fact, it was made in 2008 after such attacks. Abahlali baseMjondolo (AbM) contested the reference to migrants as 'illegal immigrants':

> There is only one human race. Our struggle and every struggle is to put the human being at the centre of society, starting with the worst off [sic]. An action can be illegal. A person cannot be illegal. A person is a person wherever they may find themselves. If you live in a settlement you are from that settlement and you are a neighbour and a comrade in that settlement (http://abahlali.org/node/3582).

Apparent 'foreigners' then should not be treated differently from anyone else, as people have been living side by side for years and faced the same problems; only in this way can a nation of human beings be conceived. Abahlali have been organising systematically against xenophobic violence in the communities in which they have a presence and have been engaging in joint political actions with and organisation of Congolese migrants in Durban. We have in the statement above a complete rethinking of rights as applicable to all and not only to some, to formal citizens. In fact, Abahlali attempt to maintain in their politics the axiom which Badiou (2008) has consistently stressed: 'There is One World Only'. In this manner they are rethinking and providing new political content to both democracy and nation in South Africa. Their statement re-affirms the universality of humanity in the contemporary context and attempts to build a political practice on this principle. In fact, during the major outbreak of xenophobic violence in 2008, the areas where Abahlali had political influence did not experience xenophobic violence (Neocosmos 2010). This was because Abahlali had already engaged in anti-xenophobic politics as a matter of principle and also because specific measures were taken to avoid such violence. Today Abahlali organise political events with the Congolese Solidarity Campaign which organises African migrants in Durban. In their own words Abahlali note that this kind of principled politics has resulted in oppression by power:

> We have been working to build a politic [sic] from below that accepts

each person as a person and each comrade as a comrade without regard to where they were born or what language they speak. In this struggle we have faced constant attack from the state, the ruling party and others. We have been attacked for having members from the Eastern Cape, members born in other countries and Indian members. We have always stood firm against these attacks (http://abahlali.org/node/14685/#more-14685).

Nevertheless, despite the predictable violence of identity politics unleashed by the state (which is a regular occurrence in Durban in particular), the fight against the scourge of xenophobia, wherever it may exist, requires a principled statement of the kind proposed by Abahlali to guide political action. It is these collective popular politics which ensure that everyone is treated in the same way irrespective of social location (origins, young/old, male/female, ethnicity, etc.) which has made Abahlali's politics popular among the masses of the poor in Durban in particular and which have drawn to themselves the repression of the state and the opprobrium of the dogmatic left as they refuse as a matter of principle to enter into patronage relations (Gibson 2011).

It should be noted first that each one of these statements is directly linked to a struggle for emancipation – they make no sense outside of this struggle; and second each statement illustrates a dialectic, a dialectic which is both embedded in the particular and emanates from it while also putting forward a very similar conception of the universal, namely 'a person is a person'. Emanating from a struggle against slavery, a struggle for economic equality and a struggle against xenophobia all three are clearly located in the particular while at the same time transcend it. It is this process, which can be termed dialectical, and which defines the character of a particular singular form of emancipatory politics. This subjectivity is what the French philosopher, Alain Badiou, calls an 'immanent exception'. It is both located in a particular culture, in society as well as exceeding it so that it is not reducible to it. Emancipatory politics can only be thought dialectically in this sense.

4. Rethinking uBuntu Dialectically

In conclusion I would like to suggest that it may also be possible to rethink the South African concept of *uBuntu* dialectically rather than as a simple feature of culture, however ethically appealing that may seem. Briefly, the notion of *uBuntu* refers to the much-celebrated idea of social interdependence ('I exist because you exist') in African cultures (we must be careful to distinguish existence from being). As it is predominantly understood, *uBuntu* is reduced to a cultural (ethno-) philosophical practice more or less undermined by colonialism/apartheid and more or less adhered to. It follows that in circumstances where this practice has been reduced, if it is to revive, it has to be taught like all cultures (e.g., Praeg and Magadla 2014: 101). Of course, the attraction of such a view is its proposed alternative to Western individualism. Yet the simple reduction of complex African conceptions to an (ethno-) philosophical notion that 'I exist *because of others*' (p. 96) effaces the centrality of political potentiality in African thought – i.e. the understanding that such a conception of mutual interdependence is not given but must be struggled for by a political practice – in favour of an anthropological notion of culture. It thus may become fully compatible with a communitarian politics of identity. Drucilla Cornell, on the other hand, is at pains to stress the centrality of agency in the idea of *uBuntu*. She sees it as 'an important ideal and value in the day-to-day life of South Africa' (Cornell 2014: 180). She continues by stressing that:

> It defends itself as a new ethical way of being human together, we need to judge it then, not simply because it is African or South African, but because of the philosophical project it offers of solidarity ... uBuntu is itself an anticapitalist ideal and ... capitalism cannot be rendered consistent with it (p. 180).

Cornell is at pains to defend *uBuntu* against Western liberal conceptions and to argue that what these miss 'is precisely the activism inherent in making a difference. In this manner, *uBuntu* is said to have an ideal edge. There is no end to the struggle to bring about a human world and to become an individual person who makes a difference within it' (Cornell and Van Marle 2015: 2). Yet at the same time, *uBuntu* can easily collapse into identitarian communitarianism if it is idealised, i.e. considered as a lost ideal ethical tradition. The point is not to think of *uBuntu* as a lost ideal or morality but as a real possibility for excessive thought that can only exist when it governs a collective thought-practice – a politics, not an ethics. If it is to be politicised it must be re-constituted precisely as an innovation, as a radical beginning that cannot be inferred from the past.

It may also be useful to make a parallel with the idea of equality as understood by Jacques Rancière. The point for him is not to think of emancipatory struggle as one for future equality (*uBuntu*), but the collective coming together must itself be founded on equality, or as he puts it 'people do not come together in order to realise a future equality; a certain kind of equality is realised by the act of coming together' (Rancière 2012: 207 [my translation]). If there is no 'coming together' i.e. no collective politics, there is no equality. This is precisely what the Haitian *Bossales* attempted to achieve in their collective practice and what has emphatically not been achieved in South Africa with the exception of Abahlali. Abahlali's universal humanism is founded on a number of conceptions but not collectively on *uBuntu*. *UBuntu* may have inspired the agency of some individuals while others may have been inspired by liberation theology or Marxism; the point however is that such beliefs are not in any way sufficient in themselves to define an emancipatory politics. *UBuntu* unfortunately has so far not been at the centre of an anti-capitalist emancipatory politics in South Africa. In fact, the conviviality it extols is no substitute for politics; the danger is that *uBuntu*, read as an *existing* feature of culture, can lead to one version or other of communitarianism.

More precisely perhaps, it is important to note that *uBuntu* refers to a cultural ethic regarding individual existence in relation to others; it does not of itself prescribe equality in the same way that another common tradition in Southern Africa – 'a chief is a chief by his people' – does not prescribe democracy. In order for either to enable the thought of egalitarianism and democracy, such a belief would need to be embedded within a collective political practice and transformed into a prescription so that sociality, mutual recognition and respect are transcended so as to constitute a politics. In fact, if time is taken to refer to popular struggles expressed in cultural subjectivities, it can be noticed that, during the colonial and apartheid periods, these were regularly directed to re-establishing popular control over the institution of the chieftaincy that had now produced chiefs 'by the colonial state'.

We therefore return to the question of state power struggles which I mentioned at the beginning of this chapter. Both the Council of Commoners in Lesotho and the Mountain Movement in Mpondoland activated a potential in African culture for the democratic accountability of the chieftaincy. Although these movements differed fundamentally in their reactions to the state's attack on the idea that 'a chief is a chief by his people', they each emphasised the potentially political character of African culture. A new thought of democracy emanated in each case from a political struggle against oppression. Thus, in the absence of its activation in politics where it takes a prescriptive form, the slogan that 'a chief is a chief by his people' remains politically empty and purely moral. The same is the case with *uBuntu*. It is only organised collective action – i.e., politics – that can give life to culture by making its statements prescriptive. All politics (i.e. collective organised thought practice), if it is to be emancipatory, must exhibit a dialectic of expressive and excessive thought. The absence of the dialectic implies the absence of a politics.

5. Concluding Remarks

I have attempted to shift the discussion of African cultures from an emphasis on identity to a focus on what I believe are latent ideas of universality. Their latent or potential character suggests that they must be activated and it is my contention that this can only happen in collective struggle during which the oppressed are the main contributors to the development of new theoretical concepts, for they, and they alone, are the makers of universal history. I believe that this is an urgent task if we wish to contribute to the creation of a new world where war must be minimised for it never fundamentally resolves contradictions. In order to avoid misunderstanding, I must state clearly that I am not thinking in terms of a notion of 'many universalisms' nor, indeed, in terms of 'human uniformity'. Let me explain: to maintain that there are several universalisms clearly means that there are various ways of grasping universal humanity in thought depending on cultural contexts. But this does not mean that all these conceptions are of equal value for, some – and in particular the Western liberal conception of Man – are simply false because they exclude 'barbarians' variously described. Western liberal 'universalism' excluded the colonised, supposedly inferior 'races' (and sexual minorities), in brief the non-European 'Other', and continues to do so. There may be other conceptions of humanity that are also exclusionary, and to consider all these as universalisms is to pander to their own views of themselves and thereby to give them legitimacy from within a crude relativist position. Moreover, to follow this procedure is to uncritically prioritise cultural differences, the overwhelming majority of which are hierarchically structured. African universalist statements are only 'potentially' emancipatory if they are valid 'for all' without exception.

The point is that there are features of humanity as a whole that exist independently of culture. Pre-eminent among these are language, thought and reason. The liberal racist European denial of the 'reasonable other' is purely a mark of its imputed superiority; it cannot be taken as a legitimate indication of its humanism. Reason was not an invention of the Enlightenment. In order to speak from the point of reason, *not from the point of another reason* – in fact there is only one reason in the absence of which we would not be able to comprehend what Khun-Anup (the Egyptian eloquent peasant) is saying in 3,000 BCE – I hold precisely that it is fundamental to think from the point of the excluded and the oppressed. But to do that they must be allowed to speak in their own name for they are fully capable of doing so. This is what I meant by insisting on the fact that 'people think' (Neocosmos 2016). The oppressed are able to think universal human equality precisely because they are excluded from it, the oppressors who do the excluding equate themselves with humanity. As Lewis Gordon (2019) puts it in his now famous expression, the point then is 'to shift the geography of reason' and he continues 'in shifting the geography of reason, reason itself is shifted from a closed to an open, relational commitment'.[5]

If we are not to collapse into a Hobbesian 'war of all against all', there must of necessity be an overriding norm to which all agree to subordinate their interests. It is this norm which must emphasise human universality. In the recent past this was referred to as 'the public good' or 'the common good' and was consciously conceived and defended (to a greater or lesser extent) by some states in a manner that tried to take into account the interests of the less powerful groups. Today this notion is no longer part of public discourse whether in Africa or in the world as a whole. Moreover today, such a conception must necessarily be subordinated to the welfare of humanity as a whole – not least because of greater interconnectedness – which is in grave danger of being permanently damaged in what has been called the 'Anthropocene'. This suggests the utmost importance of the centrality of universal humanity along with its ultimate dependence upon nature in emancipatory political thought. The thinking of excluded and (neo-)colonised people is thus of great importance here as are their early cultural cosmologies which are invariably universalistic in form. It is no longer sufficient to refer exclusively to partial interests. It is indeed the future of humanity as a whole that is at stake today, threatened as it is by the growing possibility of wars, the continued plunder of the planet's natural resources and the destruction or dismembering of national states by totally unbridled capitalism. It is my view that only an idea of human equality can consistently underpin such universalism. Human equality, of course, can make no sense if it is assumed that everyone is the same, if differences are glossed over. Differences are what make the idea of human equality possible. Yet the recognition of differences, whose importance it is necessary to assert in order to avoid state coercive creation of a spurious uniformity, cannot be conflated with or conceived as exclusively enabling identity politics. Unfortunately, these latter views are overwhelmingly dominant in social thought today including in the dominant conception of 'politics'.

The rise of new forms of fascism worldwide (mistakenly called 'populism' in the international media) is a typical example of this trend. To reduce all politics to the politics of difference is to replace human emancipation by the supposed freedom of one group at the expense of others. Such is the central idea of all identity politics. To insist on identities as the foundation of politics, however much one does so in combination with others and however much they are seen as evolving historically, is to contribute to enabling the conditions for more coercive practices and wars. It should be apparent that identity politics are statist in essence, which does not mean that only state agents deploy them. I have argued here that the potential for a politics of emancipation is frequently already in existence in a latent form in many African cultures and apparent within proverbs and sayings. These provide the potential for a new subjective dialectic of emancipation, but it must be understood that these potentials themselves need to be activated collectively in political practice if they are to have tangible effects. Africa can indeed show the way forward to the rest of the World. Alternative modes of politics are then potentially available among the people, but in the absence of collective political activation, they will remain museum pieces of African cultures to be included in edited collections of cultural idioms.

Endnotes

[1] This text is a revised version of the keynote address to the African Potentials Seminar held in Makhanda (Grahamstown) 25 November 2017.

[2] For a recent discussion see, e.g., Mignolo (2011). Decolonial theory is typically of Latin American extraction, a descendent of dependency theory, although this time not structuralist, but rather concerned with subjectivities, in particular, knowledges and their production. For these perspectives, the history of the South was made in the West. For a critique of such a viewpoint see Cabral's notion of 'return to the source', namely learning from the resisting masses who have not been assimilated into Western thought (e.g., Cabral 1980).

[3] See the *Mail & Guardian*, 24 February–1 March 2012, South Africa.

[4] For the full text and a detailed discussion of these statements see Neocosmos 2016, chapter 1.

[5] See Interview with Lewis Gordon

(https://www.newframe.com/shifting-geography-reason).

Acknowledgement

This work was supported by JSPS KAKENHI Grant Number JP16H06318.

References

Aristide, J.-B. (1992) *Tout moun se moun – Tout homme est un homme*, Paris: Seuil.

Badiou, A. (2008) 'The communist hypothesis', *New Left Review*, No. 49, pp. 29–42.

Barthélemy, G. (1991) *L'univers rural haïtien: Le pays en dehors*, Paris: L'Harmattan.

——— (2000) *Créoles – bossales: Conflit en Haïti*, Petit Bourg, Guadeloupe: Ibis Rouge Editions.

Cabral, A. (1980) *Unity and Struggle*, Nairobi: Heinemann.

Césaire, A. (1972) *Discourse on Colonialism*, New York: Monthly Review Press.

Cornell, D (2014) *Law and Revolution in South Africa*, New York: Fordham University Press.

Cornell, D and Van Marle, K. (2015) 'Ubuntu feminism: Tentative reflections', *Verbum et Ecclesia*, Vol. 36, No. 2, a1444 (https://doi.org/10.4102/ve.v36i2.1444) (accessed: 11 November 2020).

De Sousa Santos, B (2014) *Epistemologies of the South: Justice against Epistemicide*, London and New York: Routledge.

Edgar, D. (1988) *Prophets with Honour: A documentary History of Lekhotla la Bafo*, Johannesburg: Ravan.

Fick, C, (1990) *The Making of Haiti: The Saint Domingue Revolution from Below*, Knoxville: The University of Tennessee Press.

Gibson, N. (2011) *Fanonian Practices in South Africa*, Pietermaritzburg: UKZN Press.

Gordon, L. (2019) 'Shifting the geography of reason', interview with Lewis Gordon, *New Frame*, 21 January 2019 (https://www.newframe.com/shifting-geography-reason) (accessed: 11 November 2020).

Hallward, P. (2007) *Damming the Flood: Haiti, Aristide and the Politics of Containment*, London: Verso.

Lacey, M. (1981) *Working for Boroko*, Johannesburg: Ravan Press.

Lodge, T. (1983) *Black Politics in South Africa*, Johannesburg: Ravan Press.

Mamdani, M. (1996) *Citizen and Subject: Contemporary Africa and the Legacy of Late Colonialism*, London: James Currey.

Mignolo, W. (2011) 'Epistemic disobedience and the decolonial option: A manifesto', *Transmodernity*, Vol. 1, Issue 2 (https://escholarship.org/uc/item/62j3w283) (accessed: 11 November 2020).

Neocosmos, M. (1987) 'The agrarian question in Swaziland: Some observations on historical commoditisation and the post-colonial state', in M. Neocosmos (ed.) *Social Relations in Rural Swaziland: Critical Analyses*, Kwaluseni: Social Science Research Unit, University of Swaziland, pp.81–125.

———— (1995) 'Towards a history of nationalities in southern Africa', *Working Paper* 95.6, Centre for Development Research, Copenhagen (http://thinkingafricarhodesuniversity.blogspot.com/2012/04/ethnicity-state-and-democracy-in.html) (accessed: 11 November 2020).

———— (2010) *From 'Foreign Natives' to 'Native Foreigners': Explaining Xenophobia in Post-apartheid South Africa*, Dakar: CODESRIA (http://www.codesria.org/IMG/pdf/Neocosmos_From_Foreign_Native_to-2.pdf) (accessed: 11 November 2020).

———— (2016) *Thinking Freedom in Africa: Toward a Theory of Emancipatory Politics*, Johannesburg: Wits UP.

Nesbitt, N. (2008) *Universal Emancipation: The Haitian Revolution and the Radical Enlightenment*, Charlottesville and London: University of Virginia Press.

Praeg, L. and Magadla, S. (eds) (2014) *Ubuntu: Curating the Archive*, Pietermaritzburg: UKZN Press.

Rancière, J. (2012) *La méthode de L'égalité: Entretien avec L. Jeanpierre et D. Zabunyan*, Paris: Bayard.

Sekyi-Otu, A. (2018) *Left Universalism: Africa-centric Essays*, London: Routledge.

Segar, J. (1989) *Fruits of Apartheid: Experiencing 'Independence' in a Transkei Village*, Bellville: Anthropos.

Shemsw Bak (2016) Smi n skhty pn (The Tale of the Eloquent Peasant), San Francisco: Per Ankh.

Trouillot, M-R. (1980) 'Review of M. Lundhal *Peasants and Poverty: A Study of Haiti*', *Journal of Peasant Studies*, Vol. 8, No. 1, pp. 112–25.

Vail, L. (ed.) (1989) *The Creation of Tribalism in Southern Africa*, London: James Currey.

Index

278

extraversion 1–13, 16, 27, 29, 53, 100–1

in Somalia 113–6

state building as 113–6

F

failed state 100, 102, 104, 115

failure/s 7, 45, 69, 101, 104, 107, 113–4, 155, 158–9, 166, 169, 172, 242, 265

farmer/s 8, 71–2, 75, 77–80, 86, 91–2, 94, 124–5, 132, 134, 137, 205

FDI *see* foreign direct investment

Federal Government of Somalia (FGS) 99, 114

flexibility 7–9, 121–2, 168, 181–96

and negotiability in the African land tenure system 123–4

force/s (fighting) 4, 16–21, 23, 27, 39, 42–4, 110–1, 161, 163

Forces Républicaines de Côte d'Ivoire (FRCI) 18–9

foreign direct investment (FDI) 129–31

forestry 125, 133

formal institutions 3, 99

formalisation 3, 131, 133, 137

fragmentation 99

diversification and 50–2

framework/s 1, 74, 81–2, 85, 87, 100, 131, 169

new 80–3

fratricide 148, 151

FRCI *see Forces Républicaines de Côte d'Ivoire*

futurity 237–8

fynbos 69, 88

G

Gbagbo 3–4, 15–25

genealogy/ies 212, 216–8

geographical indication (GI) 83, 93

Ghana 126–7, 135, 137, 236

global citizenship 10–11, 203–20

COVID-19 and the emergent 215–9

global governance 185, 204

global market/s 5, 74, 88

images of local knowledge in a 86–93

Global North 1, 45, 51, 54, 240

Global South 41–4, 52, 227–9, 240, 242

globalisation 88, 111, 125, 181

Government of Southern Sudan (GOSS) 163–4, 166

in the African land tenure system 123–4

New Sudan Council of Churches (NSCC) 149–50, 152

NGO *see* non-governmental organisations

Nicaragua 42, 51

nomadic global citizenship 10, 203–20

    COVID-19 and the emergent 215–9

nomadic identities 204–5, 207, 211, 216

nomadic subjectivity 10, 203–4, 207, 211, 216

non-governmental organisation (NGO) 9, 45, 49, 51, 54, 153, 158, 160, 164–5, 168, 170, 185–8, 190, 192–3

non-institutionalised informality 6, 100

non-intervention 41, 43–4, 51, 53

non-state actor/s (NSA) 4–5, 7, 35–62, 104, 112, 185

North America 51, 101, 170

NSA *see* non-state actors

NSCC *see* New Sudan Council of Churches

O

OAU *see* Organisation of African Unity

One World Government 204, 207–8

oppression 12, 17, 204, 213–4, 257, 261, 264, 266, 270

Organisation for Security and Cooperation in Europe (OSCE) 45–7

Organisation of African Unity (OAU) 26, 47

Ouattara 3–4, 17–22, 24

P

pastoralism 151, 167

path dependency 9, 181–96

patronage 131, 258, 267

Pax Christi 155, 158

peace agreement 17, 133, 155, 166

peacebuilding 9, 28, 121, 147, 152, 155–6, 162, 164–72

peace from below 8–9, 147–76

    limits of 155–63

    and peace from above 167–71

    Wunlit Dinka–Nuer Peace and Reconciliation Conference (1999) and 147–52

287

United Nations (UN) 3, 15, 22, 25–8, 41–2, 45, 52, 111
    a 'proxy' for the nations of Africa? 25–8
United Nations Charter 19–20, 24, 46, 48–9
United Nations Firearms Protocol 48, 54
United Nations Operation in Côte d'Ivoire (UNOCI) 3, 15–31
United Nations Peacekeeping Operation (UN PKO) 4, 15–16, 20–1, 26–9
    intervention by the 16–9
United Nations Small Arms Programme of Action 48, 54
universalism/s 12, 204, 253–275
universality 3, 13, 253–4, 256, 261–2, 266, 271–2
UNOCI *see* United Nations Operation in Côte d'Ivoire
UN PKO *see* United Nations Peacekeeping Operation
UN Security Council *see* Security Council
Upper Nile 147, 149, 165–6
urbanisation 129, 135

V

violence 7, 18–9, 22, 35, 37, 40, 44, 52, 121–2, 125, 133, 135, 151, 157, 161, 163, 166, 205, 207, 253, 262, 266–7

W

war of liberation 147–8
Wassenaar Arrangement (SALW) 45–6, 48
weak institutions 11, 100, 228, 239–40, 242
West Africa/n 4, 26–27, 230
Western ideas and mechanisms 5, 54
Western Nuer 9, 147, 151
white (people) 71, 73, 80, 84, 91, 160–1, 187, 205
World Bank 124, 239–40
World Health Organization (WHO) 183, 186, 228
Wunlit 9, 147–8
Wunlit Dinka–Nuer West Bank Peace and Reconciliation Conference 9, 147–155, 172

X

xenophobia 11, 17, 206, 228, 231, 265, 267

Z